VICTORIANS IN THEORY

MANCHESTER
UNIVERSITY PRESS

Victorians in theory

From Derrida to Browning

JOHN SCHAD

MANCHESTER UNIVERSITY PRESS
Manchester and New York

distributed exclusively in the USA by St. Martin's Press

Published by Manchester University Press
Oxford Road, Manchester M13 9NR, UK
and Room 400, 175 Fifth Avenue, New York, NY 10010, USA
http://www.man.ac.uk/mup

Distributed exclusively in the USA by
St. Martin's Press, Inc., 175 Fifth Avenue, New York, NY 10010, USA

Distributed exclusively in Canada by
UBC Press, University of British Columbia, 6344 Memorial Road, Vancouver, BC, Canada V6T 1Z2

British Library Cataloguing-in-Publication Data
A catalogue record for this book is available from the British Library

Library of Congress Cataloging-in-Publication Data applied for

ISBN 0 7190 5134 7 *hardback*

First published 1999

05 04 03 02 01 00 99 10 9 8 7 6 5 4 3 2 1

Typeset in 9.5/12.5pt Palatino
by Action Publishing Technology Limited, Gloucester
Printed in Great Britain
by Bookcraft (Bath) Ltd, Midsomer Norton

...draw your own conclusions and hug the theory closely.
(Charles Dickens, letter to G. H. Lewes, 1838)

...who still
Goes floating ...
Across the theoretic flood from France ...
(Elizabeth Barrett Browning, *Aurora Leigh*, 1857)

... don't promise too much Mr Theorist.
(Conan Doyle, *The Sign of Four*, 1890)

To Ischmael Murdockhy
who reads Tennyson in the midst of civil war

Contents

	Acknowledgements	*page* ix
	Introduction: 'between two worlds'	1
1	**'The Lowest Room': Christina Rossetti through Irigaray's *Speculum***	6
	Other than writing	6
	Before the door	10
	The medium of glass	14
	Optics	19
	Looking-glass theology	22
	Turning	28
	Fire	34
2	**The buried lives of silence: Foucault after Arnold**	42
	Headless saints	42
	The life of life	48
	Between two bodies	56
	Holy city of the plague	61
	Face after face	68
3	***À Dieu:* from Browning, from Derrida**	79
	Towards an exhalation	79
	Greek endings	79
	Monstrous angels	84
	Eating words	90
	A grammatologist's funeral	92

Spectres of Sludge, or Mr Derrida the Medium 95
Things that go thump 95
Mourning becomes 99
SA/Ba 104

4 'No one dreams': where Hopkins was, there Lacan will be 116

God's sleep 116
God's (m)Other 120
Wo Es war 129
Knock, knock 133
Footing it 137

5 'The ends of being': between *Aurora Leigh* and Hélène Cixous 149

Ends 149
Deserts 155
Gospels 159
Ecclesia 164

Index 175

Acknowledgements

I began this book upon taking up a University of Wales Research Fellowship within the Department of English at Swansea – this is my first debt. Important in this connection was James Davies; for the second time in my career he had been instrumental in my getting an absolutely crucial break. My time at Swansea and the early work on this book was greatly enhanced by the exciting intellectual environment cultivated by Steve Vine, Laurent Milesi and others. The latter work on the book has been done since coming to the Department of English and Drama at Loughborough; I must here record my enormous gratitude to all my colleagues for their support and friendship. I am especially indebted to Marion Shaw – I could not imagine a better head of department.

I must also mention Matthew Frost of Manchester University Press: first, to applaud the amazingly good taste he showed in commissioning this book; and second, to thank him for his patience in waiting for me to complete it. During this time a number of friends have kindly read and commented on various parts of the book – heroic work indeed. In particular, I must thank: Andrew Bennett, John Bowen, Alison Chapman, Tim Clark, Patricia Ingham, W. David Shaw, Jeremy Tambling and Terry Wright. Other friends have simply been supportive and, in many ways, inspirational – in particular, Roger Ebbatson, Robin Hamilton, Kevin Mills, Neil Rowlands, Martin York and fellow members of that cryptic church the Christian Literary Studies Group.

Inspirational in quite different ways was my father, Dick S(c)had (1930–1996) – he took the 'c' out and I put it back – characteristically, he did not mind. He is, I think, to blame for my obsession with quotation and, indeed, misquotation. I blame my mother for everything else.

Finally, there is Bethan and Thomas who are both looking forward to being five on Wednesday. Without these two this book would have been finished some time ago but then so might I. I would certainly be finished without Katie, whose name I have finally learnt to spell since writing the acknowledgements for my first book. She has not read a word of what follows and doesn't really intend to; nevertheless, I somehow always feel she knows every word.

As they say, the frailties in what follows are all my own – I hope you don't notice too many.

An early version of part of Chapter 4 appeared in *Victorian Poetry*. I am grateful for permission to reprint.

John Schad
Loughborough University

Introduction: 'between two worlds'

> Wandering between two worlds, one dead,
> The other powerless to be born ...
> (Matthew Arnold, 'Stanzas from the Grande Chartreuse')[1]

I would like to claim that this book arose directly out of current critical-cum-theoretical trends and an acute sense of how these trends should develop; such a claim, though, would be something of a lie. It is true that this study is enormously indebted to those who have read Victorian poetry theoretically – in particular, Isobel Armstrong, Yopie Prins, W. David Shaw and Herbert F. Tucker; equally important are those who have read poststructuralist theory poetically – in particular, James Bernauer, Malcolm Bowie, Jane Gallop and Nick Royle; still more important are those who have, at times, done both – in particular J. Hillis Miller. However, for all the influence of the critical community, this book primarily issues from a shambolic process of interpretive hunches, accidents of reading and idiosyncratic habits of thought. That, at least, is how it seems to me. The best way to introduce *Victorians in Theory* is, I think, by describing this process.

The project began as a conventional study of Victorian poetry. I wanted to know how far Victorian poets were concerned with the very ideas of language, words and meaning; I wanted to know in what ways they imagined, or dreamt, these ideas. I then felt it necessary to compare these imaginings or dreams with those of another set of writers who fascinated me – namely, the Francophone poststructuralists. At this point I soon found that I was not so much applying the theory to the poetry as reading the two discourses alongside each other. I was, quite simply, comparing and contrasting, but that is not quite what theoretical critics usually do. I was not just using the theory to reread the poetry; I was also and at the same time using the poetry to reread the theory. The relationship between the two bodies of writing could no longer be seen as that of text and metatext but rather as genuinely intertextual. I was trying to read both ways, back and forth, to pay equally close attention to both poet and theorist. I found myself – to adapt Derrida's phrase – reading with two hands.[2] This meant that, at times, I was almost reading the poetry as theory and the theory as poetry – or, to be more precise, as a tissue of metaphors or moments of rhetorical blindness and insight. Many of these moments were only discernible in the light of the peculiarly Victorian discourses of the poetry. For example, I noticed the angels in Derrida's work because there are so many in Browning; again, I could not help but locate the hell within Irigaray's *Speculum* when reading it in relation to Rossetti; or then again, Cixous's apocalyptic only surfaced whilst setting her against *Aurora Leigh.* Importantly, these were metaphors of which the theorist – for all her/his self-consciousness – was not fully aware. In such cases – to adapt a phrase of Christopher Norris's – the poetry seems to have the courage of theory's own metaphors,[3] to know the theorists better than they know themselves.

The theorists, of course, have often seen their writing as, primarily, a tissue of metaphors; in this sense, I was only reading in the way they ask to be read. Cixous, for instance, writes, 'I let myself be carried off by the poetic word'; Foucault remarks, 'I have never written anything but fictions'; Derrida declares that 'deconstruction is itself a literary text to be read like other texts'.[4] Conversely, Victorian poetry knows itself to be, in many respects, a quasi-theoretical discourse. Driven to the cultural margins by the double assault of Utilitarianism and the novel, the poetry of the mid nineteenth century was forced to occupy a critical, or metatextual, space. 'Try as it might,' writes Joseph Bristow, 'Victorian poetry could not assert itself as a primary discourse'; 'the history of Victorian poetry', remarks Isobel Armstrong, 'is the gradual assent to self-reflexive art'.[5] As Bernard Richards comments, 'it would be possible to glean a whole history of poetic theory from the works themselves'.[6] Arthur Hallam testifies to such reflexivity when, in 1831, he writes that 'modern poetry [is characterised by] ... that return of the mind upon itself'.[7] Armstrong goes still further, asserting that 'the Victorian dramatic poem is not the dialogue of the mind with itself so much as the dialogue of the poem with itself'.[8] 'Our interest', declares Browning's Bishop Bloughram, '[is] on the dangerous edge of things';[9] that edge is, in part, a theoretical edge.

It is for this reason that the poetry so often overlaps with the theory; the fact remains, however, that this study wanders between two quite different worlds. In so doing it must risk entering an intertextual no man's land, a space that does not quite belong to either the poet or the theorist. In this space I find myself at times discussing a third and almost ghostly figure or text. Between Hopkins and Lacan there emerges that no man's land *The Waste Land*; between Derrida and Browning there appears the spectre of Martin Luther; between Irigaray and Rossetti I come across Lewis Carroll's Alice. At times this figure would come into view were we reading just one of the two writers. There are, however, occasions when I am discussing figures, texts or tropes which only become apparent as an effect or trick of the unique dynamics of the specific pairing, or dialogue, that I have set up. And set it up I have, in the sense that nothing absolutely insists that Browning, say, should be read alongside Derrida, or Irigaray with Rossetti, and so on; though I always sought to make the pairings as likely as possible, they are all haunted by the fact that they might have been otherwise. For this reason each pairing, each chapter, is unnerved by an apprehension that it is, in some sense, arbitrary – in some sense a trick of interpretive ingenuity. After all, much of this study is concerned with accidents of meaning which take place between two bodies of writing that are usually thought of as being separated by language, genre and period. In this sense, I am involved in an experiment of reading, an experiment which is best described as an extended verison of the seventeenth-century poetic conceit, the elaborate comparison of apparently dissimilar objects. Such an experiment is in the very spirit of the dangerous edge that is Victorian poetry; it is also in the spirit, or rather letter, of poststructuralist intertextuality. If all texts are haunted by every other text, then in reading seemingly unlike texts together I am not so much making connections as discovering them; the accidents of meaning are accidents waiting to happen.

Such accidents do, of course, place some strain on a conventional sense of literary history – there is something unusual in suggesting, as I do, that Hopkins anticipates the First World War that so concerns *The Waste Land* that so concerns Lacan in 'The Insistence of the Letter'. The logic or poetic of such a transhistorical reading is, however, internal to both Victorian and poststructuralist writing. The poststructuralists are plagued by the possibility that they are merely repeating the nineteenth century, that they too are Victorians, 'other Victorians' in Foucault's terms.[10] Foucault himself remarks, in 1969, that there are 'those who believe we can continue to situate our present discontinuities within the historical and transcendental tradition of the nineteenth century'.[11] One such believer is Barthes: 'for the last hundred years', he writes, 'we have been living in repetition'; another might just be Derrida, whose discussion of 'the specters of Marx' – he who is, for Derrida, the very (dis)embodiment of the nineteenth century's historicotranscendental tradition – issues in the question: 'what exactly is the difference between one century and the next?'[12] The next century is also on the mind of the Victorians: 'Each century', wrote Dickens, '[is] more amazed by the century following it than by all the centuries before.'[13] The nineteenth century is more than capable of thinking and, indeed, writing the twentieth; in Oscar Wilde's *Dorian Gray* (1891) Dorian declares: 'I forgot I was in the nineteenth century.'[14] In this moment he is only a Victorian in theory.

It is such moments of forgetting that this study seeks to remember. Such moments do not take place outside of history; on the contrary, they are a simple fact of history, a simple fact of the history of forgetting, a history of poetic and theoretical imaginations. This particular history does, of course, take place within or alongside the more familiar histories of wars, revolutions, acts of parliament, literary movements and individual human lives. All these histories make their presence felt in this book. Indeed, one imperative of reading theory as a text in its own right is to bring it to the bar of its own historical contexts; this I have attempted to do. In wandering between two worlds, though constantly struck by similarities I am no less conscious of difference; I am conscious, in Derrida's words, of 'crossing between ... two phantoms of witnesses who will never come down to the same'.[15]

Notes

1 *The Poems of Matthew Arnold*, ed. Miriam Allott (London: Longman, 1979), 288.85–6.

2 Jacques Derrida, *Positions*, tr. Alan Bass (London: Athlone, 1981), 6 / *Positions* (Paris: Minuit, 1972), 4.

3 See Christopher Norris, *Deconstruction: Theory and Practice* (London: Routledge, 1982), 64.

4 'An Exchange with Hélène Cixous', in Verena Andermatt Conley, *Hélène Cixous: Writing the Feminine* (Lincoln: University of Nebraska Press, 1984), 151–2; Michel Foucault, 'The History of Sexuality' [Finas interview], *Power/Knowledge: Selected Interviews and Other Writings, 1972–1977*, ed. Colin Gordon (Brighton: Harvester, 1980), 193; Jacques Derrida, 'Deconstruction and the Other', in Richard Kearney, *Dialogues with Contemporary Continental Thinkers* (Manchester: Manchester University Press, 1984), 125.

5 Joseph Bristow, *The Victorian Poet: Poetics and Persona* (London: Croom Helm, 1987), 22; Isobel Armstrong, *Victorian Poetry: Poetry, Poetics and Politics* (London: Routledge, 1993), 8.

6 Bernard Richards, *English Poetry of the Victorian Period* (London: Longman, 1988), 18.

7 Arthur Hallam, 'Review of Tennyson's *Poems, Chiefly Lyrical*' [August 1831], reprinted in J. Jump (ed.), *Tennyson: The Critical Heritage* (London: Routledge and Kegan Paul, 1967), 41.

8 Armstrong, *Victorian Poetry*, 14.

9 *Robert Browning: The Poems*, ed. John Pettigrew and Thomas J. Collins, 2 vols (Harmondsworth: Penguin, 1981), 1.627.395.

10 See Michel Foucault, *The History of Sexuality: An Introduction*, tr. Robert Hurley (Harmondsworth: Penguin, 1976), 3–13 / *La Volonté de savoir* (Paris: Gallimard, 1976), 9–22.

11 Michel Foucault, 'What Is an Author?', in *Language, Countermemory, Practice*, ed. Donald F. Bouchard (Ithaca: Cornell University Press, 1977), 120 / 'Qu'est-ce qu'un auteur?', *Bulletin de la Société Française de Philosophie*, 63 (1969), 81.

12 Roland Barthes, 'From Work to Text', in *Image–Music–Text*, ed. Stephen Heath (London: Collins, 1977), 156 / 'De l'oeuvre au texte', in *Ouvres complètes*, 2 vols (Paris: Seuil, 1994), 2.1211; Jacques Derrida, *Specters of Marx: The State of the Debt, the Work of Mourning, and the New International*, tr. Peggy Kamuf (London: Routledge, 1994), 39 / *Spectres de Marx: L'État de la dette, le travail du deuil et la Nouvelle Internationale* (Paris: Galilée, 1993), 71.

13 Charles Dickens, *The Uncommercial Traveller and Reprinted Pieces* (Oxford: Oxford University Press, 1958), 132.

14 Oscar Wilde, *The Picture of Dorian Gray* (Harmondsworth: Penguin, 1949), 87.

15 Geoff Bennington and Jacques Derrida, *Jacques Derrida* (Chicago: Chicago University Press, 1993), 315 / *Jacques Derrida* (Paris: Seuil, 1991), 278.

1

'The Lowest Room': Christina Rossetti through Irigaray's *Speculum*

Other than writing

> Socrates tells us that men – *hoi anthropoi* – sex unspecified – live underground, in a dwelling formed like a cave. Ground, dwelling, cave ... all these terms can be read more or less as ... the *hystera*.
>
> (Luce Irigaray, *Speculum*)[1]

> So now in patience I possess
> My soul year after tedious year,
> Content to take the lowest place,
> The place assigned me here.
>
> (Christina Rossetti, 'The Lowest Room')[2]

For both Irigaray and Rossetti a woman's place, or rather the place that is woman, is below. Irigaray rereads Plato's *antre* (cave) as *ventre* (womb); Rossetti invites us to reread her 'room' in exactly the same, rhyming way. Witness the woman's body that is the buried subject of 'The Lowest Room'; concerned as it is with *The Iliad* – it was originally entitled 'A Fight over the Body of Homer' – this is a poem about a poem about a fight over the body of *Helen*. However, the poem's account of *The Iliad* and its 'men of men' (52) is so intensely male – so hom(m)eric, as it were – that Helen is buried, overlooked. The poem's passive, spinster speaker is not, then, alone in the lowest room but effectively joined there by Helen; she is the fallen and erring woman whom we here may read but only *between* the lines that describe the poem's married sister as she who 'stumble[s] like to fall' (20) and allows 'her needle [to] err' (89). Rossetti's lowest room – shared as it is with Helen – is, in Irigaray's terms, not just *un antre* (a cave) but also *entre* (between,

between the lines). But then for Irigaray this is inevitable since 'the feminine', she claims, 'must [always] be deciphered as inter-dict [*inter-dit*]', as at once both prohibited and located 'between the lines' (22/20). It is no accident that Rosetti's speaker describes her life as 'Line graven on line and stroke on stroke' (267).

According to Irigaray, initially women writers can only write lines upon lines, lines already written – already written by men: 'There is,' she declares, 'in an initial phase, perhaps only one "path", the one historically assigned to the feminine: that of *mimicry*.'[3] That Rossetti followed this path is almost a critical truism; as Dolores Rosenblum comments, 'her poems are deliberately echoic'[4] – most obviously of Dante, Petrarch, Maturin and, of course, the Bible. Mimicry is not, though, for Rossetti, merely an initial strategy and neither, in truth, is it for Irigaray. Although she describes 'playful repetition' as merely a means to 'make "visible" ... the cover-up of a possible operation of the feminine in language'[5] there is a sense in which the repetition is itself the operation of the feminine. This is particularly true of the repetition of the words of other writers; both Rossetti and Irigaray quote excessively. Whole sections of *Speculum* are nothing but quotation; likewise, remove the Bible from Rossetti's poetry and it would become, as her brother William Michael speculated, 'something approaching a vacuum'.[6] In quoting so extensively both writers explore a writing that is, in a sense, not writing at all. In 'Would that I were a turnip white' (3.298–301) Rossetti wearily expresses the desire to endure anything 'rather than writing' (12) and indeed in her poems it is often as if she is *quoting* 'rather than writing'. 'I cannot write the words I said' (1.65.130) but only, as it were, the words that others have said. Rossetti is, very conspicuously, doing something other than writing as it had been understood since the Romantics – writing, that is, as a primary, creative act.[7] In *Speculum* Irigaray is even more determined to be doing something other than writing. Just as Derrida's *Of Grammatology* [1967] announces 'The End of the Book and the Beginning of Writing' so, seven years later, Irigaray's *Speculum* announces the end of writing and the beginning of quotation.

Of course, coming from an Anglo-Italian family, Rossetti is always, in a sense, doing something other than writing English – hers is an Italicised English in more senses than one. Indeed, to some extent she is the figure of 'Enrica' (1865), that Italian woman in England whom the poem views from the perspective of 'we Englishwoman':

> … our tongue grew sweeter in her mouth.
>
> (1.193.4)

To return to Irigaray, Enrica's Italicised English deciphers the feminine as 'inter-dit', for what lies between these words is the prohibited desire *of* women *for* women: 'our tongue … in her mouth'. We here read between not only the words but also the lips – female lips; this reading between, as Irigaray would point out, mimics the operation of the gynaecologist's speculum. What, then, lies between the lines of 'Enrica' is Rossetti's lowest room/womb – 'she found us', the poem concludes, 'Deep at our deepest'. The logic at work here anticipates the word-playing (il)logic of *Speculum*, where 'entre' shades, or descends, into not only 'antre' but also 'ventre', and 'the *cryptic*' (191/238) shades, or descends, into 'the crypt' (195/243, 282/351).

Since caves, wombs and crypts all exclude the light, it is clear that the riddles between the lines of *Speculum* challenge what Irigaray identifies as photocentrism – the representation of truth as light, and light as the *'anchor or origin'* (256/318). That light is also challenged in Rossetti, albeit occasionally, is no surprise; for the Victorians combined explicit reverence for light and sight with an acute awareness of their frailties. At the same time as Ruskin was declaring that the 'Sun is God', solar physicists were spreading fears that the sun was cooling;[8] moveover, extensive scientific work on the physiology of the eye was making obvious the unreliability of vision.[9] As Susan Horton observes, the 'Victorians [became] increasing[ly] uncertain … of the visual as a ground for truth'.[10] It is intriguing that, in *The Face of the Deep*, Rossetti should write of the 'analysis of light' in the strict, spectral sense of the dissection, or undoing, of light – a theme that develops as she goes on to ask 'whether the sun is passing away' and then to confess, as a sin, her desire 'to watch an eclipse'.[11]

Such undoing of light is never, though, so explicit in Rossetti's poetry, where it may only be read between, or rather within, the lines – lines such as 'And change was written on the sun' (3.77.15); 'His yoke [is] easy and *His burden light*' (3.24.2: my italics); and, 'To be all as *the sun fails* not to smile' (3.323.13: my italics). This last line makes vulnerable what is, otherwise, a perfectly standard photocentric formulation. In the poem 'A Martyr' another such formulation – 'As blossoms to the sun I turn to thee' – is troubled, or complicated:

> Lord, stand by me
> As once by lonely Paul in his distress.
> As blossoms to the sun I turn to thee.
>
> (2.161.71–3)

Seduced as we are into misreading the 'blossoms' as an analogue of Paul (who was, of course, blinded by light) we read, quite literally, between the lines – we make a connection that does not exist. As a result, the sun to which the martyr (re)turns becomes a blinding light.

The logic, or *theo*logic, of a blinding light is always, of course, paradoxical – implying, as it does, a believer who desires the light only in order to see it no more. But this paradox is only part of a more general theological disregard for the seeing subject; elsewhere Rossetti enjoins us to 'walk by faith *in lieu* of sight' (my italics).[12] In comparison, Irigaray's critique of sight and light looks somewhat cautious: '[it is] better', she writes, 'to be misled by fakes [the shadows of the cave] than to lose one's sight by opening the eyes to the flame of truth' (276/343). Such preservation of the seeing subject, the Cartesian eye/I, is a long way from Rossetti's sun-blinded martyr; it is also a long way from Irigaray's own insistence that the female subject 'knows nothing (of herself)' (345/432). There is, however, one important sense in which *Speculum* is an exercise in knowing nothing (of herself); since her first name is *Luce* (literally, 'light'), Irigaray, in composing her critique of light, is gradually making herself unnameable and thus unknowable. To quote Rossetti: 'nameless … / I go to the dark land' (1.178.540–1). To use Irigaray's own words, she is putting herself outside 'the economy of truth, of proper meaning and proper nouns' (274/341). In this respect *Luce* Irigaray comes close again to *Christ*ina Rossetti; just as one reluctantly bears the Roman name for light, so the other reluctantly bears the Christian name for God – in 'Three Stages' (1848) Rossetti declares 'it is an empty name / I long for' (3.232.14–15). But, for Irigaray, there *is* no empty name since all names, she argues, belong to the false economy of self-identity and presence; thus it is that Irigaray looks to the figure of *la mystérique,* that mystic-cum-hysteric who seeks 'an abyss that swallows up … all names' (194/242).

Before the door

In Rossetti's poetry the place of namelessness is not the abyss but the threshold – that (non-)place which, as neither inside nor outside, resists categories and names. Its importance to Rossetti is evident in the very titles of her poems: witness 'The Convent Threshold' (1858), 'Shut Out' (1856) and 'Behold, I stand at the door and knock' (1851). There are, in fact, so many doors in Rossetti's verse as almost to recreate her experience of London as 'a cityfull of … doors'.[13]

The threshold's analogue, within Irigaray's Platonic schema, is the passage which goes between the cave and the world above; it is, writes Irigaray, 'neither outside not inside … [but] Between … Between … Between' (246/305–6). Frustrating 'all dichotomies, categorical differences, [and] clear-cut distinctions', this passage, remarks Irigaray, is usually 'forgotton'. But what makes it so *un*forgotten in Rossetti is precisely this resistance to category. In 'Noble Sisters', for instance, the 'nameless man … / Who loitered round our door' (1.34.45–6) is a would-be lover of one sister whom the other claims, falsely, is married – the 'nameless man' thus has a nameless desire, one that falls between the respective names of courtship and adultery. Likewise, in 'The Ghost's Petition' (1864) the 'someone standing out on the landing / [who] Shook the door like a puff of air' (1.146.26–7) is the ghost, a threshold figure who blurs the distinction between living and dead.

The key threshold figure for Rossetti is, though, Christ – he who not only stands at the threshold between man and God but declares, 'Behold, I stand at the door, and knock' (Revelation 3.20). This declaration is a constant theme of both Rossetti's work and her life. Not only does it provide the title for one poem and the scene for another ('Despised and Rejected' (1868)), but when Holman Hunt visualised it in his painting *The Light of the World* (1851–53) Rossetti sat as one of the models for Christ's face.[14] In allowing her dark, female features to be converted into the fair, male face of Hunt's Christ, Rossetti plays the part of Irigaray's specularised woman – woman as the mirror in which man sees only a negative of himself. But Rossetti does not forget that the mirror is female; in her poetry the Christ at the door is always, in a sense, herself – not *The Light of the World*'s enLightened woman but, more nearly, what Irigaray calls 'the other woman'. In 'Despised and Rejected' the voice that, Christlike, cries 'Open thy door' (19) is characterised by darkness ('all night long [it] ... spake' (38)), concavity (he is a 'hollow friend' (7)) and, above all, blood: 'On the morrow / I saw upon ... / ... my door / The mark of blood for evermore' (55–8). In 'The Convent Threshold' (1858) the figure at the door is even further from Holman Hunt's specularised woman: once again there is blood on the threshold; this time, however, the cry is not simply that 'My feet bleed' but that 'my lily feet are soiled ... / With scarlet mud which tells a tale / ... of guilt' (1.62.7–9). Since 'my sheets are red' (117), is this the guilt of menstruation? Since 'You sinned with me a pleasant sin' (51), is this the guilt of a 'scarlet' woman? Or, then again, is it the guilt of incest? 'There's blood between us, love, my love, / There's father's blood' (1–2). If incest, this poem *fore*tells a tale of guilt: the tale of Freudian psychoanalysis. Like Freud's early case-studies,[15] the poem links the scene of incest to both the work of the unconscious ('tell ... what I dreamed last night' (85)) and such classic symptoms of hysteria as insomnia ('how long until my sleep begin' (56)) and sobbing ('My pillow is damp' (117)).

It is not only Freud's hysteric into which Rossetti's threshold figure shades; there is also Irigaray's *mystérique*. From the threshold, Rossetti's speaker has both a beatific vision of paradise – 'I see the far-off city grand' (18) – and an almost excremental vision of 'the off-scouring of the world' (27). Likewise, Irigaray's *mystérique* not only knows ecstasy but also 'has been so often humiliated ... [that] every particle in her being seems but ... *waste, refuse*' (199/248). What, though, distinguishes the *mystérique* is that she reverses specularisation – the crucified and bleeding Christ is *her* looking-glass: 'I see myself', she declares, 'in ... his wound' (200/249). Moreover, she is so taken up by this reflection, so 'transformed into Him', that she 'loses all sense of corporeal boundary' (201/250). As Margaret Whitford writes, '[though] the house of the male subject is closed [for] Irigaray ... one characteristic of women's sexual bodies is that they are precisely not closed'.[16] This is not, though, quite the case in *Speculum*, where woman is located not only within, and as, a cave but also behind a hymenal 'wall-curtain [that] ... forms an *impermeable* barrier' (282/351).

The house of Irigaray's female body is not as open as Whitford believes. There is, in other words, a door in Irigaray's cave; it is, however, encoded as a series of textual clues. Witness the 'hinge' that is a woman caught between two men (22/21) and that set of 'keys' which litter the text: 'the key to the mystery of femininity' (20/18), the 'key passage' between the cave and the world above (246/305), and the 'keystone' that is the philosopher's sun (267/332). Just as Irigaray locates a mirror deep-buried in the unconscious of Western philosophy, so *Speculum*, read alongside Rossetti, discloses a hidden door. Irigaray's difficulty in recognising that door becomes obvious on the one occasion it is made explicit: 'the girl-child', she enigmatically declares, '[is] imprisoned behind the door of the house' (327/409). Doors, for Irigaray, mean imprisonment; so for her to see the door in her cave would be to view the material, maternal space of the cave as a prison, a place to escape – and that is precisely the old, Platonic myth she seeks to undo.

By contrast, Rossetti seems to be forever seeing doors that limit, or mark boundaries, and she does so even when playing the part of a *mystérique.* In 'The Convent Threshold', at the height of her hystericised piety, the door persists: 'Today, whilst it is called today / Kneel, wrestle, *knock,* do violence, pray' (47–8: my italics). Again, in a poem written thirty years later, Rossetti's piety is still marked by the door – '[I] kneel down before / That ever-open door' (2.304.17–18). But here the door marks not just the corporeal boundary that, for Irigaray's *mystérique,* dissolves – it marks also a social boundary. In seeing herself kneeling before a door Rossetti conjures up what Stallybrass and White identify as an extremely potent, almost emblematic, Victorian scene – that of the maid kneeling to clear the doorstep.[17] To return to 'The Convent Threshold': 'my … feet are soiled with mud / … I seek … to wash the spot' (7–14).

Whilst Holman Hunt substitutes for the Christ that stands at the door a Christ-ina who sits, Rossetti herself may substitute a maid that kneels. In so doing, she effectively joins two moments within *Speculum* that Irigaray herself seems not quite to link – namely, Engels's claim that 'within the family … the wife represents the *proletariat*' (121/151) and her own claim that the suffering Son is 'that most female of men' (199/249). The obvious, syllogistic implication that Christ is also 'that most *proletarian* of men' soon presses upon us once we return to Rossetti. For instance, the poem 'Behold, I stand at the door and knock' (3.27–8) draws on Matthew's Gospel (25.31–46) to make the Christ at the door a man in flight from 'the Workhouse' (14).

What, though, makes the maid the key, or paradigmatic, worker-at-the-door is that she exists, as Jane Gallop writes, '[both] ... "within the family" and "outside the family"'.[18] In other words, she may be located on both sides of the door at once and thereby mimics Rossetti's Christ, who is to be found not only outside the door ('Behold, I stand') but also inside: 'Who knocketh at His door / He welcomes evermore' (2.303.15–16). (To compound the conundrum, Rossetti also recalls that 'O Christ ... Thou ... [art] Thyself the Door' (3.31.1–13).)[19] The sense of being, simultaneously, on both sides of a door is a recurring impossibility in Rosseti's poetry: 'I lock my door upon myself, / And ... wall / Self from myself' (1.226.7–9). Such a sense is, perhaps, bound to recur in the work of one who seems always to doubt her salvation and describes a Christian sensibility as the apprehension of 'the two worlds, visible and invisible, ... as double against each other'.[20] This double vision finds riddling expression in 'I Lord, thy foolish sinner' (2.199), where, as the speaker contemplates the final judgement, she expresses her fear at 'hav[ing] to stand / ... on Either Hand' (25–6) of Christ – Christ the door, of course; a prospect punningly and suggestively reproduced by the phrase: 'dare a*dore*' (6: my italics). The trick or illusion of being on both sides of the door of phonetic difference (the door that here hinges on 'a') is reworked in 'I know you not' (1856). Here the experience of being purely and simply outside – 'Who is This That shuts the door' (3.32.33) – is complicated by the oddly capitalised 'This That', which seems, semantically as well as phonetically, to look two ways at once.

To do so is, of course, an optical impossibility; as Irigaray writes, 'to see both the front and back of things *in conjunction* ... the [whole] field of optics would have to be overturned' (337/422). This does not, though, concern Irigaray, for whom the science of sight has always been limited by the idealist inclinations of Western thought, most obviously in the Simile of the Cave.[21] The intended force of the Simile, argues Irigaray, is that everything we see is, ultimately, a mere shadow or reflection of the realm of ideal forms and it is this which we should seek to apprehend; of no importance to Plato is the material support for these shadows and reflections – the wall in the cave, the pools of water above ground. However, in *Speculum*, to get to 'the back of things', to the back or material support of the image, is precisely Irigaray's concern. And this concern is, to some extent, anticipated in Rossetti's work by her fascination with both sides of the door, a door that may be read or misread as, variously, a mirror ('she smil[es] at the door' (3.136.24)), a screen ('the sun casts his latest beam' on 'the Western door' (3.182.64–5)) or simply something to be stared at: 'thirsting ... eyes / Watch the slow door' (1.46.10–11).

Of course, to undertake what Irigaray herself describes as 'a crazy journey through the looking glass' (353/442–3) and thus uncover a whole realm of 'reversal ... [and] topsy-turviness' (277/345) is, in part, to rewrite Lewis Carroll's *Through the Looking-Glass*. As Elizabeth Grosz writes, 'Alice ... acts as a metaphor for the woman who, like Irigaray ..., steps beyond her role as the reflective other for man.'[22] Much the same might be said of Rossetti's 'Alice', or at least the enigmatic figure who goes by that name in '4th May Morning' (3.340). Here the speaker sends across London a carrier pigeon, a 'well-known Eros' (as it is called), to 'give a kiss to dark-locked Alice' (6–19). Since the Alice of John Tenniel's contemporary illustrations was blonde whilst Rossetti, like the real-life Alice (Alice Liddell), was brunette, it is as if this other, dark-locked Alice has been wrested from Tenniel's male gaze[23] and made into the likeness of the poet herself. Rossetti, in other words, apears to kiss her own reflection; the 'well-known Eros' thus becomes that *un*known Eros which Irigaray calls 'the desire of/for women' (144/179), the realm of female auto-homo-eroticism. If Rossetti's Alice has, like her namesake, passed through a looking-glass, that glass is what Irigaray calls a '*hymen* of glass' (294/462: my italics).

The medium of glass

The penetration of the mirror in Rossetti's poetry is often an eroticised movement; at times, though, the penetration is unwanted, even incestuous. Incest certainly plays an important role in Irigaray's analysis of the mirror, but in her case it is 'unrecognised incest' (343/463)[24] – that general 'évolution vers le père' (43/40), or *père*-version, which is inscribed not only in Freud's account of the girl-child but in all Western representation (310/387). Time and again, argues Irigaray, our culture so privileges the paternal term – for example, Light or Spirit – as to turn the maternal, opposing term (for example, Darkness or Body) into a negative 'mirror of the same'. As Irigaray puts it, '"she" is always already … a matrix for reproducing images of him [the father]' (345/432). Indeed, so prior is this *père*-version, this predetermination to mirror the father, that the act of penetration is actually forbidden by the father: 'by freezing the path that would lead back to her he [succeeds in] … re-producing himself in that … hymen' (351/440). The father, that is, wants 'un hymen de glace' (462), a hymen of glass and ice. By contrast, Irigaray wants to see the hymenal looking-glass break and melt, to be penetrated: in 'penetration', she writes, 'one [that is, the Father] may not find oneself always and eternally the same' (351/440). In the moment of penetration, it seems, *le hymen de glace* melts to flesh and blood, thus revealing the materiality of the mirror. *Speculum* dreams the same dream as Lewis Carroll's Alice:

> 'Let's pretend the glass has got all soft like gauze, so that we can get through.' … And certainly the glass was beginning to melt away, like a bright silvery mist.[25]

Carroll's journey, however, is read very differently by Rossetti; for her, the penetration of the mirror seems to issue not so much in a mist as in blood. If Irigaray's concern is the tain of the mirror, Rossetti's concern is the bloody stain, or taint of the tain. 'What would I give … / To wash the stain … again' (1.142.7–9), cries one speaker; 'this selfsame stain … / To wash', echoes another (1.62.12–14); whilst still another talks of 'a home defiled / … [by] shameful sights and sounds that taint the air' (3.27.19–20). What makes these stains, or taints, into a kind of tain is that they reflect, albeit secretly, a father's sexual advances: 'that selfsame stain' is, of course, the 'father's blood' (1.61.12, 2). Though 'her look [may] / Show … forth her passion like a glass' (1.202.97–8), her guilt – also like a glass – shows forth *his* passion. That is certainly the case for Rossetti's latest biographer, Jan Marsh, who argues that 'Christina['s] … pervasive sense of sin[, secrecy and] … self-loathing', along with her nervous breakdown at fourteen and other circumstantial evidence, all suggest paternal incest.[26] Its shadow certainly falls across 'Repining' (1847), a poem composed just two years after Rossetti's breakdown and which describes a young woman whose longing for a lover is finally answered, but not as she expected:

> one night, when the moon-light
> Turned all the trees to silver white,
> She heard, what ne'er she heard before,
> A steady hand undo the door.
>
> (3.18.21–4)

If this last line hints at an intra-mural, familial love, the next line almost spells out the very name of such love within, or between, the words 'since' and 'set':

> the nightingale s*ince set* of sun
> Her throbbing music had not done.
>
> (25–6: my italics)

What alerts us to this *inter-dit* is the reference to the nightingale, the bird into which the mythological Philomela is transformed after being raped by her brother-in-law. What is more, having had her tongue cut out to prevent her telling anyone, Philomela wove the crime into her tapestry. 'The wind', we later read, 'it seemed to tell, not understood, / Strange secrets' (214–16); Rossetti, it seems, does likewise.

Irigaray's rhetorical question, *'who is aware that perversion has always already taken place?'* (310/387), may just have an answer: Rossetti. The 'strange secrets' that she herself tells *are*, perhaps, 'understood'; they do, perhaps, suggest that she is aware of a purely symbolic paternal incest. However, Rossetti's secrets also seem to witness to an incest, or at least an unwanted penetration, that is bloody and actual. Whether or not this was ever her own experience, her involvement in the 'reform' or prostitutes brought her into vivid and daily contact with the historical fact of female violation. By contrast, Irigaray seems to so privilege the symbolic *père*-version of patriarchy as to lose sight of the actual *père*-version of incest. Ironically, she thus repeats, in part, Freud's controversial (mis)interpretation of the female hysteric's claims of abuse – claims he attributed to an unconscious desire for her father.

In this sense Irigaray is herself *père*-verted, is herself always already turned towards the father – in her case 'the father of psychoanalysis' (40/44). And this is true even as, in her pursuit of 'the other woman', she seeks to pass beyond the looking-glass woman of Freudian psychoanalysis. Irigaray speaks not only about Freud but also both *to* him: 'your insistence on proving' (39/43), and even *as* him: 'I, Freud, am here to tell you' (15/12). Given that

Irigaray and Freud are separated by not only a looking-glass but death, *Speculum* at times becomes a kind of séance – Irigaray the medium and Freud the conjured spirit. Irigaray does nor forget the etymological link between 'speculum' and 'spectre'; not does she neglect the *glas* (the 'death-knell') in *glace* – 1974 is also the year of Derrida's *Glas.* What Irigaray calls the 'theatre of [Plato's] ... cave' (355/445) – with its illusions, curtains, props, magicians, darkness and seated audience – has, of course, all the theatre of the séance (literally, 'sitting'). As Irigaray remarks, Plato's 'cave ... breed[s] nothing but ghosts' (282/351).

The point is one that Derrida makes, albeit obliquely, in *Dissemination* [1972]. However, the ghosts that the two theorists see are not quite the same – nor, as Margaret Homans observes, are their responses.[27] For Derrida, the cave's ghosts are to be celebrated – 'the copy of a copy' is, for him, 'a phantom of no flesh ... or past'[28] and thus, reversing Plato's intention, denies any original truth. By contrast, Irigaray is highly suspicious of what she sees as the disembodied 'revenant' who, as in Plato's Simile, returns not to stay in the cave/womb but rather to call other prisoners to the light. Such ghosts are, therefore, 'washed of their uterine contaminants' (282/352) and that is precisely Irigaray's problem with Derrida's ghostly copies – his 'phantom[s] ... without [either] death, birth, or presence'.[29] Derrida is celebrating, argues Homans, a system of reproduction that invisibilises the body and, in particular, the maternal body.

When Irigaray uses the phrase 'derrière le miroir' (455/363) we may not, then, read 'Derri*da* le miroir' – a play on words that Derrida himself exploited when contributing to the 1975 series *Derrière le miroir.*[30] For all Derrida's influence on Irigaray his name is, in *Speculum*, a conspicuous absence – at best, therefore, a ghostly presence. He is, perhaps, banished for perpetuating a philosophical tradition of ghost-making that Irigaray is determined to expose as patriarchal. This is not to say that Irigaray simply abandons this tradition; rather, she hints at a female counter-tradition of ghosts: 'la terre/mère' (185/148), 'she [who] knows how to re-turn (upon herself)' (134/166) is, quite literally, a revenant. She is, however, the only ghost that Irigaray does not suspect.

This suspicion of ghosts is shared by Rossetti. It is true that her lowest room also breeds spectres – hence 'The Ghost's Petition' (1864), 'The Hour and the Ghost' (1856), 'The Poor Ghost'

(1863) and so on. Nevertheless, like Irigaray, she remains at one remove from her ghosts. 'I have', she declares, 'a friend in ghost-land' (3.268.1), as if to say she herself does not live there. Indeed, whilst both her brothers shared the contemporary enthusiasm for séances, Rossetti herself was extremely distrustful of any kind of spiritualism.[31] In this she was, as Marsh observes, at one with the women in her circle; was her distrust, then, motivated by not just piety but also an intuitive feminist-materialism? She certainly writes of 'spirits that ... our fleshly ear is [too] dull [to hear]' (3.165.12–13) – a line to be placed alongside Irigaray's remark that the specularised woman is not only a mirror that reflects but an 'eardrum [that] duplicat[es]' (141/176). Just as the mirror in question is concave and womb-like so the ear is, as Derrida notes, vagina-like.[32] If it is true that most spirits *are* 'cleansed of their uterine contaminants' it is no surprise that Rossetti's fleshly ear cannot hear them.

But there may be spirits which that ear might just hear – for Irigaray does hint at ghosts, or revenants, that do retain their debt to the body. And indeed, if it is true that Rossetti believed in Soul Sleep[33] (that the soul remains, with the body, in the grave until Judgement Day), then she subscribed to a belief which, for some Victorians, represented an almost *fleshly* theology of ghosts.[34] Ghosts, they argued, were souls who are tied to their bodies. Something of this materialism is hinted at in the poem that opens 'I seek among the living & I seek / Among the dead for some to love' (3.320); in echoing the angel's words to the women who came to Christ's empty tomb ('"Why seek ye the living among the dead?"' (Luke 24.5)), the poem conjures up the most famous cave-bred revenant of all – he who, with his wounds still visible, was *not* 'purged of ... [his] associations with ... the "body"' (282/352). That body is maternal in that Christ's wounds encode, for Rossetti, a kind of female opening, or womb: 'Open Thy bleeding Side and let me in' (3.246.12). The Christ revenant is '*un*washed of its uterine contaminants'. So too is the revenant subject of 'A Chilly Night' (3.247), a poem written just a year later in 1856; this time, indeed, it is 'my Mother's ghost' (3) – even so, the female body and, in particular, the womb (the place of becoming flesh) is once again encoded, here as the mother's 'mouth' and the daughter's 'flesh ... on ... bones':

She opened her mouth and spoke
...
While my flesh crept on my bones.

(27–9)

In writing of 'my Mother's ghost' almost thirty years before her mother's actual death, Rossetti renders her mother at once, as it were, both living and dead. The poem's ghostly mother is, in other words, a revenant who not only returns to her daughter but also, like Irigaray's *terre/mère*, 're-turn[s] (upon herself)'. In this she anticipates that ghost who, in a poem composed two years later, in 1858, returns to her own house: 'When I was dead, my spirit turned / To seek [my] ... familiar room' (1–29); returning to a house now occupied by others, this ghost is, in a sense, both host and guest. To put it another way, the 'I' here plays both medium and ghost, and that is precisely what Rossetti does whenever she gives a voice to her own dead self. This she does several times in *Goblin Market and Other Poems* (1862): witness 'Remember', 'After Death', 'Song' and 'Dead before Death'. The same spiritualist conceit is reworked, through the medium of glass, in 'Mirrors of Life and Death' (2.75). The poem combines looking in the mirror and talking with the dead – the ghost, once again, is Rossetti herself, her own reflection: 'I see / Darkly as in a glass / ... shadows pass, / And talk with me' (1–5).

Giving a voice to the dead became almost a reality for Rossetti in the diary she kept on her mother's behalf during her last, infirm years. Rossetti sustained this ventriloquy, as Alison Chapman has pointed out, even to the point of death:

> the night over, no rally: unconsciousness at last ... Mr Nash prayed beside my bed-side, but I knew it not(?)[35]

Here Rossetti, we might say, *is* the ghost whom she sought thirty years before in 'A Chilly Night' – her 'mother's ghost.' By contrast, though *Speculum* does hint at a maternal revenant, that '*terre/mère*' who returns to herself, Irigaray appears doomed to be the *father's* ghost: 'I, Freud'.

Optics

> taking the eye of a man recently dead ... a piece of white paper must be placed at the back of the eye to form a screen

for the reflection of objects outside.

(Descartes, *Dioptrics*)[36]

Rossetti's daughterly concern with the 'I' of a woman recently dead is paralleled by Irigaray's philosophical concern with Descartes's 'eye of a man recently dead'. Indeed, the whole point of Irigaray's critique of Descartes is that his analysis of the seeing eye, as a screen or mirror, betrays the truth about the thinking 'I', Descartes's *cogito ergo sum.* This thinking subject, argues Irigaray, is just like sight in that it too is a trick performed by a mirror; Descartes, however, insists that the 'I' simply thinks himself into being. As Irigrary herself puts it, 'the notion that, like a mirror, he might reflect and be reflected ... is in some sense denied' (149/186).

Just as Descartes penetrates the eye of a man recently dead so, in *Speculum,* Irigaray penetrates both the 'eye' and the 'I' of the philosopher who, it is implied, is always already dead (see 350/438). Irigaray thus discovers not only the (m)other in whom the thinking, philosophical 'I' sees himself reflected (183/229) but also the 'cavelike [womb-like] socket' (312/389) at the 'back of th[e] ... eye' (336/421). Through the looking-glass of the philosopher's eye/I is the female body. And the way through is provided by an opening which Irigaray compares to the dark mirror at the centre of the eye, the pupil (328/410). By using, though, the Greek word for 'pupil', namely *kore,* Irigaray invokes, as Philippa Berry points out, 'the myth of the ... goddess Kore, the maiden (otherwise known as Persephone) whose identity was mysteriously divided between the roles of daughter (to the earth goddess Demeter) and bride (to Hades or Death)'.[37] If the way through the I/eye is the way of not just *kore* but Kore then it is a way marked by Hades, by the underworld of death.

This much Rossetti knows well; her writing from the perspective of the dead reads just like an exploration of the other side of the 'I'. Irigaray also, it seems, knows how death and, in particular, the death drive divides and thus opens up the 'I': she writes of 'the death drives that the eye (of) consciousness refuses to recognise' (55/63).

Such refusal is, and is not, to be found in 'Death' (1848), a poem about a mother recently buried which ends with:

> It is not death ye see ...
> It is the second birth

but opens with:

> 'The grave-worm revels now'
> ... on ... eyes so dead.
>
> (3.156–7)

The poem ends, we might say, with 'the [philosopher's] eye [that] will not suffer the introduction of dead flesh' (303/378) but begins with a mother's eye that *is* dead flesh. At one moment the poem fixes us with the looking-glass eye of philosophy – the 'ye' of the philosophical 'ye see' reflecting, like a pupil, the e*ye* of the reader; at another moment, the poem glimpses the fleshly eyeball behind that looking-glass.

How far Rossetti is actually conscious of such Irigarayan distinctions is difficult to determine. There is, though, no doubting their presence in her writing – here, for Irigaray's 'optics of Truth' (362/454), we may read Rossetti's 'supernaturalized' eyes;[38] likewise, for Irigaray's 'bodily vision' (312/389), we may read Rossetti's 'the vulgar optic' (3.223.4). These distinctions certainly played a prominent part in Victorian aesthetics – witness: Ruskin's principle of the non-analytical 'innocent eye'; Dickens's satirical reference, in *Hard Times*, to Mr Sleary's glass eye as the 'fixed eye of Philosophy'; and the period's scientific fascination with the physiology of the eye.[39] If, though, the Victorians in general had reason to consider the fleshy materiality of the eye, Rossetti in particular had reason to do so – in 1870 she contracted Graves' disease, a thyroid disorder which left her with bulging eyes.

Given the name of the disease, Rossetti's relationship to the eye is marked by death in much the same punning way as is Irigaray's: for 'Graves', that is, read 'Kore' – the bride of Hades. But what distinguishes the two is that whilst the *kore* represents for Irigaray a dark opening to the concave back of the eye, the disease exaggerates the eye's convex surface. And when Rossetti considers the eye she does seem to see a mirror rather than an opening. In '"Look on this picture and on this"' (3.254) her male speaker declares of one woman, 'oh those hazel eyes a devil is dancing in' (5), and to another (called Eva) he remarks, 'a pitiless fiend is in your eyes' (64); he is, we infer, in both cases seeing his own, devilish reflection. The suggestion that we are in Eden, with the devil being reflected in the eye of not Eva but Eve, is punningly replayed in 'Later Life' (1881) – here we read that 'Eve had for *pupil* the enquiring snake' (2.144.3: my italics). For Rossetti, it seems, the pupil is a spiritual looking-glass that holds up to the beholder the truth about herself. Rossetti's subtext is, of course, Christ's rhetorical question: 'And why beholdest thou the mote that is in thy brother's eye, but considereth not the beam that is in thine own eye?' (Matthew 7.3). For Christ the dark spot in the other's eye is only ever a mirror and one in which I *should* recognise myself and my own blindness. At work, then, in Rossetti's dissection of the pupil is a New Testament version of the specular logic that Irigaray condemns; for Rossetti there is an ethical mirror in the eye that ought never to be finally penetrated.

Looking-glass theology

Though Rossetti's theology may, in this case, forbid any passage through the looking-glass, in other ways theology takes her straight into that 'state of reversal' which specularisation entails but always conceals. For instance, Christ's promise of a time when the 'first shall be last and the last shall be first' (Matthew 19.30) parallels the double meaning of *hystera* as both 'womb' *and* 'last'. As Homans observes, 'the men [in the cave] ... mistake ... first for last, origin for end'.[40] Again, Irigaray's description of the cave as a place in which 'everything has been set upside down' (363) mirrors what was said of the early Christians: 'these that have turned the world upside down are come hither also' (Acts 17.6). An inverted world is also part of the doctrine of Judgement Day; for then it is that 'all deep secrets shall be shown, / And many last be first' (1.207.278–9). If, as Irigaray writes, 'the cave .. will ... set you walking on your hands' (244/302), so will Judgement Day; or at least so it seems in 'I Lord' (2.199), where Christ's injunction that Rossetti 'stand upon [her] feet' is succeeded by a vision of that time 'When I / Shall die and have to stand / Helpless on Either Hand' (24–6). Tricking us into envisaging a handstand, Rossetti smuggles an inverted body into heaven; she who elsewhere aspires to be 'His likeness' (2.238.19) here presents God with a carnivalised reflection of himself. 'What ... confusion would result', writes Irigaray, 'if God were to perceive himself ... the wrong way up, thus losing an immutable awareness of ... right and left' (331/413–14). That is, though, precisely what we suspect may happen, in so far as we misread Rossetti as 'stand[ing] ... on Either Hand' *of God* – on both sides of him, that is. 'What if', asks Irigaray, 'God is unaware of all that [his] specula(riza)tion owes to inversion?'; in Rossetti's verse, it seems, he *is* aware.

'It must ... not be known,' continues Irigaray, 'how much the procreation of the "son", of the logos ... owes to inversion' (310/387). However, something of this debt does seem to be known in 'Herself a rose' (2.238), which, in describing the Virgin Mary as 'Christ's mirror she of grace and truth' (16), not only reveals the maternal mirror by which the son is reproduced but hints, through the inverted syntax, at something of the inversions entailed. As Lewis Carroll's Alice remarks, in '"Looking-glass House ... words go the wrong way"'.[41] Indeed, in the case of 'Christ's mirror' it is also sexual relations that go the wrong way, since the poem ends with Christ addressing Mary as not just 'Mother' but also 'Spouse'. As Irigaray declares, 'Once [God is] caught in the becoming of a looking-glass game, his Being will suffer innumerable, unpredictable transformations' (331/414). These transformations, however, *are* predicted by Rossetti's Anglo-Catholicism, according to which Mary is not just Christ's mother but also, as the Queen of Heaven, his bride. Irigaray errs, then, in so far as she implies that the Incarnation necessarily elides the role of the maternal mirror and its inversions in the reproduction of Being. To be sure, what Irigaray calls 'Being without ... copulation' (184/230) may well be implied by the Virgin Birth, but in Rossetti's poem Christ only addresses Mary as mother after he has addressed her as spouse – some kind of copulation *is* being suggested. Christ thus enters into a relationship to 'his [own] likeness' which exceeds the sterile specularity that, according to Irigaray, is the fate of all subjects, each of whom 'covet[s] above all ... to be united with ... [their own] *image* ... [only to find that] the glass ... separates [them]' (189–90/236). Since Christ's mirror-spouse becomes a mother, the glass, it seems, does not separate them – it *is* penetrated.

The sexual scene within the looking-glass world of Rossetti's theology is not simply a marital, parental coupling. As with Christ and his mother–spouse, Rossetti's primal scene is always already complicated by the strange inversions of the Holy Family; and these inversions are, in turn, never quite free from what Irigaray sees as the incestual *père*-versions of Western thought. That is, in part, the coded message of '"I have a message unto thee"' (1855); here the ventriloquised voice of the flowers who 'tell of God's unimagined love' not only mirrors the imaginable love of parents overseen but also gives that scene an unimaginable, incestual twist:

> 'Better you had not seen us
> But shared the blind man's night,
> Better you had not scented
> Our incense [incest?] of delight.'
>
> (3.240.99–102)

God's unimagined love is again reflected in the topsy-turvy world of sexual inversion in the, appropriately *un*published, poem 'Young Death' (1865). It concerns a young woman's ascent to heaven; however, described as both 'God's daughter' and 'Christ's bride', the young woman is at the centre of a strangely eroticised scene in which she 'pleasure[s]' her father and marries her brother:

> Life not lost but treasured,
> God Almighty pleasured,
> God's daughter fetched and carried,
> Christ's bride betrothed and married.
> ...
> She shall sit down to supper,
> New bathed from head to feet.
>
> (3.296.18–24)

Eroticised though she is, the young woman remains dead. The looking-glass world of Rossetti's theologised sexual scene is here marked not only by *père*-version but by the body of a woman recently dead. But then if, as Elisabeth Bronfen has argued, Western art characteristically aestheticises the female corpse,[42] a woman is bound to see herself represented as dead – death *is* her mirror. As Rossetti writes in 'Passing and Glassing' (2.117), 'All things that pass / Are woman's looking-glass' (1–2). This observation is reworked in Rossetti's short story 'Commonplace', whose heroine is relieved, upon reaching 30, to find 'her mirror bore witness to no glaring accession of age having come upon her in a single night'.[43] Rossetti here begs, albeit very simply, the question of the mirror's relationship to time, and in so doing anticipates Irigaray's abstruse insistence that we should not overlook the 'time [albeit 'almost nonexistent'] it takes for ... reflection' (288/359) – the time, presumably, it takes for light to travel to and from the mirror. For Irigaray, of course, mirror-time or the 'time of (re)production' (356/446) is related to the time of the womb – she writes of 'the mother's function ... as [the] space-time of (re)production'. By contrast, Rossetti – for whom passing is glassing – sees the time of the mirror as more nearly the time of dying. According to Rosenblum, the many dead women of Rossetti's poems are always, in the Pre-Raphaelite mode, spectacles – like Snow White they occupy, writes Rosenblum, 'a glass coffin'.[44] But then so did many middle-class Victorian women who, as luxury objects of consumption, were often set behind the metaphorical glass coffin of the shop window. The glass, in fact, became literal within that most famous of Victorian glass enclosures, the 1851 Great Exhibition – here, as Andrew Miller writes, 'woman ... oscillate from one side of the display glass to the other, from [being ideal viewers to] being objects viewed'.[45]

A Victorian woman's life, or rather death, on the other side of glass was not necessarily the wonderland encountered by Alice. Carroll's looking-glass world is, in fact, the specific target of Rossetti's prose story *Speaking Likenesses* (1874); and, as U. C. Knoepflmacher observes, its most 'anti-Carrollian' moment[46] is that in which the young Flora finds herself shut in a room which is

> lined throughout with looking-glasses [producing] not merely ... reflections, but reflections of reflections, and reflections of reflections and reflections.[47]

Here the time of the mirror is not just that of death but, more specifically, that of infinity. The same might be said of 'A Royal Princess' (1851), where 'All my walls are lost in mirrors' (1.149.10), or, again, of Rossetti's poem on the death of her nephew, 'Michael F. M. Rossetti' (1883), to whom, we read, 'Eternity holds up her lookingglass' (3.48.9). At such moments Rossetti's looking-glass coffin comes under the sign of philosophy for, like Irigaray's Plato, that coffin attempts 'to push ... the projection ... back into infinity. Into the eternal elsewhere ... [where] the screen ... is hidden away' (356/446).

According to Irigaray, what makes the mirror seem to disappear into infinity is philosophy's dream of absolute Being, an essence which seeks to conceal its dependence on reproduction, or reflection. And there is no doubt that Rossetti's poetry is, in part, driven by the pretensions of being. Witness the insistent 'be' not only of 'I dreamed that love would be and be and be' (3.236.3) but also of 'Be Best Beloved' (3.278.8); witness too 'I am even I' (2.123.14) and, indeed, 'I who am myself cannot but be myself.'[48] This last assertion is part of a commentary upon the divine 'I AM THAT I AM' (Exodus 3.14), and it is right to interpret Rossetti's confidence in being as confidence of *divine* being. This confidence is, in turn, one that Irigaray would relate to what she calls the '*unity, totality,* [*and*] *entity of one … that abstains from any conjunction whatever*' (312/390) – such being is, necessarily, 'Being without … copulation'. So far, so far Rossetti, whose sense of being – 'I who am myself' – does indeed appear related to being single, to being celibate. However, equally important in this connection is – to quote 'My Dream' – 'being dead' (1.39.32). For instance, in 'After Death' (1849) the dead speaker foregrounds the being of being dead to the extent of ending the penultimate line with 'and very sweet it is'. Again, in 'Ellen Middleton' (1848) the female subject, this time 'a lone wife', asks: '– is this death?' (3.158.12); in so doing she comes close to challenging Irigaray's suggestion that 'the body of the mother' 'eludes the question, "what is?"' (161/201). The first question of ontology is, for Rossetti, posed by the last experience – one's own death; it is as if in this experience the fact of being is, somehow, most insistent. Indeed, in 'The Thread of Life' 'to be' is not 'to have', nor even 'to do', but rather 'to *have* been':

> I am not what I have nor what I do;
> But what I was I am …
>
> (2.123.13–14)

The same conceit is at work in Irigaray's reference to 'the ex-sistence of the "subject"' (133/165); however, whilst Irigaray thus seeks to show how death undermines the pretensions of being, for Rossetti death is the mirror in which being sees itself. After all, if non-being is the inversion of being then being dead is (in a sense) being-in-the-mirror – the point at which being is both reproduced and inverted. Note how, in that meditation on death, 'Passing and Glassing' (2.117), being is not only doubled but made, as it were, to go backwards – the poem's very last two words are 'be was': 'that which shall be was'. Here Rossetti comes close to glossing Irigaray's passing and wholly unexplained reference to 'that speculum (of) death' (356/446).

Rossetti comes even closer through the familiar metaphor of 'the bitter cup of death' (1.186.66); a cup that is glazed and, with a concave base, is like a speculum in that it not only reflects and inverts but also, of course, dilates lips (144/180). Rossetti has a sustained interest in the cup and thus develops, in effect, an *un*developed theme in *Speculum*, where the cup appears but only to disappear. Witness, for instance, Irigaray's passing assertion that 'the burning glass enflames all that falls into its chalice' (144/180);[49] or again, her cryptic declaration that 'bloody calvary ... or an in(de)finite liquid ... opens the cup of its chalice even in Absolute Mind' (222/275–6). Irigaray alludes, in part, to the eucharistic chalice, that cup of Christ's infinite blood; his chalice thus becomes, for her, a speculum. Irigaray takes the cup from Christ's lips to dilate her own. It is a sleight-of-hand that is at once both demystifying and feminist – a strategy we might expect of Irigaray but not, necessarily, of Rossetti. Consider, though, the very end of Rossetti's 'A Better Resurrection' (1857); here the speaker aspires to become 'A royal cup for Him my King', crying 'O Jesus, drink of me' (1.68.23–4). In so doing she not only mirrors back to Christ his own eucharistic injunction (to drink of *him*) but also thereby addresses him as a mother (a breast-feeding mother); she becomes, for him, a cup that is also a maternal mirror. Though the cup is held up to *his* lips we are more aware of *her* body, and it is in this sense that the cup passes from him to her.

Another cup of Christ's that passes into Rossetti's hands is the purely metaphorical cup of death, or suffering, of which Christ speaks in Gesthemane. 'Let this cup pass from me', he prays (Matthew 26.39), and so it does in that Rossetti and her speakers frequently seek to drink from it: 'who next shall drink the trembling cup...?' (1.216.66–8). The answer, it seems, are the martyrs who long that 'we may drink of Jesus' cup' (1.184.42).

According to Irigaray, because women are the living reminders of birth and, therefore, death they become the representative representation of death; for the same reason, she argues, 'women [have] no possible symbol ... of their *own* death drives'.[50] Gesthemane, however, seems to offer Rossetti, and her martyrs, just such a symbol; and with it she is able to reimagine even the political in terms of the feminine. Or at least that is the case in 'The German–French Campaign. 1870–1871', where the act of drinking the cup of death is the act of a female polis: 'Who next', we read, 'shall drink the trembling cup … / After [Sister] France?' (1.214.66–8).

Turning

Female suicide as an act of transgression or empowerment marks a number of Rossetti's poems – most obviously 'A Study. (A Soul.)' (1854), which invokes the figure of the 'indomitable' Cleopatra. The unnamed 'she' of the poem 'stands', we read, 'like Cleopatra … when she felt the aspic writhing in her hand' (3.226.2–4). Four times we read 'She stands' – she stands, as it were, on the edge, and in doing so stands *for* another classical model of female suicide – namely, Sappho. Rossetti's interest in Sappho is most conspicuous in the poem 'What Sappho would have said had her leap cured instead of killing her' (1848).

Rossetti, who usually stood when writing[51] – writing or even writ*h*ing, we might say, with the aspic of a pen in her hand – frequently imagines *herself* as standing on the edge. This is, of course, a very different Rossetti from the one who sits in the lowest room. In one poem she chooses 'to stand upon the brink / Of the deep grave' (3.299.5–6); in another she asserts 'it is mere / Madness to stand for ever on the brink' (3.319.6–7). Nevertheless, that is precisely how Rossetti seems to see herself in 'Autumn' (1858), where she who dwells alone is said to '"grieve … / Uplifted, like a beacon, on her tower"' (1.145.53–4). The tower or the brink means, for Rossetti, both terror and risk: the terror of 'Towering above her sex with horrid height' (3.300.8) and the risk of falling – in 'Goblin Market' (1859) Laura, struck by hysteria, is 'cast down headlong' (1.24.520). Rossetti, however, does not abandon the tower, nor the dream of overlooking the world, precisely *because* this dream sets her 'above her sex'; through it she acquires that phallic value of verticality which, in Western culture, so often characterises the privileged position of the subject.

It is, though, a position whose verticality Rossetti, like Irigaray, is prepared to parody:

> Like the watchtower of a town
> Which an earthquake shatters down,
> Like a lightning-stricken mast,
> Like an uprooted tree,

Like a foam-topped waterspout
Cast headlong in the sea,
She fell at last.

(1.24.514.–21)

With the long deferral of the main clause ('She fell'), Rossetti's syntax parodies Laura's experience – the end of the sentence falling from the dizzy, conceptual height of grand simile, or sameness ('Like ... Like ... Like ... Like'). It is as if, like prisoners escaping Plato's cave, we are – as Irigaray puts it – 'swinging from the chandelier-Idea' (271/337). For Irigaray, the Platonic ascent from shadow to light 'implies a jump ... which cannot be [effected] without ... [the] risk [that] one may lose ... one's balance' (273/340). Though Irigaray repeatedly refuses this jump, *Speculum* remains fascinated with the experience of vertigo. Just as Irigaray 'flirts with the philosophers'[52] so her dizzying syntax and dazzling logic flirts with the danger of losing balance; 'swinging from the chandelier-Idea' is, presumably, intoxicating – certainly more addictive than Irigaray admits. Indeed, there is a sense in which the play of her own language does commit her to the (il)logic of the Platonic jump. Though she dismisses the philosopher's claim that, in the ascent from shadow, 'there [always] remains a *leap* that one will not ...make in one's lifetime' (341/427), Irigaray twice foregrounds, in relation to 'woman', the formulation *'pas encore'* (207/166, 287/232) – not only 'not yet' but also, punningly, 'step again', one more step. The step over the brink?

Or again, is it more nearly that 'certain step of the dance' of which Derrida writes, just two years before, at the end of 'Différance'?[53] There is, certainly, a dance as well as a step encoded in *Speculum* – witness the 'pirouette(s)' (238/295), the 'dance of difference' (247/306) and *'les chassés-croisés'* (a dance step) (374/300). But, for Irigaray, dance is not simply the name of affirmation; hers is the dance of Plato's prisoner – a dance, for the most part, choreographed by the philosopher and only in part an act of resistance. Like the 'dancing ... philosophic bear' of which Rossetti writes (2.168.1, 11), Plato's prisoner dances to his master's tune. Note that the prisoner's turn from wall to sun is an *'authoriz[ed] ...* pirouette' (261/324), authorised by Plato. Note too that the ascent from the cave entails a series of *chassés-croisés*, or substitutions (of, say, shadow for thing), 'which will not be noticed' (300/374).[54]

Within philosophy's 'theater of the identical' (138/171) 'the dance of difference' will be choreographed to the point of invisibility. It is true that, for Plato's prisoner, the bewildering effect of turning towards a dazzling light means that 'ne sait-il plus tres bien sur quel pied danser' (343/276); the philosopher, however, refuses to countenance this dance of bewilderment. Interestingly, Gillian Gill's translation almost repeats that blindness by omitting the dance trope.[55]

Irigaray herself is not so blind. For, like Derrida, she seems to see in the dance within philosophy the potential to exceed the logic of the same; she writes, that is, of a 'dream choreography', one which 'recast[s] the roles that history has laid down for "subject" and "object"' (138/171). She writes too of 'ce choréisme', a dance-ism or, as Gill translates, a 'distortion' in which 'the danger would … be of losing one's bearings' (340/425). This dance-ism is the dance of the prisoner who does not know which way to turn – having turned towards the sun he then makes as if to turn back. This is precisely the dilemma that besets Rossetti, who resists the myth of the cave but does so, like Irigaray, from within – from within her lowest room. Rossetti certainly read and reread Plato but her influential brother, Dante Gabriel, also read Walter Pater and was much swayed by his critique of Plato's insistence on 'the One'.[56] Christina, more like Pater, is in *two* minds: whilst one poem begins 'Press onward … / Up out of shadows into very light' (3.55.1, 10), in another 'her face', we read, 'is steadfast toward the shadowy land' (3.226.5). Again, though Rossetti declares that 'Man yearneth (as the heliotrope / For ever seeks the sun)' (3.279.3–4), and was herself declared to be a 'Heliotrope',[57] there is still at times a refusal to leave the cave for the sun:

> I half turn to go yet turning stay.
>
> (1.37.4)

If Rossetti both turns and yet does not turn to the sun then she not only challenges philosophy's 'solar tropism' (261/324) (its privileging of the metaphor of light) but also disputes the trajectory of all metaphors. For turning is the trope for trope (*tropos* meaning 'turn'); in both turning and yet not turning Rossetti turns against tropism itself. And tropism, according to Irigaray, is one of philosophy's most cherished dreams – she refers to it as the 'dream of … analogy [and] … comparison' (27/27), that disembodying dream by which, in Plato's Simile, 'the *hystera* is made [mere] metaphor' (247/306).

The dance of one who will never quite turn round, whether performed by Rossetti or by Plato's prisoner, is – for Irigaray – a dance against philosophy. Of course, if the bewildered pirouetting of Plato's prisoner is a trope for Irigaray's critique of tropism then *Speculum* becomes paradoxical. It demonstrates what Paul de Man describes as the inevitability of 'reentering a system of tropes at the very moment we claim to escape from it'.[58] 'We all', observes the narrator of *Middlemarch* (1871–72), 'get our thoughts entangled in metaphors'[59] – even, as here, when one attempts to escape them. This double bind is particularly at work in the Platonic injunction 'Don't turn back!' – an injunction that Irigaray mimics throughout *Speculum*: 'One must walk ... toward the "sun"'; 'it [is] imperative that there be no going back' (314/392). To turn back to the wall may well be to escape the turn to the sun that is, within philosophy, the characteristic movement of metaphor; however, it is also to *become* a metaphor for anyone who has ever been told *not to turn back*. That this includes such figures as Orpheus, Lot's wife, and the disciple whom Christ enjoins to turn his hand to the plough only becomes obvious when we too turn back – back to the nineteenth century, to Rossetti's poetry. For whilst these three figures have no discernible place in *Speculum*, they are Rossetti's familiars: 'I ... / Would ... not / ... with Lot's wife cast back a faithless look', claims one lover (2.89.4); 'once we looked back together / With our hands upon the plough' (3.220.101–2), confesses another. By contrast, Irigaray looks back alone, seemingly unaware of those who, metaphorically, turn with her. But then Irigaray writes not verse but prose, and whilst 'prose' derives from the Latin word *prosa*, meaning 'straightforward', 'verse' derives from *versus*, originally meaning 'the turn of the plough' and only latterly naming the turn of the line of a poem. In this sense Rossetti's writing is forever turning back on itself to an extent that Irigaray's can never do, for all her striving after a convoluted and 'double syntax'. Rossetti's writing is also, and for the same reason, forever turning back to the earth to an extent that Irigaray's, again, can never do – notwithstanding her scorn for those who 'turn ... the earth over rather than turn ... back to it' (352/441).

To 'look back ... with our hands on the plough' is, of course, to risk departing from the straightforward and, thus, to 'Look ... back without control' (3.267.5) – without control of not only the plough but also, perhaps, one's mind. For 'delirium' comes from *delirare*, literally 'to depart from the ridge between furrows'. Having begun 'my walk of life', writes Rossetti, 'I [soon] grew half delirious' (3.343.1).

If to depart, or step out of line, is to transgress then to look back, not to look where you are going, is both to lose control and to loosen it. Witness Lot's wife, who, in looking back to Sodom and Gomorrah, violates an angel's injunction (Genesis 19.17, 26). Though Rossetti's 'Monna Innominata' claims not to look back with Lot's wife, her fateful turning *is* inscribed in '"Faint yet Pursuing"' (3.54). Here the escape from the burning cities of Sodom and Gomorrah is faintly replayed in the injunction to 'press onward … press upward' and the reference to 'fire with mounting fire' (1–5); thus, the rather strange declaration that

> Man's lot of death has turned to life his lot
>
> (13)

entails, as a kind of underthought, the assertion:

> … has turned to *salt* the *wife of* Lot.

In 'Only Believe' (1858) Rossetti herself seems to glance back to Sodom, or at least to the biblical formulation 'men [lying] with men' (Romans 1.26) – a formulation encoded in the poem's cryptic phrase: 'man with man, lie with lie' (3.275.48). This she reworks in another poem of 1858, as 'Man with man, truth with lie' (2.294.14).

Mindful as she is of Lot's wife, Rossetti's account of looking back possesses a transgressive force that Irigaray's never has; Rossetti's turning around entails a revolution in precisely the political sense that Irigaray's turning does not. Rossetti not only turns away from the 'dream of analogy and sameness' but enters the nightmare of history. For instance, although the Risorgimento (the revolutionary movement for unification in Rossetti's native Italy) becomes, at times, an analogue for the rise of women[60] there is still a sense of historical event. Hence 'The Massacre of Perugia' (1859), written in response to the brutal suppression of the citizens of Perugia by Papal States troops. By contrast, though *Speculum* does include references to 'revolution' (for example, 142/176) the word has little to do with history. Irigaray employs Marxist terms not to refer to the condition of the working-classes under the historical fact of capitalism but, rather, to describe women under the discursive system of psychoanalysis. For example, with a glance at the alienation of labour, she writes that 'woman … in the work of engendering the child … becomes the anonymous worker, the machine in the service of a master-proprietor who will put his trademark upon the finished product' (23/21). Though Irigaray claims that she is simply exploring the *'economic infrastructure [which] governs Freud's conception of the role of women'* (121/150) there is a sense in which the role of women governs Irigaray's conception of economics. As she herself observes, in *Speculum* it is 'the sense of history [which] … undergo[es] … revolution' (142/176) – it revolves, or turns into a trope. Irigaray complains that, in Plato, 'hystera is made metaphor', but in *Speculum* history is made metaphor.

This is most obvious in the case of revolution, which, in *Speculum*, is never purely and simply a historical category – we are never allowed to forget the revolution of the earth. What so interests Irigaray is that, in the sixteenth century, this latter revolution was itself subjected to revolution, the Copernican revolution – the discovery that the planetary system centred not on the earth but on the sun. Irigaray's ambition is to disrupt male philosophy's appropriation of heliocentric cosmology to justify a logocentric account of truth; in this account 'the [male] subject … becomes the "sun" … around [which] … things turn' (133–4/165–6) – 'the … fixed, frozen … keystone [sun]' of Western photology (267/332). Irigaray dreams a quite different cosmology, asking how philosophy might be refashioned 'if the earth … turned upon herself' (133/165). Though Irigaray is never explicit, it is as if she dreams of a pre-Copernican cosmology. This is particularly true of the chapter on *la mystérique* in which, as Berry argues, 'Irigaray [generally] … evokes … the time of the late middle ages.'[61]

This same time is also a conspicuous feature of Rossetti's work, heavily influenced as it is by the Pre-Raphaelites. Their nostalgia for the time before Raphael (1483–1520) may, indeed, be read as an unacknowledged nostalgia for the time before Copernicus (1473–1543), a time before the sun became, as it were, fixed, frozen and central. The Pre-Raphaelite rejection of the classical rules of art certainly entailed a marked de-centring of light: 'Why should the highest light be always on the principal figure?', asks Holman

Hunt; whilst Ford Madox Brown's avowed intent is 'to insure the peculiar look of *light all round*'.[62]

For all her photocentrism, Rossetti goes even further than the Pre-Raphaelites – at times not only drawing attention away from the sun but also positively turning towards the earth. It is not, she writes, the 'motion of the sun [that is] … in question, but only the revolution of the earth'.[63] 'Should I', she asks, 'turn with yearning eyes, / Turn earthwards?' (1.63.75–6); 'Earth', she declares, 'beneath her crust … / Nurses fire unfelt, unseen' (2.212.1–3). In turning to the earth that does itself turn and, moreover, turns out to *be* herself – Rossetti also nurses unseen fire – it is as if the earth has indeed, as Irigaray dreams, somehow 'turned upon herself'. What is more, in turning to the inner fire of the earth, Rossetti anticipates someting of the internalised fire of Irigaray's *miroir ardent*, or burning glass – the fire produced by a calculated turning, or angling, of a concave mirror. Irigaray quotes Ruysbroeck the Admirable:

> Take a concave mirror and put it next to a dry and inflammable material; then expose the mirror to the rays of the sun; the dry material will catch fire and burn because of the heat of the sun and the concavity of the mirror.
>
> (191/238)

Fire

Speculum is, as Berry observes, a '"fire book"'; 'Irigaray['s] … objective', continues Berry, 'is … to set philosophical speculation figuratively on fire',[64] 'to expose it to the very fires of the desire of/for woman' (144/179) that philosophy both entails and yet denies. Philosophy, for Irigaray, is a trick performed not just by mirrors but by fire. She refers us, once again, to Plato's cave:

> there where we expect to find the … matrix of a logos immutable in the certainty of its own light, fires and mirrors are beginning to radiate, sapping the evidence of reason at its base!
>
> (144/179)

Though philosophers play with fire they will not admit to it: 'Reason', declares Irigaray, 'is the result of systems of mirrors that ensure a steady illumination … but one without *heat* … [It] has banished not only the darkness of night but also the fires of noon'

(148/184). The sun, in truth, is too hot for philosophy to handle – in particular, it is too hot for any city or state, such as Plato's Republic, that is founded upon philosophy:

> the sun ... joins together with a burning glass ... and sets the fleet of a whole nation aflame, and must therefore topple from its place as model by which to establish the eternal laws of the City.
> (148/184–5)

Irigaray here celebrates, it seems, the sun's capacity to burn, to mean something radically different from pure, disembodied reason. This way, however, danger lies. For though Plato's city may be undone by the sun becoming fire, by reason becoming desire or spirit, Hitler's city – the Nazi polis – positively embraced fire and spirit. In the Holocaust (literally, 'total burning') not just a fleet but a whole nation was set aflame, the nation of Israel. As Berry observes, 'the fieriness of Irigaray's revisioning of Plato's cave ... [draws on] Heidegger's [concern with] ... the fire of *Geist*, or spirit, [which] ... often [appears] in contexts where the political results of Nazism – in the fires of the Holocaust – are tragically prefigured'.[65] Irigaray does, admittedly, hint at these fires: 'one will rightly suspect', she writes, 'any perspective ... that ... claims ... to have rightfully taken over ... th[e] concave mirror's incandescent hearth' (144/179). Nevertheless, as Berry argues, Irigaray never explicitly addresses 'the dilemna she has inherited from Heidegger'.[66]

But then, as a postmodern believer, or *mystérique*, Irigaray's account of fire has no hell, and what was the Holocaust if not hell? By contrast, as a Victorian believer and the daughter of a Dante scholar, Rossetti's poetics of fire always entails hell as a terrible reality. The book that Rossetti's father wrote on Platonic love, all copies of which were burnt, may have quite literally set philosophy on fire; however, this was not the Heideggerian fire of spirit but rather the biblical fire of hell – Rossetti's mother burnt the book for fear it would endanger her immortal soul.[67] Rossetti's Irigarayan question, 'When will fire break up her screen?' (2.212.8), is, significantly, asked in 'Advent', a poem about the fires of judgement. Likewise, Rossetti's Irigarayan yoking of 'glass and fire' takes place within that 'sea of glass and fire' (1.62.13) which, in Revelation (20.10), neighbours 'the lake of [hell-]fire'. The total burning that was the Holocaust is here dimly foreshadowed by the hellish aspect of Rossetti's own *miroir ardent*. This same total burning is more obviously spelt out in 'An "Immurata" Sister', where she cries:

> Kindle, flash, my soul …
> Thou whole burnt-offering!
>
> (2.121.26–7)

Here, through the (il)logic of whole self-sacrifice, Rossetti's theology of fire entails her own total negation. It is not, though, the 'negative … totality' of which Irigaray writes (215/268) in connection with the polis, or state. Indeed, Rossetti's poem is about defying or cheating the totality of the state, for Rossetti invokes that mythological *immurata* sister, Antigone – the very next poem in *A Pageant and Other Poems* (1881) begins 'My brother's blood … doth cry' (2.121). And, as Irigaray reminds us, it is Antigone who, when condemned to be immured alive in a tomb, commits suicide, thus escaping death at the hands of the state. What makes this myth so important is that, according to Irigaray, all women are, in a sense, condemned to death-by-the-state, or at least by the Platonic-cum-Hegelian principle of totality which informs the state:

> The/a woman … is … torn apart, drawn and quartered in the service of … unit(y) …
>
> (240/298)

It may well be that Rossetti's *immurata* sister, as a kind of Antigone, in some sense escapes this death by totality. However, unlike Irigaray, Rossetti does not see such death – death by the state's negative totality – as totally negative. (To do so would, of course, be merely to repeat that totality.) Instead, for Rossetti, death-by-the-state may always be redeemed by the figure of the martyr. As she writes of the church-as-bride, in the 'fires of martyrdom … she set[s] up mirrors whereby to fashion herself after Christ's likeness'.[68] For Rossetti the fires of state-death, as endured by the martyr, not only turns the she-church into the likeness of Christ but also conjures up another such likeness:

> [In the] furnace-fire voluminous,
> One like God's son will walk with us.
>
> (1.183.5–6)

The allusion is to the uncanny fourth figure in King

Nebuchadnezzar's fiery furnace: 'Did we not cast three men ... into the ... fire? ... Lo, I see four ... and ... the fourth is like the Son of God' (Daniel 4.24.–5).

This fourth figure is, of course, conventionally (mis)interpreted not as *like* Christ but rather *as* Christ. However, reading the figure through *Speculum*, we may just interpret 'him' as *her*, as the maternal 'fourth' that lies within all 'trinities':

> [In] the essential *trinity* structure [of] ... subject ... object, instrument-copula ... [or] Father, Son and Holy Ghost ... the womb of mother-nature enables the (male) one to join up with the (so-called) other in the matrix of a discourse. [Therefore] it will ... be possible, by playing upon negativity, to extend this so-called family circle to include four terms, four members. The fourth, by its absence, its dumbness, its death, [and] ... glass smooths out the exchanges between the three others.
>
> (233–4/290)

For Irigaray, the fourth figure in the furnace would be 'like the Son of God' because she is, in a sense, his (m)other.

Whether Irigaray would be right or not, the fact remains that the fourth figure complicates, albeit from within, the fixed and 'essential *trinity* structure' of Western totality. Indeed, for Irigaray, son and mother are always to be linked by their common distance from the father, the very source of philosophical totality: 'the son', writes Irigaray, 'is still too close to the earth/mother, too absorbed in her world of passions ... to serve as standard for measuring the father's ideal speculations' (148/185). It is not, though, just that the son is absorbed in the mother's passions – for what Irigaray does not seem to know is that the mother is also absorbed in the Son's Passion. Her death, that is, shades into Christ's, for they both die deaths that are to be repeated: Christ through the breaking of bread and wine, the mother through that wild vengeance of which irigaray writes at the very end of *Speculum*:

> Imagine then that someone ... rouses these prisoners who have been freed of their chains at the very moment that the philosopher ... has sat down among them, in his old place. Don't you think that if they 'catch the offender, they would put him to death?
>
> No question, he said.'
>
> All that remains to be known is whether what they caught was not already dead ... And whether in this fight they did anything but

tear themselves apart. Making blood flow … blood that recalls a very ancient relationship with the mother. Repeating a murder that has probably already taken place.

What, then, might all this mean? First, that when Rossetti writes about Christ's Spirit ('God's son who walks with us'), she is also, unwittingly, writing about the dead mother – he is, as it were, the ghost of the mother's ghost. Second, that when Irigaray writes about the already dead mother she is also, again unwittingly, writing about the crucified Christ. For instance, the murder at the end of *Speculum* recreates the crucifixion of Christ in that in both cases we might say of the murderers, 'they know not what they do' (Luke 23.34).

So much for answers. The question is: which murder comes first? Which is the originary blood-letting? For Irigaray it is the mother's, for Rossetti it is Christ's – for the two writers there is no question. The question is only for us who read between them.

Notes

1 Luce Irigaray, *Speculum of the other Woman*, tr. Gillian C. Gill (Ithaca: Cornell University Press, 1985), 243 / *Speculum de l'autre femme* (Paris: Minuit, 1977), 301. Subsequent page references will appear parenthetically in the text and are to the English translation followed by the French reference; this order is reversed when I quote the French.

2 *The Complete Poems of Christina Rossetti*, ed. R. W. Crump, 3 vols (Baton Rouge: Lousiana State University Press, 1979–90), 1.207.269–72. Subsequent references will appear parenthetically in the text and are to volume, page and line. The date of the poem's composition, when it is known, usually appears in parenthesis.

3 Luce Irigaray, *This Sex Which Is Not One*, tr. Catherine Porter with Carolyn Burke (Ithaca: Cornell University Press, 1985), 76 / *Ce Sexe qui n'en est pas un* (Paris: Minuit, 1977), 73.

4 Dolores Rosenblum, *Christina Rossetti: The Poetry of Endurance* (Carbondale and Edwardsville: Southern Illinois University Press, 1986), 2.

5 Irigaray, *This Sex*, 76 / *Ce Sexe*, 74.

6 William M. Rossetti, Preface to *The Poetical Works of Christina Rossetti*, ed. William Michael Rossetti (London: Macmillan, 1904), xii. Further testimony to the sheer extent of Rossetti's 'debt' to the Bible is Nilda Jiminez's *The Bible and the Poetry of Christina Rossetti: A Concordance* (Westport, CT: Greenwood Press, 1979).

7 'Would I were a turnip white' is, significantly, from Rossetti's story *Maude*, where the female characters are playing a game of *bout rimés* – a game in which poems are written to accommodate certain predetermined rhymes. I am grateful to Alison Chapman for pointing this out.

8 John Ruskin, unpublished letter to E. R. Milnes, 19 November 1862, cited in

D. Birch, '"The Sun is God": Ruskin's Solar Mythology', in J. B. Bullen (ed.), *The Sun is God: Painting, Literature and Mythology in the Nineteenth Century* (Oxford: Clarendon Press, 1989), 112. For discussion of fears regarding the sun's cooling, see Gillian Beer, '"The Death of the Sun": Victorian Solar Physics and Solar Myth', *ibid.*, 159.

9 Susan R. Horton, 'Were They Having Fun Yet? Victorian Optical Gadgetry, Modernist Selves', in Carol T. Christ and John O. Jordan, *Victorian Literature and the Victorian Visual Imagination* (Berkeley: California University Press, 1996), 3.

10 *Ibid.*, 8.

11 Christina Rossetti, *The Face of the Deep: A Devotional Commentary on the Apocalypse* (London: SPCK, 1892), 39, 214, 231.

12 Christina Rossetti, *Letter and Spirit: Notes on the Commandments* (London: SPCK, 1883), 11.

13 Christina Rossetti, *Time Flies: A Reading Diary* (London: SPCK, 1885), 98.

14 For further discussion of Rossetti and the feminisation of Christ see Virginia Sickbert, 'Dissident Voices in Christina Rossetti's Poetry', unpublished Ph.D. thesis, State University of New York, 1990.

15 See, in particular, the essay on 'Dora' [1905] in Sigmund Freud, *Case Histories 1: 'Dora' and 'Little Hans'*, The Pelican Freud Library, vol. 8 (London: Penguin, 1977).

16 Margaret Whitford, *Luce Irigaray: Philosophy in the Feminine* (London: Routledge, 1991), 159.

17 See Peter Stallybrass and Allon White, *The Politics and Poetics of Transgression* (London: Methuen, 1986), 151, 154.

18 Jane Gallop, *Feminism and Psychoanalysis* (London: Macmillan, 1982), 146.

19 She alludes to Christ's declaration, '"I am the door"' (John 7.9).

20 *Letter and Spirit*, 131. The phrase 'double against each other' is first used by Rossetti in 'From House to Home' (1858).

21 See Plato, *The Republic*, tr. H. D. P. Lee (Harmondsworth: Penguin, 1955), 278–86.

22 Elizabeth Grosz, *Sexual Subversions: Three French Feminists* (Sydney: Allen and Unwin, 1989), 131.

23 Interestingly, the girl that Carroll himself draws to decorate the manuscript copy of 'Alice's Adventures Under Ground' is dark-haired.

24 My translation.

25 Lewis Carroll, *Alice's Adventures in Wonderland and Through the Looking Glass*, ed. Roger Lancelyn Green (Oxford: Oxford University Press, 1971), 127–8.

26 Jan Marsh, *Christina Rossetti: A Literary Biography* (London: Jonathan Cape, 1994), 258–60.

27 See Margaret Homans, 'The Woman in the Cave: Recent Feminist Fictions and the Classical Underworld,' *Contemporary Literature*, 29 (1988), 382–3.

28 Jacques Derrida, *Dissemination*, tr. Barbara Johnson (London: Athlone, 1981), 206.

29 *Ibid.*

30 Derrida's contribution, '+R (Into the Bargain)', appeared in *Derrière le miroir* (no. 214, May 1975, Éditions Maeght) and was subsequently reprinted in Jacques Derrida, *The Truth in Painting* (Chicago: University of Chicago Press, 1987), 149–82.

31 See Marsh, *Christina Rossetti*, 343.
32 Jacques Derrida, *The Margins of Philosophy*. tr. Alan Bass (London: Harvester Wheatsheaf, 1982), xiv, n. 6.
33 See Jerome J. McGann, 'The Religious Poetry of Christina Rossetti', *Critical Inquiry*, 10 (1983), 127–45.
34 Soul Sleep (perceived by many as a materialist heresy) was, for example, crucial to Isaac Taylor's claim, in his *Physical Theory of Another Life* (1836), that ghosts were 'the dead ... yearn[ing] after their lost corporeality'. See Linda E. Marshall's excellent 'What the Dead Are Doing Underground: Hades and Heaven in the Writings of Christina Rossetti', *The Victorian Newsletter*, 40 (1987), 57.
35 See Alison Chapman, 'Father's Place, Mother's Space: Identity, Italy and the Maternal in Christina Rossetti's Poetry,' in Mary Arsenau *et al.* (eds), *Christina Rossetti* (Athens: Ohio University Press, 1999). The diary entry appears in William Michael Rossetti (ed.), *The Family Letters of Christina Georgina Rossetti* (London: Brown, Langham and Co., 1908), 232.
36 See Irigaray, *Speculum*, 183, n. 1.
37 Philippa Berry, 'The Burning Glass: Paradoxes of Feminist Revelation in *Speculum*', in Carolyn Burke *et al.* (ed.), *Engaging with Irigaray: Feminist Philosophy and Modern European Thought* (New York: Columbia University Press, 1994), 232.
38 See Rossetti, *The Face of the Deep*, 116.
39 For Ruskin, 'the whole technical power of painting depends on our recovery of what may be called the *innocence of the eye* ... a sort of childish perception of these flat stains of colour ... without consciousness of what they signify' – quoted in E. H. Gombrich, *Art and Illusion: A Study in the Psychology of Pictorial Representation* (New York: State University of New York, 1993), 250; Charles Dickens, *Hard Times* [1854] (Harmondsworth: Penguin, 1969), 83; see Christ and Jordan, *Victorian Literature*, 3.
40 Homans, 'The Woman in the Cave', 383.
41 Carroll, *Alice's Adventures*, 127.
42 See Elisabeth Bronfen, *Over Her Dead Body: Death, Femininity and the Aesthetic* (Manchester: Manchester University Press, 1992).
43 Quoted in Marsh, *Christina Rossetti*, 255.
44 *Christina Rossetti*, 127.
45 Andrew H. Miller, *Novels Behind Glass: Commodity Culture and Victorian Narrative* (Cambridge: Cambridge University Press, 1995), 64; Miller also remarks, albeit without quite explaining himself, that 'the Exhibition inspired several male observers to imagine the display of British women under glass' (10).
46 See Knoepflmacher's excellent essay 'Avenging Alice: Christina Rossetti and Lewis Carroll', *Nineteenth Century Literature*, 41 (1996), 320.
47 Jan Marsh (ed.), *Christina Rossetti: Poems and Prose* (London: Everyman, 1994), 330–2.
48 Rossetti, *The Face of the Deep*, 47.
49 My translation.
50 See Whitford, *Luce Irigaray*, 121, 105.
51 See W. M. Rossetti, Preface to *Poetical Works*, lxix.
52 Grosz, *Sexual Subversions*, 182.
53 See Derrida, *The Margins of Philosophy*, 27.

54 My translation.
55 Gill translates the phrase as: 'he is probably completely at sea now' (344).
56 See Marsh, *Christina Rossetti*, 319, 357; see W. D. Shaw, *The Lucid Veil: Poetic Truth in the Victorian Age* (London: Athlone Press, 1987), 168–70.
57 See Marsh, *Christina Rossetti*, 132.
58 Paul de Man, *The Rhetoric of Romanticism* (New York: Columbia University Press, 1984), 72.
59 George Eliot, *Middlemarch*, ed. Rosemary Ashton (Harmondsworth: Penguin, 1994), 85.
60 See, for example, 'Mother Country' (1866 – 1.222), which, at one and the same time, suggests both Italy and the cause of women: 'It rises, that land' (10). For further discussion of Rossetti's reading of Italy as a maternal space, see Chapman, 'Father's Place, Mother's Space'.
61 Berry, 'The Burning Glass', 240.
62 W. H. Hunt, *Pre-Raphaelitism and the Pre-Raphaelite Brotherhood* (London, 1905), 88; *The Pre-Raphaelites*, catalogue of the 1984 Tate Gallery Exhibition, 124.
63 Rossetti, *Time Flies*, 34.
64 Berry, 'The Burning Glass', 231–2.
65 *Ibid.*, 237.
66 *Ibid.*, 238. I am, as is obvious by now, greatly indebted to Berry's fine essay.
67 See Marsh, *Christina Rossetti*, 150; and Angela Leighton, *Victorian Women Poets: Writing Against the Heart* (London: Harvester Wheatsheaf, 1992), 119.
68 Rossetti, *The Face of the Deep*, 436.

2

The buried lives of silence: Foucault after Arnold

Headless saints

> The Sea of Faith
> Was once, too, at the full, and round earth's shore
> Lay like the folds of a bright girdle furled.
> But now I only hear
> Its melancholy, long, withdrawing roar.
>
> (Matthew Arnold, 'Dover Beach')[1]

> man is a recent invention ... the effect of a change in the fundamental arrangements of knowledge ... if those arrangements were to disappear ... then one can certainly wager that man would be erased, like a face drawn in the sand at the edge of the sea.
>
> (Michel Foucault, *The Order of Things*)[2]

In 1851 Arnold describes a sea that is going out; in 1966 Foucault wagers on a sea that is coming in.[3] It is, in a sense, the same sea and the same beach. For, in 'Dover Beach', as faith retreats so man emerges: 'we are here' (35), concludes the poem. In 'Dover Beach' we doubt therefore we are; for Arnold, man *is* the doubting subject; as we read in 'Empedocles upon Etna' (1849–52), 'man doubt[s]' (I.ii.88). And it is this same man, man produced by the retreat of faith, who is threatened with disappearance on Foucault's beach a hundred years later – as Foucault observes, 'it is in the death of God that [man] speaks, thinks and exists' (*OT*, 385/396). What threatens this man is, in a sense, a returning sea of faith; after all, its incoming is a matter not of certainty but rather of a 'wager' that recalls Pascal's famous wager on the existence of God.[4] The very first words of *Madness and Civilisation* [1961][5] are Pascal's and, as Foucault himself observes, *The Order* is 'an echo' of the earlier work (xxiv). Indeed, the sea with which *The Order* closes is an echo of the cryptic equations of sea and sacred madness, ship and holy fool, with which *Madness* opens:

> Something new appears in the imaginary landscape of the Renaissance ... the Ship of Fools ... pilgrimage boats ... [with] cargoes of madmen ... It is for the other world that the madman sets sail ... that great uncertainty external to everything.
>
> (*MC*, 7–11/18–22)

Though the ship of fools is part of the Great Confinement and sails 'in search of reason' (9/20) it is, for Foucault, not only an instrument of civilisation but also a figure of liberation. These ships of fools are, after all, a 'dream fleet' (8/19) with 'highly symbolic cargo' (9/20), an effect of Foucault's own imaginary landscape.[6] *Madness* opens, then, with not just a pilgrimage but also what Foucault calls, somewhat cryptically, a 'counter-pilgrimage' (10/21) – a voyage or 'tide of madness' (17/27) that runs counter to Foucault's seeming secularism. Foucault goes on, in *Madness,* to speak positively of 'Christian unreason', recalling us to 'the great theme of the madness of the Cross' and 'the scandal of Christian faith' (78–9/170–1). Like the incoming sea at the end of *The Order*, the 'tide of madness' at the beginning of *Madness* runs into a wild and scandalous sea of faith.[7]

This sea that Foucault never names and yet, in a sense, sails is, ironically, the sea that Arnold names but never sails; and this is precisely because of its wild unreason. Just as his prose resolutely opposes the supernaturalism of orthodox Christianity so his poetry is wary of the madness of the sea of faith.[8] In 'Dover Beach' this madness is confined to the 'melancholy' of the sea's withdrawing roar; but in the later poem 'St Brandan' (1859–60) Arnold describes a sea marked by a faith that is conspicuously mad:

> Saint Brandan sails the northern main;
> ...
> So late! – such storm! The Saint is mad!
>
> (1–4)

St Brandan's sea of faith is distinguished not just by madness but also by being a 'sea without human shore' – this stormy sea of faith has no Dover beach, no human limit, no 'we are here', and in this it is more nearly Foucault's man-erasing sea. Indeed, the man erased is, in both cases, styled as a murderer of God. 'Man', writes

Foucault, 'has killed God ... what Nietzsche's thought heralds is the end of [t]his murderer' (*OT*, 385/396); likewise, the one human figure that St Brandan encounters is the 'traitor Judas' (20), that 'murderer' of Christ whose disappearance concludes the poem: 'St Brandan ... looked, and lo ... / ... no Judas there!' (73–6). These seas are seas of strangely negative faith – negative to the point of enacting a kind of revenge on humanity itself.

This revenge, however, is a signifier of not simply the scandal of faith but also its sheer theatricality. For both writers, the revenge in question is intensely theatrical. In 'Dover Beach' there is, in the reference to Sophocles, a reference to the Greek theatre of revenge – the sea's 'eternal note of sadness' was 'heard', we read, by 'Sophocles long ago' (15). Likewise, at the end of *The Order*, the erasure of God's 'murderer' like a face in the sand will coincide, it is announced, with 'the return of masks' (385/396–7).

The theatrical illusion of the mask, the illusion that we have faces, is, for Foucault, never more potent than at the point of death – not just the death of man but death *per se.* In the modern world 'death', writes Foucault, 'is constitutive of singularity; ... in ... death, the dull, common life becomes an individuality ... death gives a face'[9] or rather the illusion of a face. Arnold seems to echo this in 'Tristram and Iseult' (1849–52) when Tristram declares, of Iseult, that 'she seems one dying in a mask' (III.75). Similarly masked, in 'Sohrab and Rustrum' (1852–53), is Sohrab, who dies at the hand of his own father who has mistaken him for someone else. Just as, for Nietzsche, language begs the question 'who speaks?'[10] so, for both Foucault and Arnold, death begs the question 'who dies?'

The answer, it seems, is always more than one. In a strange sense Iseult dies *with* her masked persona and, likewise, Sohrab dies *with* the 'someone else' for whom his father mistook him. For Arnold the mask worn at death is not, primarily, to do with the illusion of individuality but rather the riddling, philosophical intuition that the 'I' never dies, that 'I' can only ever die with or as someone else.[11] Modern death is not necessarily the privatised affair that Foucault describes. This seems particularly true of those deaths that Arnold locates in sand, as if he finds in the desert a trope for the strangely othered space of dying. At the end of 'The Function of Criticism' (1864) it is not 'I' but '*we* [who] shall die in the wilderness' (my italics).[12] Again, it is in sand, 'bloody sand', that Sohrab dies not only *as* another but *with* another – 'the lion', we read, '[also] comes ... to die upon the sand' (526). Many more are imagined to die shared deaths on the sands of Dover beach, that 'darkling plain ... / Where ignorant armies clash by night'. Even the suicidal Hamlet, he who would die the absolutely private death of 'self-slaughter', strays into the public space of Arnold's sands: in 'The Youth of Man' (1852), as Arnold looks, across 'hamlet and copse', he talks of those who, growing old, 'see, for a moment ... like the desert / In its weary, unprofitable length, / Their faded, ignoble lives' (108–11). Encoded here is, of course, Hamlet's 'how weary, stale, flat, and unprofitable'.[13]

These words, which Hamlet speaks when all alone, are no longer his own, they have been appropriated; the private space of soliloquy is no more possible than that of self-slaughter. For Arnold, the chief significance of Hamlet is that he is never on his own, that he is always plural. Just as there are 'hamlets' (82) in 'The Scholar Gypsy' so there are Hamlets in Arnold's imagination. The most obvious is the 'half mad' (I.i.23) and suicidal philosopher Empedocles, but he must rub shoulders with those 'whose common theme', to quote Shakespeare's Hamlet, 'is death of fathers'.[14] This includes not only Aegyptus, the prince who, in 'Merope', seeks to revenge his royal father's death, but also Arnold himself, who, after the replacement of his dead father as Rugby's headmaster, writes to Clough: 'But thou'dst not think, Horatio, how ill it is here.'[15]

Whilst Arnold uses Hamlet to explore the frailties of individuation Foucault uses Hamlet, not dissimilarly, to write the history of madness, or what he calls his 'archeology of ... silence', the silence of reason on the subject of madness (*MC*, xiii). Describing how the nineteenth-century asylum's rule-by-observation limits 'madness ... [to] that part of itself which is visible', Foucault evokes the dying words of Hamlet by adding: 'All the rest is reduced to silence' (*MC*, 250/507).[16] If Arnold's Hamlet articulates that which *is here* ('how ill it is here') Foucault's Hamlet articulates that which is *not* here – or at least that which is invisible. Arnold's privileging of 'the here' has already been encountered: 'we are *here*', 'no Judas [is] *there*'; witness too his cry 'What ... life is here!' (270.14) and the question 'what am I, that I am here?' (304.66). Again, whilst Shakespeare's *Hamlet* begins with 'Who's there?', 'Empedocles on Etna' or, if you will, Arnold's *Hamlet* begins with a speech that concludes with 'Who's here?' (I.i.28). In 1867 Arnold writes 'What *is there*, is for me the only question' (my italics)[17] and yet in his modernised *Hamlet* there is, it seems, no there, no elsewhere – a theme echoed, in another poem, by the strange line: 'What else is all these waters are' (500.133). Such waters run, presumably, into St Brandan's 'sea without shore', that sea without an outside that also washes up in those earlier poems which speak, respectively, of 'some false, impossible shore' (285.69) and 'an infinitely distant land' (290.74).

Such infinite recession anticipates, in some ways, Foucault's discussion of man's origin as an 'ever-receding ... horizon' (*OT*, 332/343). There is, however, just a hint that this horizon may be reached, that there *is* an elsewhere; for 'thought', continues Foucault, 'advances with dove-like steps towards ... the ... horizon'. Though such steps suggest infinitely slow progress they also, and paradoxically, recall the biblical moment in which Noah learns that the waters of the Flood have begun to recede – the moment in which a dove walks rather than flies. Changing his metaphor, but still talking of infinite recession, Foucault adds that 'le désert croît' (345) – 'the desert increases' (334); given, however, the dove that walks we might also misread that 'the desert believes' (*le désert croit*).

For all its seeming scepticism there is within Foucault's writing, certainly his early writing, a strange subtextual topography that includes a desert as well as a sea of faith. The desert, for Foucault, is the site of holy madness – in particular, the holy madness of St Anthony; Foucault not only writes an essay on Flaubert's *The Temptation of St Anthony*[18] but in *Madness* he identifies 'the sleep of unreason' with 'the desert of Bosch's Saint Anthony' (280/550). Indeed, there is a sense in which the Foucault of *Madness* is himself a kind of St Anthony since just a few pages later he describes his exploration of 'the madness ... of art' as 'our mixed vocation of apostle and exegete' (288/557). Foucault the apostle and 'exegete' (literally, 'one who leads out') presumably leads out to a desert of holy madness. If so, he gives a very different account of the wilderness of criticism that so concerns Arnold; whilst Arnold sees it as a place to which we, as critics or exegetes, are doomed Foucault sees it as a place to which we are positively called. However, what both seem to glimpse in the desert is, strangely, not isolation but community. Though St Anthony was a hermit 'his desert', writes Foucault, 'was infinitely populous' (280/550). Likewise, Arnold finds company in that direct descendant of the community of desert hermits, the monastery; in 'Stanzas from the Grande Chartreuse' (1851–55) Arnold argues that, within the haste and noise of modernity, the only space afforded to doubt is, paradoxically, the desert community of faith:

> 'Fenced early in this cloistral round
> Of reverie, of shade, of prayer,
> ...
> – Pass, banners, pass, and bugles, cease;
> And leave our *desert* to its peace!'
>
> (205–10: my italics)

For all their talk of estrangement and doubt, both Arnold and Foucault find themselves, at times, within a community of faith – even the community of saints. In 'Tristram and Iseult' Arnold suddenly, and without explanation, addresses his readers as 'Dear Saints' (III.112); equally startling is David Halperin's recent title, *Saint Foucault: Towards a Gay Hagiography.*[19] Halperin makes very little of this title but there is a sense in which Foucault does see something of himself in St Anthony, a saint who 'achieves... saintliness... through the dangerous space of books'.[20] It is, of course, Foucault who points out that the conventional figure of the Author may be viewed as a latter-day saint: 'modern criticism', he writes, 'uses methods similar to those that Christian exegetes employed when trying to prove the value of a text by its author's saintliness'.[21]

Growing up as a Catholic in France, Foucault could hardly avoid saints; of Poitiers he writes:

> Such is the city where I was born: decapitated saints, book in hand, watch to assure that justice is just ... That is where I inherited my wisdom.[22]

That is also where Foucault inherited his madness for he too is a headless saint in that, though christened Paul Michel Foucault, he chose not to use 'Paul'[23] – the name of not only his father but also that most authorial and authoritative of saints. Foucault's often-stated desire for anonymity, for namelessness, begins with this deletion, with Foucault as the author who dare not speak his Christian name, or rather the Christian name for Author. What Foucault is left with is, of course, Michel – still a saint's name but one that is also a question: in its original, Jewish form (Micheal) it means 'who is like God?' As not Paul but Michel, Foucault takes the saint's name that is, in a sense, not a name.

In so doing he replays something of Arnold's poem 'The Divinity' (1863?), which tells the story of St Bernard, whose heterodox declaration that '"God of ... his attributes is made"' has not been heeded:

> This message no Saint preaches ...
> 'Tis in the desert, now and heretofore.
>
> (5, 13–14)

The one exception to this rule is, of course, the poet himself; as the increasingly well-known voice of liberal theology he *is*, as it were, this 'no Saint ... in the desert', this no name in the sand. Indeed, just a year later, in 'The Function of Criticism', Arnold not only locates himself 'in the wilderness' but, in a bizarre digression, rages against the mere deletion of a Christian name. Quoting a newspaper report concerning a murderer whom the paper describes as 'a girl named Wragg', Arnold declares that 'the girl's [seemingly] superfluous Christian name [has been] lopped off ... [by] straightforward [Anglo-Saxon] vigour'.[24] This, though, is precisely what happens to Arnold's own Christian name when, just two years later, he describes 'Matthew Arnold' as 'that pecular Semitico-Saxon mixture which makes the typical Englishman';[25] in so doing Arnold confronts his readers with the non-Christian character of their so-called Christian names. Like Foucault, Arnold challenges his Christian prehistory at the point of his name. And just as Foucault's decapitation of 'Paul' leaves the theological question 'who is God?' so Arnold's Judaisation of Matthew begs the political question: 'And we, then, what are we? What is England?'[26]

The life of life

> And we shall feel the agony of thirst,
> The ineffable longing for the life of life.
>
> (Arnold, 'Empedocles on Etna', II.356–7)

Arnold and Foucault are both concerned with not just questions but also the very nature of questions – they beg, if you like, the question of the question. In the sixties Foucault sees the question as part of what he calls 'the confused sleep of dialectics'[27] – that

Socratic process of debate by which Western philosophy has traditionally structured itself; in the seventies Foucault identifies the question with juridical interrogation and the culture of discipline – indeed, where the English translation of *Discipline and Punish* reads 'juridical torture' the original reads 'la question'.[28] Such concerns may seem, at first, to be lost on Arnold, who tends towards dialectical, oppositional thought (witness *Culture and Anarchy*, 'Hebraism and Hellenism') and describes 'living by ideas' as the ability 'to be ... carried ... to the opposite side of the question'.[29] There is, however, a sense in which for Arnold – or at least Arnold the poet – the opposite side of the question is, like the other side of the mirror, a ludic and dreamy space; if to question is, as Foucault claims, to sleep is it also 'perchance to dream?'[30] The strange poem 'A Dream' (1849–53) begins 'Was it a dream?' and in so doing not only questions the act of dreaming but also dreams the act of questioning. Arnold here explores the unconscious of the question, the confused sleep of dialectics. And this he does elsewhere by transposing the scene of question-and-answer to the dreamy world of the sea-shore: in one poem 'he asks what waves ... / ... have swelled, / ... and gone' (485.69–72), in another the 'waves an answer made' (553.68) and in still another the speaker grows 'sick of asking / ... [as] / At this vessel's prow I stand' (149.1–3). By so defamiliarising the act of questioning Arnold, like Foucault, questions the question. And that is what Arnold quite literally does in 'Euphrosyne' (1850?), where he not only asks 'Why should they ask if truth be there?' (4) but follows this with 'Truth – what is truth?', the very question that Pilate puts to Christ as part of his brutal interrogation (John 18.38). Like the later Foucault, the poem returns the question to the culture of discipline.

It also, though, returns us to Arnold's earlier poem 'Shakespeare' (1844), which, reflecting the early Victorians' almost complete failure to produce a biography of the bard, declares:

> Others abide our question. Thou art free.
> We ask and ask – [and yet] Thou smilest and art still,
> Out-topping knowledge.
>
> (1–3)

Just as Pilate's question of truth was 'answered' by the silence of Christ so here the biographer's question is met with the silence of Shakespeare – or rather silence and a smile. There is, it seems, a long and various history to the silence and laughter with which Foucault, towards the end of *The Order*, 'answers' what he calls the 'anthropological question':

> To all those who still … ask themselves questions about what man is … we can answer only with a philosophical laugh – which means, to a certain extent, a silent one.
>
> (343/353)

Foucault's laugh returns the reader to the very beginning of *The Order*: 'this book', we there read, 'first arose out of laughter'; the last laugh is, then, philosophical in precisely the return-to-origin sense that Foucault would not intend. It is also philosophical in the Socratic sense of being provocative and superior; if we the readers are so naively 'anthropological' as still to ask questions about man then Foucault's laugh carries the sneering message with which he plays in *The Archeology of Knowledge* [1969], namely: '"I'm … laughing *at you*"' (my italics).[31] The silent answer has, however, a history that is not just philosophical, or anti-philosophical; as Arnold reminds us, this history is also stubbornly biographical, it has to do with human lives: Shakespeare's buried life and Christ's tortured life, lives that still beg the anthropological question.

Foucault's laughing response to this question belongs, of course, to the high-structuralist moment of 1966 and Foucault himself admits that it took the political events of 1968 to jolt him out of a narrow and quasi-scientific concentration on discourse.[32] However, whilst Foucault's laughter may be forgetful of human lives, the curious silence of that laughter is not so forgetful; in Foucault's work silence has a memory. This is never more obvious than when Foucault speaks, in *Madness*, of his attempt 'to write the archeology of … silence' (xiii); a phrase that bears witness to Foucault's sense of the sheer density of silence – what we might call, after Arnold, the buried life of silence, or rather the lives that are buried in silence. The silence which concerns Foucault is, he argues, never far from the near-silence of the confessional, the silence of *lives*, lives buried in narratives of guilt. Foucault's argument is a historical one: in the intensely moralised asylum of the nineteenth century 'the [literal] absence of language', he writes, 'has its correlative in the exposure of confession' (*MC*, 262/517). The cultural silence surrounding madness is only extended by the near-silence of confession.

It is no accident that as Foucault writes the archaeology of this silence – which he does, in effect, throughout his career – so he also writes his own confession, his own buried life. Foucault, of course, is no stranger to the confessional narrative – writing an introduction to one, *Moi Pierre Rivière*, and echoing the title of another, Sartre's *Les Mots* (1964), in his own *Les Mots et les choses* (1966). 'I have always', declares Foucault, 'wanted my books to be fragments from an autobiography.'[33] And this is true in not just the very broad sense that Foucault suffered from mental illness and had a police record. Witness too the close similarity between the very end of *The Order* and Foucault's account of his wartime childhood:

> the impression of fulfilment … of end makes us believe that something new is about to begin, something we glimpse only as a thin line of light low on the horizon …
>
> (*OT*, 384/396)

> To have lived as an adolescent in a situation that had to end, that had to lead to another world … was to have the impression of spending one's entire childhood in the night, waiting for dawn.[34]

Even as Foucault announces that man is in the process of disappearing, 'Foucault' himself is in the process of appearing. This paradox is replayed at the beginning of *The Archeology*, where, at the same time as celebrating the effacement he finds in writing, Foucault might almost be 'confessing' to the fleeting pleasures of an urban sexual encounter:[35]

> in writing … I [am] … preparing a labyrinth into which I can venture … opening up underground passages … in which I can lose myself and appear at last to eyes that I will never have to meet again.
>
> (*AK*, 17/28)

At such moments, where Foucault's philosophy becomes autobiography, reason is ambushed by life – logos, if you will, is ambushed by pathos. And it is, as Derrida argues, pathos which realises the silence that so concerns Foucault:

> the silence of madness is not *said*, cannot be said in the logos of this book [*Madness and Civilisation*], but is indirectly, metaphorically, made present by its *pathos*.[36]

This pathos, I would add, is at times the pathos of Foucault's life – indeed, for the later Foucault life *is* pathos in the sense of being pathological; as he writes in *The Clinic*, 'the idea of a disease attacking life [from outside] must [for modern medicine] be replaced by the much denser notion of *pathological life*' (153/156).

This notion is very precisely anticipated by Arnold's reference to 'this strange disease of modern life' (366.203); indeed, the intuition that life is disruptive or critical – in every sense of the word – runs throughout Arnold's work. For though he declares that 'poetry is at bottom a criticism of life'[37] there is always a sense that life itself is also, for Arnold, a kind of criticism. This possibility is most obviously encoded in his talk of 'the buried life', with its implication of a dark and hidden biography that radically undermines the poet's official life. The poem 'The Buried Life' (1849–52) seems to promise precisely this; its references to 'lips unchained', 'unspeakable desire', and 'this heart which beats / So wild' (28–53) anticipate something of that late-Victorian genre, the sexual confession. In short, for 'The Buried Life' read Walter's *My Secret Life* (1888); or even Foucault's not-so-secret life for, strange though it may seem, we here find something of the anonymous homoerotic encounter:

> I knew the mass of men concealed
> Their thoughts, for fear that if revealed
> They would with other men be met.
>
> (16–18)

The next line ('With blank indifference, or with blame reproved') buries the sexual suggestion but only for it to resurface later in the poem:

> But, often, in the world's most crowded streets,
> ...
> There rises an unspeakable desire
>
> (45–7)

and later in Arnold's career:

> So on the sea of life, alas!
> Man meets man – meets, and quits again.
>
> (520.47–8)

What connects these fragments is not just 'life' but the trope of life-as-sea; 'The Buried Life' ends by running into the sea of life as it concludes with the couplet: 'The hills where his life rose, / And the sea where it goes' (96–7). That this buried life that is also a sea might name the buried life of sodomy is a conceit which recurs in 'A Dream' (1849–53); the poem culminates in a subterranean 'river of life' that encodes a reference to those burning cities of the plains, Sodom and Gomorrah:[38]

> the river of Life
> ...
> Black under cliffs it raced [till] ...
> Soon ...
> ... us burning plains,
> Bristled with cities, us the sea received.
>
> (32–7)

Life again seems to gesture towards sodomy in 'To a Republican Friend, 1848' – namely Clough; here, with a verbal daring typical of Arnold's relationship to Clough,[39] the phrase 'Man's fundamental life' (4) buries within its etymology (*fundus* meaning 'anus') the cryptogram 'man's anal life'. According to Susan Walsh, a similar though wholly unconscious cryptogram is to be found in Arnold's peculiar outburst against what he saw as the 'grossness' of Anglo-Saxon surnames; reminding us of Arnold's familiarity with the homoerotic cultural life of the Greeks, Walsh suggests that for 'Higginbottom, Stiggins, Bugg!' we may read 'Higginbottom, Stiggins, buggery!'[40]

When, in addition to all this, Arnold writes, in 'Tristram and Iseult', of 'a love they dare not name' (I.150) there is an uncanny sense in which Lord Alfred Douglas's famous definition of homoerotic desire has already been written. Likewise, given that Arnold's buried life comes close to naming this unnameable love there is a sense in which Foucault's sexual life has also already been written. But then that is precisely the point of Foucault's chapter 'We Other Victorians', where, rejecting the Freudian account of the Victorians as sexually repressed, Foucault argues that we do not differ from the Victorians, that we are 'only' other, or more, Victorians.[41]

For all its articulation of a sexual life buried *in* silence, Arnold's buried life has also to do with the buried life *of* silence. In particular, Arnold's poetry is concerned with the moment at which life and silence meet, that moment at which it is impossible to distinguish between the biography of the writer and the biography, as it were, of silence. This moment is, for Foucault as well as Arnold, the moment of silent reading; in both cases it is the writer's reading life that threatens to disappear into the life of silence. Note how, in *The Order*, Foucault first reveals himself reading – 'this book ... arose out of a passage in Borges, [and] out of [my] laughter ... as I read the passage' – and then reminds us of the silence of this reading: '[with] the ... Renaissance ... [and] printing [came also] ... a literature no longer created for the voice' (xv, 38 / xx, 47). Likewise, in Arnold's poetry the silent life of reading enters both punningly, as a buried life:

> Is my page here? Come, turn me to the fire!
> ...
> To-night my page shall keep me company
>
> (218.298–310)

and literally, as Empedocles describes the dying life of a philosopher:

> We search out dead men's words ...
> ...
>   But still, as we proceed
>   The mass swells more and more
>   Of volumes yet to read
> ...
> Our hair grows grey, our eyes ... dim ..., our heat is tamed.
>
> (I.ii.326–36)

Later in 'Empedocles' the life of reading is even more nearly a dying life and at the same time the stage direction gives the *silence* of reading a life of its own:

>   I alone
> Am dead to life and joy, therefore I read
> In all things my own deadness.
>
> [*A long silence.*]
>
> (II.320–2)

In this long silence we might well read Arnold's deadness, or rather that deadness-to-come in which he will give up writing poetry for criticism and the silent world of reading, that wilderness in which he will expect to die. Empedocles' long silence has, though, a life that is not only theatrical but philosophical, or anti-philosophical – for this is Descartes in reverse: 'I am dead therefore I read' being a bizarre reversal of 'I think therefore I am'.

It is, in a sense, as if we are already witnessing Foucault's inaugural lecture at the Collège de France in 1970. Here Foucault presents his lecture not just as theatre – he speaks of the 'provisional theatre of ... [my] work' – but also as an implicitly anti-Cartesian theatre: the burden of his lecture being not 'I think therefore I am' but 'I speak therefore I am not'. As Foucault declares, quoting Samuel Beckett, 'words say me'.[42] What makes this performance still closer to Empedocles' silent theatre of inverted philosophy is that Foucault is very deliberately rehearsing what he had only recently described as Deleuze's *theatrum philosophicum* – a staging of thought in which 'philosophy', writes Foucault, '[is] a [silent] theatre of mime' and the 'laughter of the [word-playing, truth-bending] Sophist tears through the mask of Socrates'.[43] Empedocles has, of course, been 'banished' by the 'sophists' (I.i.122), so when he delcares 'I am not therefore I read' it is as if the laughter of the Sophists breaks through the mask of Descartes.

The resemblance between Empedocles' theatrical silence and Deleuze's theatre of mime extends to the way the life of silence describes, in both cases, a kind of after-life. Empedocles' long silence testifies, of course, to the living death of 'reading in all things my own deadness'. Likewise, Deleuze's theatre is dominated by relations between bodies, relations that Foucault calls 'phantasms' and that, in his own theatre, become more nearly phantoms as he conjures up 'a nameless voice speaking ... long before me'.[44] Foucault, indeed, goes so far as to reimagine the space of discourse as a curious kind of heaven: the institutional declaration that 'a place has been made ready' for Foucault's discourse echoes Christ's '"I go to prepare a place for you"' (John 14.2); the quotation of Beckett's 'before the door that opens'[45] echoes Christ's 'I have set before thee an open door ... a door ... in heaven' (Revelation 3.8–4.1).

If Empedocles' and Foucault's respective theatres of silence only hint at an after-life, Arnold's 'Bacchanalia; or, The New Age' (1864–67) establishes the conceit. For here, as the old age ends it 'clear[s] ... a stage' for what the speaker calls 'the after-silence sweet' (34, 13) only for that after-silence to become an appalling after-life, a space in which the dead not only live on but fight on:

the dead-age
Did now its silent warfare [continue to] wage.

(19–20)

Though both silent and violent this staged after-life is still, like Foucault's theatre, dimly recognisable as the heaven of the Bible – a heaven that *is* both silent and violent. The Book of Revelation speaks not only of a door but of a silence: 'there was silence in heaven' (8.1), and not only a silence but a war: 'And there was war in heaven' (12.17). Arnold's theatre of silence locates in Revelation a far darker heaven than does Foucault's.

Between two bodies

That Arnold, in his account of 'the New Age', should remember the war in heaven makes ready historical sense given the class 'war' in Hyde Park, the riots of 1866, which so scarred what Arnold saw as the new dawn of the 1860s.[46] By contrast, that Foucault, in his inaugural lecture, should *not* remember the war in heaven – despite being called Michel – does not make ready historical sense given that 'war' in Paris, *les événements* of 1968 which signalled the end of the optimism of the 1960s. But then, the apocalyptic space that the early Foucault is exploring, 'the void left by man's disappearance' (*OT*, 342/353), is marked not so much by war but *rumours* of war. '[In] a culture … without … author[s],' he writes, 'discourses would unfold in the anonymity of a murmur',[47] a murmur that becomes a rumour of war when Foucault reminds us of Nietzsche's assertion that 'man … would be replaced by [the warlike] superman' (*OT*, 322/333). The rumour returns when, at the very end of *Discipline*, Foucault cryptically asserts: 'we must hear the distant roar of battle' (308/315). There is, by contrast, nothing distant about the battle at the end of 'Dover Beach': 'And we are *here* … / Where … armies clash.'

For all the critical discussion of Foucault's 'warrior philosophy', for all Foucault's references to 'the philosopher's hammer'[48] and his own 'strange arsenal' (*AK*, 135/178), there is, for the most part, something muffled about Foucault's talk of war. This is certainly the case in comparison with Arnold, for whom, writing at the time of the Crimean War, there is 'something too much of war … [and] / Life [is] one perpetual fight' (419.505–6). War, for Foucault, is 'just' a rumour precisely because he sees war as almost a non-event, something that never quite happens. This is true in the biographical sense that Foucault remembers the Second World War as a kind of paralysis, or nothing:

> We saw once again that sight we had known during the German occupation: the silence of the crowd, watching and saying nothing.[49]

It is also true in the philosophical sense that, for the later Foucault, 'power is everywhere … [and] comes from everywhere' and so is never to be quite thought of as war, as a simple opposition; power, for Foucault, is 'unbalanced [and] heterogeneous'.[50]

We are, it seems, back to 'Dover Beach' and 'the confused alarms' of 'the ignorant armies that clash by night'; as Miriam Allott notes, what Arnold has in mind is the confusion of a night battle where no one knows whose side they are on. In this Arnold is drawing, claims Allott, on not only Thucydides but also the following words of John Henry Newman:

> Controversy, at least in this age, does not lie between the hosts of heaven, Michael and his angels on the one side, and the powers of evil on the other; but it is a sort of night battle, where each fights for himself.
>
> (257n.)

In Newman's version, the night battle becomes a riot of angelic neutrality, of angels not taking sides; but then angels, as sexually ambiguous figures, always already represent a radical neutrality of the body – as Foucault reminds us in his essay 'Theatrum philosophicum'. Here Foucault makes the faintest of allusions to the biblical story of the angels who stay the night in Lot's house in Sodom only to find themselves surrounded by the men of the city insisting that Lot open the door: 'to pervert Platonism,' Foucault enigmatically declares,

> we should welcome the cunning assembly [of appearances] that simulates and clamours at the door … A dead God and sodomy are the thresholds of the new metaphysical ellipse.[51]

For Foucault (or, perhaps, Michel) and his sodomised angels the confused alarms of the night are not to do with a battle but rather a savage threshold, a violent marginality or neutrality. Situated as they are between a dead God and a new metaphysical ellipse, Michel and his angels are, like Arnold in the Grande Chartreuse, 'wandering between two worlds, one dead, / The other powerless to be born' (85–6). Indeed, there is also a sense in which these angels wander between two bodies, the one male, the other female. And that is precisely Arnold's experience, for in visiting the monastery he must leave his newly-wed wife outside only to encounter, on the inside, men from whom he is also alienated, and not just by their faith but also by their sheer masculinity:[52] this 'Brotherhood austere', as he terms it, is a place of 'naked prayer – [where] / With … cries they kneel / And wrestle' (65, 38–40).

That Arnold, in the monastery, wanders between two bodies is a conceit he underwrites when, elsewhere, he gives to Wordsworth – in whose steps he is, quite literally, following – the mythological name of the double-bodied Tiresias.[53] A suggestive question of Foucault's here comes to mind: 'who can be said to have spoken … the Wanderer or his shadow? The philosopher or the first of the non-philosophers?'[54] In the case of Arnold in the Grande Chartreuse the wanderer's shadow is, it seems, not just the philosophical Wordsworth but also the non-philosophical Tiresias, non-philosophical in the sense that, as both man and woman, he gives a subversive twist to the Kantian question 'What is Man?' Indeed, Arnold's Tiresian Wordsworth is also subversive of the anthropological account of Man as the whole that is greater than the sum of its parts – Tiresias is a 'singer … less than his themes' ('The Youth of Nature', 89). When, at the end of the poem, Mother Nature speaks of 'Race after race, man after man' we cannot help but read: 'man after *Man*'.

We are led further this way by the sequel poem, 'The Youth of Man' (1852), which ridicules the notion that 'Man, man is the king of the world', claiming instead that he is constrained 'within the walls / Of an ever-narrowing world' (46–7). In so doing, however, the poem comes very close to what Foucault calls 'the analytic of finitude', that crypto-metaphysical ruse by which the emergent human sciences of the nineteenth century made man an empirical object of knowledge but also, thereby, invented man as the absolute *subject* of knowledge. As Foucault puts it, 'man's finitude is heralded … [precisely because] it also promises that very infinity it refuses' (*OT*, 313–14/324–5). Witness, in the case of Arnold's poem, the infinity tacitly claimed as the speaker declares, of his human subjects, 'Well I know what they feel! / … / Well I know what they feel!' (88, 96). Man in 'The Youth of Man' may be known but he also *knows* – he is precisely the 'strange empirico-transcendental doublet' (*OT*, 318/329) that, for Foucault, is produced by the analytic of finitude.

He is, however, also evocative of another Foucauldian doublet

– namely, 'the condemned man'; he who 'represents the symmetrical, inverted figure of the king' – particularly in having, like the medieval king, 'a double body' (*DP*, 28–9/33). Just as the king's body was held to be at once both private and symbolic, so the condemned man, argues Foucault, is somehow imagined to have one body which is purely his own and another that is subject to the law (13/19). What makes man in 'The Youth of Man' so evocative of this double body is that the prison-house monotony suggested by the 'walls of an ever-narrowing world' finds an echo in the poem's linguistic repetitions, or doubles: 'this/This'; 'man, man'; 'Lives … lives'; 'Here … Here'; 'Hush … Hush'; 'Well I know … / Well I know'; even 'murmur'. The double 'man' who haunts this double prison is Tiresias, the condemned hero of the sister poem, 'The Youth of Nature':

> When his awe-struck captors led
> The Theban seer to the spring …
> Tiresias drank and died.
>
> (43–5)

The two bodies of the condemned man also appear in 'The Sick King in Bokhara' (1847–48?), a poem which retells the Islamic story of the mullah who not only publicly accuses himself, but insists on the full punishment of death. As both accuser and accused, judge and judged, the mullah endures what Foucault sees as the doubleness of every condemned man. The mullah, however, is double in the additional sense that the king, in his admiration for the man, instructs his servants to '"lay his body in my grave"' (228); the condemned man thus takes, quite literally, the place of the king. We return to Foucault's assertion that 'in the darkest region of the political field the condemned man represents the symmetrical, inverted figure of the king'. Though, for Foucault, public execution reduces this complex mirror-relationship to a simple opposition – criminal versus sovereign (*DP*, 50/54) – in Arnold's poem the complexity persists to the point of producing an almost sacrificial relationship. The darkest region of the political field here overlaps with the religious as the condemned man becomes a type of Christ, he who also takes, in death, the place of another.

Foucault is well aware of this overlap, pointing out that the whole theory of the king's double body was 'originally close to the Christological model' (28/33). Though he does not mention this model again there is a sense in which Foucault never quite leaves it behind. In *The Order*, in parodying the invention of man as the speaking subject, Foucault declares *'Ecce Homo'* (306/317) and in so doing conjures up the Christ whom Pilate presents to the people for judgement, the Christ who in this moment is what Foucault later calls 'th[at] abstraction' the 'juridical subject' (*DP*, 13) – the condemned man as a purely legal fiction. To complete the Christological model, Foucault's assertion that 'we should analyse ... "the least [or actual] body of the condemned man"' (28/34) is, almost unwittingly, honoured with regard to Christ. For just as Foucault's tortured regicide, Damiens, is reported to have 'kissed the crucifix' (4/10) so Foucault himself seems to embrace the crucified Christ when, in *The Archeology*, his assault on the idealist history of thought leads to this:

> To whomsoever approaches that fortress ... we repeat, with a gesture that wards off all profanation: *'Noli tangere.'* But I have obstinately gone on.
>
> (203/264)

Echoing the words of the newly-resurrected Christ to Mary Magdalene – '"Touch me not"' (John 20.17) – Foucault effectively casts himself in the role of the transgressive Magdalene, one who has 'obstinately gone on' and touched the least body of Christ.

Though this moment of contact is fleeting and accidental Foucault begins *The Archeology* by warning both us and himself that his text is written 'with a rather shaky hand' and 'stumbles against what it does not mean' (17/27–8). If that includes the condemned body of Christ then Foucault is very different from Arnold, who, as if too respectful of Christ's *noli tangere*, sets out *not* to stumble into this body. Just as the King of Bokhara instructs his servants to sanitise the body of the condemned man – 'wash off all blood, set smooth each limb!' (230) – so Arnold, in his attempt to rescue religion from its materialisation in fact, is uneasy with the bloody fact of the condemned man. 'Leave ... the Cross' (277.27), he daringly declares. This cry, of course, is the cry of the new theology but it also connects with what Foucault describes as the nineteenth century's gradual invisibilising of the body of the condemned man (*DP*, 10/16) – witness, in Britain, the abolition of the pillory in 1837 and public execution in 1868. The connection becomes more obvious in *Obermann Once More*, written around

1867, where we learn that though the personified East did once '"hourly scan ... / ... [the] Cross, with ... / That nailed, thorn-crowned Man!"' (154–6) she does so no longer.

In Arnold's poetry there is one character who does not leave the cross and that is Heinrich Heine. However, as we might expect of 'this iron time / Of doubts' (241.43), Heine's cross is quite literally an *iron* cross, even an iron-ic cross, not least because Heine, 'the court jester' – as Arnold styles him elsewhere[55] – is Jewish, is dizzy and is smiling. Or at least that is how he is remembered in 'Heine's Grave' (1858–63):

> Climbing the rock which juts
> O'er the valley, the dizzily perched
> Rock – to its iron cross
> Once more thou cling'st, to the Cross
> Clingest! with smiles, with a sigh!
>
> (186–90)

Though this is the cross of a jester, the cross of 'Merry Matt', it is a cross that does not, or cannot, rid itself of the condemned man. The first condemned man is Heine himself – 'half blind, palsied, [and] in pain' (13), he suffered, as Arnold writes elsewhere, from 'a softening of the spinal marrow ... and ... for [his last] eight years ... lay helpless ... wasted almost to the proportions of a child'.[56] The second condemned man is the German Jew of which Heine is a type; with its passing reference to 'the blond / German Kaiser' (135) the poem touches darkly on the persecution of German Jews in both the nineteenth century and, almost uncannily, the twentieth. The third condemned man is Christ, another Jew who also clung to a cross with a sigh. Though the time of this poem may well be the 'iron[ic] time of doubt' Heine's iron cross still testifies to the historical time of suffering. Just like Arnold's forsaken merman, Heine's cross mournfully declares: '"'Twill be Easter-time in the world"' (103.58).

Holy city of the plague

It was Clough who first insisted that Arnold's doubt was 'transcendental doubt', an aspect of his aesthetic retreat from the world.[57] And that is certainly how Arnold stages his doubt in 'Stanzas from the Grande Chartreuse', where the act of doubting requires that he joins with the Carthusians: 'their faith, my tears ... / I come to shed them at their side' (89–90). It is not, though, for nothing that Arnold talks of 'this *iron* time of doubts'; in its context – 'Memorial Verses' (1850) – the phrase identifies Arnold's doubt with the very specific iron time of modern medicine. It was, of course, only in the nineteenth century that medical diagnosis came to be dominated by looking and touching – or, as Foucault puts it, '[by] read[ing] … at a glance the visible … organism … [and locating] the illness … exactly on the body' (*BC*, 4/2). As Arnold memorialises Goethe he very precisely evokes this methodology:

> Physician of the iron age,
> Goethe …
> …
> … read each wound …
> And struck his finger on the place,
> And said: *Thou ailest here, and here!*
>
> (17–22)

As Arnold proceeds to memorialise Wordsworth the poem not only sustains the medical analogy ('where will Europe … / Again find … healing power?' (62–3)) but glances obliquely at what is, for Foucault, the defining characteristic of modern medicine – the post-mortem dissection:

> Others will teach us how to dare,
> And against fear our *breast to steel.*
>
> (64–5; my italics)

As the iron time of doubt here shades into the iron, or steel, age of anatomo-clinical medicine so doubt becomes a kind of disease – a conceit that is echoed in later poems: 'the infection of our mental strife' (368.222), reads one; 'and palsied all our world with doubt' (575.319), reads another. Arnold, we know, is inclined to pathologise: witness 'the something that infects the world' (100.278) and, of course, 'this strange disease of modern life'; but what distinguishes Arnold's modern disease of doubt is that it is so nearly modern disease *per se.* His characterisation of doubt as 'wandering between two worlds, one dead, / The other powerless to be born' is remarkably close to Foucault on disease:

> at the beginning of the nineteenth century … disease loses its old status as an accident [extrinsic to life], and takes on the internal, constant, mobile dimension of the relation between life and death.
> (*BC*, 155/158)

Like Arnold's doubt, for Foucault, disease wanders in the space between life and death, and this space is a hidden preoccupation throughout *The Clinic.* For all its seeming materiality this study tends to confirm Barthes's identification of Orpheus (he who descends to Hades) as 'the natural hero of the theoretical endeavour'.[58] For instance, when describing the modern doctor's tendency not simply to *see* the patient's body but to *fore*see it as a dissected corpse, Foucault hints at the scene of the séance: 'these [doctors] ... who watch over men's lives [also] communicate with their death [*mort]*' (166/170) – the French, of course, allows the underthought: 'communicate with their *dead*'. If Foucault here hints at the doctor as a kind of medium then later in *The Clinic* he becomes almost an exorcist: 'because medicine', writes Foucault, 'offers modern man the obstinate, yet reassuring face of his finitude ... death is endlessly repeated, but it is also exorcized [*conjuré*]' (198/201–2). Again, the French can mean not only 'exorcised' but also its very reverse, namely 'conjured' as in conjuring ghosts. Though modern medicine may have both materialised and privatised death – '[it] left its old tragic heaven and became ... [man's] invisible truth, his visible secret' (172/176) – death, for Foucault himself, may be otherwise.

> [In] the Renaissance differences of ... fortune ... were ... effaced by [death's] ... universal gesture; it drew each irrevocably to all ... [in] dances of skeletons ... a sort of egalitarian saturnalia.
>
> (171/175)

Foucault's implication that death might yet return to this 'old tragic heaven', might once again be a point not of separation but of collectivity, is uncannily rehearsed by Foucault's own death, his death from AIDS.[59] In so dying Foucault, we may say, died the collectivised death of a medieval leper: 'in earlier times', he writes, 'one contracted leprosy against a background of great waves of collective punishment' (171/176). To die of AIDS in 1984 was to die against such a background.

That Foucault's death might return us to the collectivity of 'the old tragic heaven' makes considerable sense. For, as the historian of exclusion, Foucault had always belonged to the '"disorder[ly] ... lazar house"' (*MC*, 4/14) – that community of the excluded which is named after Lazarus, the biblical 'leper who died before the gate of the rich man and was carried straight to paradise' (7/16). The lazar house, as Foucault stresses, comes from a text that characterises the leper as a figure of not just exclusion but also salvation. Initially, Foucault ridicules the historical exploitation of this double significance: 'lepers accomplish[ed] their salvation', he writes, 'in and by their very exclusion'; however, when he discusses the nineteenth-century asylum and, in particular, Pinel's attempt to 'resume the moral enterprise of religion, exclusive of its fantastic text' (257/513), Foucault suddenly seems to mourn the exclusion of the fantastic text of heaven, and its communion of saints. Pinel's moralised religion, he writes, fails to assimilate 'the social theme of a religion in which men feel themselves brothers in the same communion'. And it is this specifically communal theme that the lazar house, by virtue of its entanglement in the fantastic text of heaven, *does* assimilate: the lazar's ascent to heaven means, for Foucault, that '[t]his exclusion offers [the lazar] … another form of communion' (7/16).

Arnold, of course, shares much of Pinel's anxiety about Christianity's fantastic text; for Arnold, Christianity had materialised itself in the fact of an objective deity who is, in truth, more nearly a symbol: 'God is … the Eternal that makes for righteousness.'[60] Such humanised Christianity might just be read as an extension of Pinel's 'neutralised asylum' (256/512), an extension of what Foucault calls 'the disciplined society' (*DP*, 198/200). To put it another way, whilst Foucault's stress on Christianity's social theme draws on the lazar, Arnold's stress on Christianity's moral theme draws on the plague, or rather that arrest of the plague which, for Foucault, is at the root of the disciplinary society:

> If … the leper gave rise to rituals of exclusion, which … provided the model for … the great Confinement, then the plague gave rise to disciplinary projects. Rather than the massive, binary division between one set of people and another, it called for multiple separations, individualizing distributions, an organization of surveillance and control … this is the utopia of the perfectly governed city.
>
> (*DP*, 198/200)

Just such a plague and just such a city feature in the humanised gospel of Arnold's 'Rugby Chapel' (1857–60). Here salvation is redefined, in effect, as the plagued but disciplined 'city of God':

> See! In the rocks of the world
> Marches the host of mankind,

...
Sore thirst plagues them ...
...
Sole they shall stray ...
...
Die one by one in the waste.

Then ...
...
Ye, like angels appear,
...
Order, courage, return.
Ye fill up the gaps ...
Strengthen the wavering line,
Stablish, continue our march,
On, to the bound of the waste,
On, to the City of God.

(171–208)

What makes this city not just perfectly governed but the site of plague is the reader's uncertainty as to where 'the City' is in relation to 'the waste', an uncertainty informed by the historical fact of urban insanitation – the mid-Victorian city was *the* site of human waste.

This fact is one that Arnold never quite forgets, even as he reimagines the City of God. Not only was 1852 the year of the Cholera Report and the Drainage and Sewerage of Towns Report, it was also the year in which Arnold's public first read that Empedocles 'could [no longer] ... / Cleanse ... the breath of poisonous streams' (115–17) and that 'Tiresias drank and died.' Arnold's insanitary City of God becomes more nearly the disciplinary utopia of Foucauldian analysis in 'Rome Sickness' (1873–75). Here, even as Arnold seems to be voicing his home sickness for Rome, the poem is haunted by the subtext of a city of not only sickness but also surveillance and control:

Unwearied ...
The incessant wanderer takes his way,
To hold the light, and reach the hand
... to all who stray!

(29–32: my italics)

As in 'Rugby Chapel', Arnold's quasi-religious dream of a holy city is also a political dream of the perfectly governed city. To put it another way, the 'incessant wanderer' and dreamer of new salvations is here shadowed, or doubled, by the figure of the policeman – he who carries a light and lays a hand upon those that stray. This double figure is, in a sense, Arnold himself: Arnold the Romantic who turns neoclassical, the poet who is also a school-inspector, and the writer who – by the time of 'Rome Sickness' – had very largely abandoned poetry for criticism. The poem, however, complicates this familiar diptych for its wanderer almost reaches a hand *to himself* – as a wanderer he is, presumably, to be numbered among 'all who stray'. For Arnold's famous 'dialogue of the mind with itself'[61] here read the dialogue of the body with itself.

'Rome Sickness' does, as a whole, exemplify this dialogue in the sense that it constitutes a return to Arnold's very first published poem, 'Alaric at Rome' (1840?) – a return that the two poems themselves imagine in terms of touch. In the first place, Rome sickness, or at least the sickness of Rome, is a key theme of the earlier poem, which declares, of the Rome besieged by Alaric, that 'strife … and sickness are within' (81). Again, the word-play between 'home' and 'Rome' inscribed in 'Rome Sickness' is a remarkably precise rebuttal to Alaric's: 'here is no echo to the sound of home' (149). In 'Alaric' the poet, addressing Rome, declares that 'hand touch thee not' (209); in 'Rome Sickness' Arnold the wanderer reaches his hand out to himself not only as 'one who stray[s]' but also as one who, over thirty years before, wrote 'Alaric'. This betrays an Arnold who, after all this time, is still writing about the same diseased city.[62] Indeed, his attempt to reach out to his younger self seems as doomed as is contact between the inhabitants of Foucault's city of plague:

> between the infected houses … is a segmented, immobile, frozen space. Each individual is fixed in his place. And, if he moves, he does so at the risk of his life, contagion or punishment.
>
> (*DP*, 195/197–8)

Whether Foucault is writing about the plague or the leper he describes 'the hand that is not stretched out' (*MC*, 7/16). In 'Rome Sickness' Arnold describes a hand that *is* reached out – reached out, in part, to his younger self; however, the space through which it moves is immobile, frozen – thirty years and still the same sick city. Arnold reaches his hand to himself as one who not only strays but stays.

Whether that hand holds on to anything is a question that is answered in the quasi-autobiographical 'The Progress of Poesy' (1864–67):

> Youth …
> … strikes the rock …
> And brings the water from the fount
> …
> The man mature with labour chops
> For the bright stream a channel grand,
> And sees not that the sacred drops
> Ran off and *vanished out of hand.*
>
> (1–8: my italics)

Arnold's hand again reaches out in vain in the later poem 'New Rome' (1874) and again it moves through the frozen space of the holy city – in particular, the frozen space of a museum. The body being reached for is 'the armless Vatican Cupid' who:

> Hangs down his beautiful head;
> For the priests have got him in prison,
> And Psyche long has been dead.
>
> (1–4)

The hand that reaches is a trick of language:

> But see …
> …
> … *The Times,* that bright Apollo
> Proclaims salvation *at hand.*
>
> (5–8: my italics)

This salvation, however, is simply the cry: '"Modernise Rome!" … Wide[n the] streets' – precisely the cry of the mid-century city-planners who widened streets both to increase surveillance and to facilitate, in emergency, the use of the military.[63] Beyond the frozen space of the Vatican there is only the frozen space of the perfectly governed city; no wonder that

> The armless Vatican Cupid
> Hangs down his head as before.
>
> (17–18)

This immobile body remains immobile – what is armless remains untouched and unmoved by what is at hand.

Face after face

What, though, has an armless body to do with hands? The buried conceit is of a body that echoes Arnold's declaration, in a letter, that 'I am fragments.'[64] In the case of the poem, however, the body is divided from itself by not just space but also time. What has an antique, classical body to do with that which is 'at hand', that which is now and cries 'Modernise!'? The time of this body (like Hamlet's body of time) is out of joint. It recalls not only Arnold's '"The day I lived in was not mine"' (573.257) but also Foucault's 'man is not contemporaneous with his [own] being' (*OT*, 335/346). Foucault does not, though, speak of a fragmented body – instead, he uses the more radical image of complete and utter shattering:

> man ... encounters [most obviously in language] ... contents and forms older than him, which he cannot master ... which, by binding him to multiple, intersecting, often mutually irreducible chronologies, scatter ... him through time, star him [*l'étoile]* at the centre of the duration of things.
>
> (331/342)

Four years later Foucault declares, 'I write to have no face'; here, as he stares at man as in a shattered glass (*étoiler* meaning to star, or crack, a pane of glass), it is as if he has already lost face. However, this starred glass carries within itself characteristic Foucauldian traces. Foucault has written before of a glass man:

> The man who imagines he is made of glass is not mad ... but he is mad if, believing he is made of glass, he thereby concludes that he is fragile, that he is in danger of breaking.
>
> (*MC*, 94/251)

Foucault has also written before of the 'large [invisible] X ... [or] St Andrew's cross' that he sees in Velázquez's *Las Meniñas* – a picture that, for Foucault, not only contains a looking-glass but also, in depicting observers, *is* a looking-glass. ('What', asks Foucault, 'are the faces that are [here] reflected?' (*OT*, 12–14/28–9).) Discernible within Foucault's starred glass are, then, traces of both madness (the man who thinks he is glass) and public execution (St Andrew's cross) – traces or signatures of Foucault himself; the starred glass that is shattered man is, in this sense, Foucault's looking-glass. He certainly sees a face in the crossed and, as it were, cracked glass of *Las Meniñas*: 'where the two lines intersect, at the centre of the X, is the gaze of the infant' (13/28). This gaze that looks out at Foucault may still be deciphered – on the cryptic basis that glass is made from sand – in the famous 'face of sand' ('visage de sable') at the very end of the book. Even as *The Order* predicts the disappearance of a face it effects the reappearance of a face. Face, it seems, will survive its own disappearance.

But then, since Foucault's man is starred it is, in a sense, inevitable that he should share, or endure, a star's capacity to survive its own extinction. As Empedocles reminds us, reflecting contemporary advances in astronomy, many of the stars we see have long since burnt out: 'And you, ye stars / ... Have you too, survived yourselves?' (276–80).

Such posthumous life is also a pertinent question for Foucault. What, he asks, will become of man after Man? 'Ought we ... to admit that ... man will return to ... serene non-existence?' (*OT*, 386/397). Foucault begs a very similar question at the end of *Discipline*; this time it is: what will become of the author once 'discourses ... unfold in the anonymity of a murmur?' Following a long newspaper quotation Foucault begins the last paragraph of his study with the announcement that 'I shall stop with this anonymous text'; however, by ending this same paragraph with that cryptic declaration, 'we must hear the distant roar of battle [*bataille*]', he ends with a noun which is also the name of that dead but, for Foucault, key author – Georges Bataille (1897–1962).[65] It is, of course, in 'What Is an Author?' [1969] that Foucault first raises the question of the function of an author's name; here, as the very last word of *Discipline*,[66] the dead author's name functions as almost a ghostly signature.

Writing just three years before, Barthes followed up his 'The Death of the Author' essay with the assertion, 'It is not that the Author may not "come back" in the Text ... but he does so as a "guest" ... no longer privileged ... his inscription is ludic.'[67] At the end of *Discipline* this ludic inscription is not so much a guest as a ghost. This haunting, this insistence of the name, may not quite be the insistence of spirit but then neither is it purely and simply Lacan's insistence of the letter.[68]

A similar haunting besets the anonymous text with which Arnold also, in a sense, stops. In the last years of his poetic career Arnold wrote not only two poems entitled 'A Nameless Epitaph' (1864–67) but also 'SS Lusitania' (1878), which does itself stop with the anonymous text of a telegram. The poem contrasts the drowning of Dante's Ulysses with the safe passage of Arnold's only surviving son:

> I dropped the book, and of my child I thought
> In his long black ship speeding night and day
> O'er those same seas; dark Teneriffe rose, fraught
> With omen; 'Oh! were that mount passed', I say.
> Then the door opens and this card is brought:
> 'Reached Cape Verde Islands, "Lusitania".'
>
> (9–14)

Though the unsigned telegram announces a safe arrival it also recalls a drowning; in this sense the telegram is another nameless epitaph. Indeed, it is an epitaph not only to Ulysses but also, in a sense, to Arnold; as Honan observes, Dante's Ulysses, in entering the Inferno to sing forever of death, 'is a lost poet'[69] – as is, by this time, Arnold. Thus haunted, twice over, by the un-signature of a dead author, Arnold's telegram is so like the last sentence of *Discipline* as to cause us to reread that sentence as yet another nameless epitaph; to locate in Foucault's anonymous text the Arnoldian 'note of sadness' ('Dover Beach', 14).

There is, for certain, a conspicuously elegiac tone within the anonymous text with which Foucault begins 'The Order of Discourse'; this time, though, it is not so much a sadness *for* the nameless as the sadness *of* the nameless, 'the nameless voice' that Foucault imagines:

> Doubling in advance everthing I am going to say, a voice would say: 'You must go on, I can't go on, you must go on, I'll go on … strange pain, strange sin … before the door that … would surprise me, if it opens.'[70]

The 'name' of this nameless voice is, appropriately, Beckett's *The Unnameable*; there is, though, still another nameless voice, this time one that doubles the very experience of being overcome by a nameless voice. It is, of course, Arnold's: 'I feel', he writes, 'a nameless sadness o'er me roll' (286.3). This is not the only occasion on which Arnold's voice doubles Foucault's experience of anonymity: '"Do not ask who I am"' (*AK*, 17/27), writes Foucault; 'ask not my name', writes Arnold (586.1). As Foucault himself remarks, 'I am no doubt not the only one who writes in order to have no face'; he is right – the later, neoclassical Arnold does too: 'the poet', he writes in 1853, '[is] most fortunate when he most entirely succeeds in effacing himself'.[71]

Foucault and Arnold most nearly come face to face when they have no faces, when they refuse to give their names. But then, for Foucault, the whole point of anonymity is precisely to make possible such face-to-face encounters – his claim to be writing to have no face is immediately prefaced by his talk of 'appear[ing] at last to eyes that I will never have to meet again' (17/28). In addition to its fleeting eroticism, this 'appearing at last' is laced with the religious tradition of coming face to face with God – a tradition that in its ascetic form, as Foucault himself knows well, [72] entails losing one's own face. True to this tradition, the face which Foucault is seeking is not, it seems, one in which he will see his own authorial face:

> How unbearable it is, in view of how much of himself everyone … thinks he is putting of 'himself' into his own discourse … how unbearable it is to cut up, analyse, combine, rearrange all these texts … without ever the transfigured face of the author appearing.
>
> (*AK*, 210/274)

It is not, though, just any authorial face that Foucault will not see; it is a *transfigured* face – something, presumably, like the face of Moses after he had seen the face of God (Exodus 35.29–35). And, of course, Moses' transfigured face is, precisely, a face that will *not* appear; for, as long as his face was shining, Moses wore a veil. Here, at the end of *The Archeology*, though there is a lack or losing of face it might just, paradoxically, be because of a divine excess of face. Foucault acknowledges something of this paradox when he describes his work, in general, as not the end of visionary experience but the beginning again; he speaks of a textual sublime in which the face of God becomes the sur*face* of discourse:

> Henceforth, the visionary experience arises from the black and white surface of printed signs, from the closed and dusty volumes that open with a flight of forgotten words.[73]

A version of just such an experience arises from Arnold's 'Tristram and Iseult' when we learn that, in his mad excursion into the moonlit woods, Tristram seeks to bathe his hot brow in a spring only to find that: '"God! tis *her* face plays in the waters bright"' (I.284). The reader cannot help but misread, albeit for a moment, 'her face' as God's; for the split second of this misreading Tristram sees the face of God – a visionary experience thus arising from the black-and-white of printed signs. It is, though, a trick, an illusion always already undermined by the 'her' that would make God female. Arnold does not, it seems, share Foucault's confidence in the textual sublime. It is no accident that Arnold remembers Moses not as one who saw God but as one who, in failing to enter the promised land, is the emblem of criticism's appalling limitations:

> the true [creative] life of literature ... is the promised land ... it will not be ours to enter, and we shall die in the wilderness.[74]

Like Foucault, Arnold experiences reading and criticism as a 'closed and dusty' world; according to Arnold, however, there is no flight of words.

This is not to suggest that, for Foucault, this textual flight is the simple ascent of a conventional sublime. Though he writes of a 'secret verticality' in literary, non-representational language[75] it is a *precipitous* verticality, of not just height but also fall. After the age of representation 'literature', writes Foucault, 'becomes merely a manifestation of a language which has no other law than that of affirming ... its own precipitous existence' (*OT*, 300/313). The radical ambiguity of this existence that offers, at once, both ascent and descent is most obviously articulated when Foucault declares:

> At this extreme limit we find a revelation that no language could have expressed outside of the abyss that engulfs it and that no fall could have ... demonstrated if it were not at the same time a conquest of the highest peak.[76]

The paradox of a fall that is also a conquest of a peak describes, very precisely, Empedocles' descent into the crater at the summit of Mount Etna:

> Receive me, save me!
>
> [*He plunges into the crater.*]
>
> (II.416)

For Foucault, to fall is to conquer; for Empedocles, to fall is to be saved. Significant in both cases is not only the theological paradox of the 'happy fall'[77] but also its Heideggerian reworking as the positive 'fallenness' of *Dasein*, of being-in-the-world.[78] Equally double in significance is what Foucault sees as philosophy's happy fall into madness, specifically the madness of Nietzsche:

> in the expiration of philosophical language a possibility inevitably arises (that upon which it falls – the face of the die; and the place into which it falls – the void in which the die is cast): the possibility of the mad philosopher.[79]

Here identified with both the fall and face of a die, philosophy's happy fall is theological in that it returns us to Pascal's wager of faith and Heideggerian in that it evokes Heidegger's talk of '*Dasein* [coming] … face to face with the thrownness of its "that it is there"'.[80] At odds, however, with all this theological and philosophical weight is the possibility of the mad philosopher that is Nietzsche – for he it is who cries: 'Come, let us kill the Spirit of Gravity!'[81] If this is what Foucault does, and we know he is prone to laughter, then Foucault's world is a weightless one in which the die will never reach the ground – it is, after all, a die cast into the void. In such a world the Pascalian wager would never be decided and Heidegger's being-as-falling become a kind of flight. It is just such a Nietzschean world that Arnold intuits[82] when, looking into the eyes of Marguerite, he writes of nothing less than 'An angelic gravity' ('A Memory Picture', 46).

Notes

1 *The Poems of Matthew Arnold*, ed. Miriam Allott (London: Longman, 1979), 256.21–5. All subsequent references appear parenthetically in the text and are, usually, to page and line. The date of the poem's composition, when known, also usually appears in parenthesis.

2 Michel Foucault, *The Order of Things: An Archeology of the Human Sciences*, unidentified collective translation (London: Tavistock, 1970), 386–7 / *Les Mots et les choses: Une archéologie des sciences humaines* (Paris: Gallimard, 1966), 398. All subsequent references will use, as an abbreviation, either *The Order* or *OT*. These will appear parenthetically in the text and are to the English translation followed by the French; this order is reversed when I quote the French. The same conventions apply to other bilingual references.

3 Foucault and Arnold have already been brought together, albeit very briefly, by one or two critics. See Linda Ray Pratt, 'Empedocles, Suicide and the Order of Things', *Victorian Poetry*, 26 (1988), 82–8; and David G. Reide, *Matthew Arnold and the Betrayal of Language* (Charlottesville: University Press of Virginia, 1989), 25–6.

4 See Blaise Pascal, *Pensées* [1662], trans. A. J. Krailsheimer (Harmondsworth: Penguin, 1966), 149–54. The importance of Pascal to Foucault may be measured by the fact that *Madness and Civilisation* was, initially, to be called 'L'Autre Tour de folie', in reference to the opening quotation from Pascal – see Didier Eribon, *Michel Foucault*, tr. Betsy Wing (London: Faber and Faber, 1993), 92.

5 Michel Foucault, *Madness and Civilisation: A History of Insanity in the Age of Reason*, tr. Richard Howard (London: Routledge, 1967) / *Histoire de la folie à l'âge classique*, 2nd revised edn (Paris: Gallimard, 1961). Abbreviated hereafter as *Madness* or *MC*.

6 In exploring the imaginative, poetic dimension of Foucault's writing, I am, in a sense, responding to Jean Baudrillard's assertion that 'Foucault's discourse is not a discourse of truth but a mythic discourse in the strong sense of the word … this writing is too beautiful to be true' – *Forget Foucault* (New York: Semiotext(e), 1987), 10–11. Foucault himself remarked in 1977 that 'I have never written anything but fictions … it is possible … to induce truthful effects with a fictional discourse' – 'The History of Sexuality' [Finas interview], *Power/Knowledge: Selected Interviews and Other Writings, 1972–1977*, ed. Colin Gordon (Brighton: Harvester, 1980), 193. As David Carroll observes, 'this … "literary" … approach to … philosophical, historical, and political issues … is not just a characteristic of [Foucault's] … 'early work", but a fundamental component of his entire critical production' – *Paraesthetics: Foucault, Lyotard, Derrida* (London: Methuen, 1987), 108.

7 Most critics have assumed that Foucault is a purely materialist thinker whose interest in the question of faith is wholly negative. There are, though, exceptions to this rule: see Mark Taylor, *De-constructing Theology* (New York: Crossroad, 1982), and also his *Erring: A Postmodern A/Theology* (Chicago: University of Chicago Press, 1984); David Chidester, 'Michel Foucault and the Study of Religion', *Religious Studies Review*, 12 (1986), 1–9; J. Bernauer, 'The Prisons of Man: An Introduction to Foucault's Negative Theology', *International Philosophical Quarterly*, 20 (1987), 365–80; Uta Liebmann Schaub, 'Foucault's Oriental Subtext', *PMLA*, 104 (1989), 306–16; and Stephen D. Moore, *Poststructuralism and the New Testament: Derrida and Foucault at the Foot of the Cross* (Minneapolis: Fortress Press, 1994).

8 Arnold is concerned with what Ruth ApRoberts calls a 'rationalisation of religion' – *Arnold and God* (Berkeley: University of California Press, 1983), 107.

9 Michel Foucault, *The Birth of the Clinic: An Archeology of Medical Perception*, tr. A. M. Sheridan (London: Routledge, 1973), 171–2 / *Naissance de la clinique: Une archéologie du regard médical* (Paris: Presses Universitaires de France, 1963), 175–6. All subsequent references will use, as abbreviation, either *The Clinic* or *BC*.

10 See *The Order*, 305/317.

11 This intuition is countered by Martin Heidegger: 'By its very essence, death is in every case mine, insofar as it "is" at all' – *Being and Time*, tr. John Macquarrie and Edward Robinson (Oxford: Blackwell, 1962), 284.

12 Matthew Arnold, 'The Function of Criticism at the Present Time', *The Complete Prose Works of Matthew Arnold*, 11 vols (Ann Arbor: University of Michigan Press, 1960–77), 3.285.

13 William Shakespeare, *Hamlet*, ed. Harold Jenkins (London: Routledge, 1982), I.ii.132–3.

14 *Ibid.*, I.ii.103–4.

15 *The Letters of Mattew Arnold to Arthur Hugh Clough*, ed. Howard Foster Lowry (London: Oxford University Press, 1957), 113.

16 Hamlet's dying words are, of course 'the rest is silence' (V.ii.363).

17 'On the Study of Celtic Literature' [1867], *Complete Prose Works*, 3.335.

18 Michel Foucault, 'Fantasia of the Library', in *Language, Counter-Memory, Practice*, ed. D. F. Bouchard (Ithaca: Cornell University Press, 1977), 87–112 / 'Un "fantastique" de bibliothèque', in *Cahiers Renaud-Barrault*, 59 (1967), 7–30.

19 David M. Halperin, *Saint Foucault: Towards a Gay Hagiography* (Oxford: Oxford University Press, 1995).

20 Foucault, 'Fantasia', 109/30.

21 Michel Foucault, 'What Is an Author?', in *Language*, 127 (translation modified) / 'Qu'est-ce qu'un Auteur?', *Bulletin de la Société Française de Philosophie*, 63 (1969), 86.

22 Postcard dated 13 August 1981 – quoted in Eribon, *Michel Foucault*, 4.

23 See David Macey, *The Lives of Michel Foucault* (London: Vintage, 1993), 12; and Eribon, *Michel Foucault*, 4–5.

24 *Complete Prose Works*, 3.273–4.

25 *Ibid.*, 3.335.

26 For a discussion of Arnold and Englishness see Julian Wolfreys, *Being English: Narratives, Idioms and Performances of National Identity* (Albany: State University of New York Press, 1994) 53–80.

27 Michel Foucault, 'A Preface to Transgression', in *Language*, 38 / 'Préface à la Transgression', *Critique*, 195–6 (1963), 758.

28 See the Translator's Note – Michel Foucault, *Discipline and Punish: The Birth of the Prison*, tr. Alan Sheridan (Harmondsworth: Penguin, 1977 / *Surveiller et punir: Naissance de la prison* (Paris: Gallimard, 1975). Abbreviated hereafter as *Discipline* or *DP*.

29 *Complete Prose Works*, 3.267. Arnold's dialectical habit of mind has been noted by a number of critics – see, in particular, Walter J. Hipple, Jr, 'Matthew Arnold, Dialectician', *University of Toronto Quarterly*, 32 (1962), 1–26; Gerhard Joseph, 'The *Antigone* as Cultural Touchstone: Matthew Arnold, Hegel, George Eliot, Virginia Woolf and Margaret Drabble', *PMLA*, 96 (1981), 22–35; and Richard Dellamora, *Masculine Desire: The Sexual Politics of Victorian Aestheticism* (Chapel Hill: University of North Carolina Press, 1990), 102.

30 'To sleep, perchance to dream' – *Hamlet*, III.i.65.

31 Michel Foucault, *The Archeology of Knowledge and the Discourse on Language*, tr. A. M. Sheridan Smith (London: Routledge, 1972), 17 / *L'Archéologie du savoir* (Paris: Gallimard, 1969), 28. Abbreviated hereafter as *The Archeology* or *AK*.

32 This point is made by, among others, Ian Hacking, 'The Archeology of Foucault', in D. C. Hoy (ed.), *Foucault: A Critical Reader* (Oxford: Blackwell, 1986), 33. For Foucault's own comments see the interview 'Truth and Power' and 'Interview with Lucette Finas', both in *Power/Knowledge.*

33 'L'Intellectuel et les pouvoirs', *La Revue Nouvelle*, 80 (October 1984), 339. For further, albeit very brief, discussion of Foucault and autobiography, see Macey, *Lives* xiv; and J. Rajchman, *Michel Foucault: The Freedom of Philosophy* (New York: Columbia University Press, 1985), 36.

34 Quoted in Allan Megill, *Prophets of Extremity: Nietzsche, Heidegger, Foucault, Derrida* (Los Angeles: University of California Press, 1985), 246.

35 Whether or not such encounters were part of Foucault's life, it was certainly part of the perception of him: as Macey writes, '[many] knew, or claim to have known, a Foucault who, clad in black leather and hung with chains, would slip out of his apartment in the rue de Vaugirard in search of anonymous sexual adventure' (*Lives*, xv).

36 Jacques Derrida, 'Cogito and the History of Madness', in *Writing and Difference*, tr. Alan Bass (London: Routledge, 1978), 37.

37 *Complete Prose Works*, 9.46.

38 Martin Bidney makes the same point in '"A Dream" as a Key to a Reverie in Matthew Arnold: Interactions of Water and Fire', *Victorian Poetry*, 26 (1988), 50. For an excellent discussion of the complex significance of 'same-sex comradeship' in Arnold's poetry see Joseph Bristow, '"Love, let us be true to one another": Matthew Arnold, Arthur Hugh Clough, and "our Aqueous Ages"', *Literature and History*, 4 (1995), 27–49.

39 Nicholas Murray describes this daring as 'undergraduate patois' which often included extensive use of foreign-language phrases – see *A Life of Matthew Arnold* (London: Sceptre, 1996), 107. As Isobel Armstrong writes, 'the letters [between Arnold and Clough] are full of half-frivolous endearments [such as] ... "You will not I know forget me" ... "Adieu and love me"' – *Victorian Poetry: Poetry, Poetics and Politics* (London: Routledge, 1993), 209.

40 Susan Walsh, 'That Arnoldian Wragg: Anarchy as Menstrosity in Victorian Social Criticism', *Victorian Literature and Culture*, 20 (1992), 221. As Park Honan demonstrates, Arnold was quite capable of obscene expletives – see *Matthew Arnold: A Life* (London: Weidenfeld and Nicolson, 1981), 59. For further discussion of the homoerotic subtext of Arnold's classical references, see Dellamora, *Masculine Desire*, 73–5.

41 See Michel Foucault, *The History of Sexuality: An Introduction* (Harmondsworth: Penguin, 1979), 1–14 / *La Volonté de savoir* (Paris: Gallimard, 1976), 9–22.

42 Michel Foucault, 'The Order of Discourse', in Robert Young (ed.), *Untying the Text: A Poststructuralist Reader* (London: Routledge, 1981), 52, 51 / *L'Ordre du discours* (Paris: Gallimard, 1971), 10, 8.

43 Michel Foucault, 'Theatrum philosophicum', in *Language*, 196 / 'Theatrum philosophicum', *Critique*, 282 (1970), 908.

44 'The Order of Discourse', 50/7.

45 *Ibid.*, 52, 51 / 9, 8.

46 This optimism is most obviously reflected in *Culture and Anarchy* (1869): 'And is not the close and bounded intellectual horizon within which we have long lived and moved now lifting up ... ? ... now the iron force of exclusion of all that is new has wonderfully yielded' – *Complete Prose Works*, 5.8–9.

47 'What Is an Author?', 138 (translation modified) / 95.

48 See, for example, Paul Veyne, 'The Final Foucault and His Ethics', *Critical Inquiry*, 20 (1993–94), 3–6; and Megill, 238. Foucault, 'Preface to Transgression', 38 / 758.

49 Quoted in Macey, *Lives*, 347.

50 *The History of Sexuality*, 93/122–3.

51 See Genesis 19.1–11; 'Theatrum philosophicum', 168, 171 / 887, 889.

52 According to C. B. Tinker and H. F. Lowry 'the whole poem should ... be read with the background of the Oxford Movement in mind' – *The Poetry of Matthew Arnold: A Commentary* (London: Oxford University Press, 1940), 252; there is also, I am suggesting, a hint of muscular Christianity.

53 The Theban prophet Tiresias had the body of a man for one part of his life and that of a woman for another.

54 'Preface to Transgression', 42/761.

55 Matthew Arnold, 'Heinrich Heine', *Complete Prose Works*, 3.115.

56 *Complete Prose Works*, 3.117.

57 See Clinton Machann and Forrest D. Burt (eds), *Matthew Arnold in His Time and Ours: Centenary Essays* (Charlottesville: University Press of Virginia, 1988), 8.

58 See Michael Holland, 'Barthes, Orpheus ...', *Paragraph*, 11 (1988), 143–74.

59 See Macey, *Lives*, 475–7; and Eribon, *Michel Foucault*, 325.

60 See *Literature and Dogma* (1873), *Complete Prose Works*, 6.152; *God and the Bible*, *ibid.*, 7.192.

61 'Preface to First Edition of *Poems*' (1853), *Complete Prose Works*, 1.4

62 This interest dates back to at least Arnold's teenage years and the 1838 poem 'Inspired by Julia Pardoe's *The City of the Sultan*' (624–7) – Pardoe's 1836 story about Constantinople as 'a city of the Plague'.

63 The poem is written in satirical response to an editorial in *The Times* of 15 April 1873 which describes the streets of Rome as 'narrow, irregular, tortuous and dirty' – see Tinker and Lowry, *The Poetry of Matthew Arnold*, 180–1. During the erection of the Crystal Palace for the Great Exhibition of 1851 the streets around Hyde Park, the site of the exhibition, were widened – as John Lucas writes, 'The official explanation was that this would give the public easier access. The truth was that the authorities were worried about the possibilities of violent demonstrations and protests against the exhibition and were advised that wider streets would make it easier for the cavalry to ride three abreast' – 'Past and Present: *Bleak House* and *A Child's History of England*', in John Schad (ed.), *Dickens Refigured* (Manchester: Manchester University Press, 1996), 147.

64 Letter to Arnold's sister 'K', *c.* July 1849 (misdated 1853), *Unpublished Letters of Matthew Arnold*, ed. A. Whitridge (New Haven: Yale University Press, 1923), 18.

65 Foucault described Bataille as 'one of the most important writers of this century' – Georges Bataille, *Ouvres complètes*, vol. 1: *Premier écrits, 1922–1940* (Paris: Gallimard, 1970), Presentation de Michel Foucault, i.

66 It is not the last word in the English translation, where, for some reason, what is a footnote in the French becomes the final sentence.

67 Roland Barthes, 'From Work to Text' [1971], in *Image–Music–Text*, ed. Stephen Heath (London: Fontana, 1977), 161 / 'De l'oeuvre au texte', *Ouvres complètes* (Paris: Seuil, 1994), 2.1215.

68 James Bernauer ends his study of Foucault with the claim that 'Foucault's work is ... ultimately ... a cry of spirit' – *Michel Foucault's Force of Flight: Toward an Ethics for Thought* (Atlantic Highlands, NJ: Humanities Press International, 1990), 184.

69 Honan, *Matthew Arnold*, 382.

70 'The Order of Discourse', 51/8.

71 *Complete Prose Works*, 1.8.

72 In the second and third volumes of his *History of Sexuality* (both published in 1984) Foucault's concern with the cultivation of subjectivity in the ancient world includes considerable discussion of Christianity's partial renunciation of the self. As Foucault puts it, 'Christian culture has developed the idea that if you want to take care of yourself in the right way you have to sacrifice yourself' – quoted in Bernauer, *Michel Foucault's Force of Flight*, 180.

73 Quoted in *ibid.*, 183.

74 'The Function of Criticism', *Complete Prose Works*, 3.285.

75 'Language to Infinity', in *Language*, 58 / 'Le langage à l'infini', *Tel Quel*, 15 (1963), 47.

76 'The Father's No', in *Language*, 71 (translation modified) / 'Le "Non" du père', *Critique*, 178 (1962), 197.

77 This is the famous *felix culpa* paradox – the belief that Adam's fall was, ultimately, a blessing since it made necessary a redemption that brought about a closer relationship between mankind and God than had existed in Eden.

78 See George Steiner, *Heidegger* (London: Fontana, 1992), 97–9. For further discussion of Foucault's debt to Heidegger see, in particular, Simon During, *Foucault and Literature: Towards a Genealogy of Literature* (London: Routledge, 1992), 19–21, 102–4; and Hubert L. Dreyfus and Paul Rabinow, *Michel Foucault: Beyond Structuralism and Hermeneutics* (Brighton: Harvester, 1982), 37–43.

79 'Preface to Transgression', 44/762.

80 Heidegger, *Being and Time*, 310.

81 Friedrich Nietzsche, *Thus Spoke Zarathustra: A Book for Everyone and No One*, tr. R. J. Hollingdale (Harmondsworth: Penguin, 1961), 68.

82 For further discussion of the unlikely relationship between Arnold and Nietzsche, see Reide, *Matthew Arnold and the Betrayal of Language*, 84–5; and Donald D. Stone, 'Arnold, Nietzsche and the "Revaluation of Values"', *Nineteenth Century Literature*, 43 (1988–89), 289–318.

3

À Dieu: from Browning, from Derrida

Towards an exhalation

Greek endings

> The dead Greek lore lies buried in the urn
> Where who seeks fire finds ashes. Ghost forsooth!
> What was the best Greece babbled of as truth?
>
> (Robert Browning, 'With Gerard de Lairesse', 1887)[1]

> ... this thought summons us to a dislocation of the Greek logos ... to depart from the Greek site ... and to move toward ... a ... speech already emitted ... inside the Greek origin, close to the other of the Greek.
>
> (Jacques Derrida, 'Violence and Metaphysics', [1964])[2]

Both Browning and Derrida characteristically seek or describe a movement away from 'the Greek origin', a movement away from the authority of reason, truth and, of course, origin. In Browning this movement becomes most obvious in 'Cleon' (1855), where the onset of Christianity, in the person of St Paul, is no less than a scandal to the Greek philosopher-poet:

> Thou canst not think a mere barbarian Jew
> As Paulus proves to be, one circumcised,
> Hath access to a secret shut from us?
> Thou wrongest our philosophy.
>
> (343–6)

'Here we see', writes Joseph Bristow, 'a critique of Arnoldian Hellenism'[3] – a critique that, later in *Men and Women*, makes a cryptic return with Bishop Blougham's passing reference to 'Greek endings'. Talking of a bygone era of faith, the Bishop declares:

> How you'd exult if I could put you back
> Six hundred years, blot out cosmogony,
> Geology, ethnology, what not,
> (Greek endings, each the little passing-bell
> That signifies some faith's about to die).
>
> (678–82)

Though Bloughram refers to sciences whose names *have* 'Greek endings' the phrase threatens to name the ending *of* the Greek, the exhaustion of all that *is* Greek, or Greek-inspired – above all, scientific rationalism. Though the passage is *about* the 'passing-bell' for religious faith it also *sounds* a 'passing-bell' for the faith that is Hellenism. Bloughram may not be able to take us *back* six hundred years, but he might just take us forward one hundred – 'forward' to Derrida's isolation of the Greek logos as the tacit faith of Western culture, a faith for which he too, most obviously in *Glas*,[4] sounds the *glas*, the passing-bell.

And just as Derrida directs us *from* the Greek *towards* the other of the Greek so Browning's movement away from Hellenism entails a movement towards Hebraism. Though often overlooked, Browning had an attachment to Hebraism which never lapsed – witness not only such poems as 'Holy Cross Day' (1855), 'Rabbi Ben Ezra' (1864) and 'Jochanan Hakkadosh' (1883) but also Browning's personal contact with Jewish writers and activists.[5] The only major Browning critic even to glance in this direction is David Shaw, who talks of 'the midrash of accumulating commentary' in 'A Death in the Desert' and remarks that 'Browning's canon, unlike the New Testament, is never closed.'[6]

As Shaw implies, this sense of unending – what Bloughram might call 'the imminent sneeze that never comes' (672) – approaches a peculiarly Jewish sense of scripture as an unfinished text, a text still awaiting its Messianic resolution. A Jewish sense of waiting and, indeed, of wandering has always been crucial to Derrida's notion of writing; in his 1964 essay on Edmond Jabès, Derrida declares that 'writing is the moment of the desert' and 'Judaism … the birth and passion of writing [*écriture*]'.[7] Such declarations are almost self-evident in the French – *écriture*, as Kevin Hart reminded us, can mean not only 'writing' but 'scripture'.

Though Derrida's interpreters have often ignored this,

Browning – like Hart – does not allow us to 'keep *écriture* completely in line with secularism'.[8] In Browning writing is a kind of scripture and scripture a kind of writing; for Browning, the Bible has little to do with what Derrida meant by 'the Book' when he declared 'The End of the Book and the Beginning of Writing'.[9] In 'Cleon' the letters of St Paul possess nothing of the authority of the Book but are a writing which is at best inconsequential and at worst subversive:

> [this] mere barbarian Jew
> He writeth, doth he? well, and he may write.
>
> (349–9)

In 'A Death in the Desert' (1864), St John's Gospel is also opened up to interrogation, this time the interrogation of Higher Criticism; contradicting his Gospel, John admits, for instance, that he 'forsook' (310) the arrested Christ. Anxious lest death will expose his Gospel to misreading, John fears that 'My book speaks on' (368); in the words of Roland Barthes, 'the Text cannot stop'.[10] This death in the desert is the death of not only *an* author but also *the* Author, the 'ending of ... [not only] his book' (658) but also *the* Book – as 'a parchment', a writing on 'three skins glued together' 2–3), John's Gospel is a book that never was, the book that never was *one*. To recall Derrida, this is a death in 'the moment of the desert' that is writing, or rather the prehistory of writing. As such, it shades into the Incarnation, that writing on skin which is the Word made flesh. Through this conceit, whose shock exceeds that of Higher Criticism, the poem sees Christ disappear into the prehistory of writing.

This is also the conceit of 'An Epistle Containing the Strange Medical Experience of Karshish, the Arab Physician' (1855); here the figure of Christ comes close to the *pharmakon*, that radically ambiguous term for writing which Derrida locates in Plato.[11] Just as *pharmakon* means, at once, 'remedy' *and* 'poison' and is related both to *pharmakeus* (magician, prisoner) and *pharmakos* (scapegoat) so

> the Nazarene
> Who wrought this cure ...
> ...
> ... the learned leech
> Perished ...
> Accused, – our learning's fate, – of wizardry ...
>
> (244–9)

As 'leech' (both remedy and, in a sense, poison), 'wizard', and 'accused' – Karshish's Christ very nearly completes the circuit of meanings which gather around the *pharmakon*. This is not, however, a simple movement from grammatology to Christology. For it is, in part, the Jewishness of Karshish's Christ that makes him so like the *pharmakon*. To the Arab physician he is 'the Nazarene' and, therefore, necessarily an accused.[12] Likewise, for the Greek Cleon, it is not Paul the Christian whose writing so 'wrongs our philosophy' but 'Paulus ... [the] Jew' (344). In Browning *écriture* is Hebraic before it is Christian. In 'How It Strikes a Contemporary' (1855) the poet who 'walked about' (42) answers well to Derrida's sense that 'the poet caught within the "error of language"' is a figure for the exilic Jew: 'the Poet and the Jew', he remarks, 'wander ... [a]utochthons only of ... writing'.[13] Browning's writerly 'man about the streets' (63) possesses, like all stereotypical 'Jewry', a 'nose / ... like an eagle's claw' (74, 52–3).

Writing and Jewishness are again two kinds of wandering in 'Childe Roland to the Dark Tower Came' (1855), a poem that almost reads like Derrida's response to Levinas:

> At the heart of the desert, in the growing wasteland, this thought, which ... makes us dream of an inconceivable process of dismantling and dispossession, ... summons us to depart from the Greek site ... and to move toward what is no longer ... a site ... but ... an *exhalation*, toward a prophetic speech already emitted ... inside the Greek origin, close to the other of the Greek.[14]

The parallels with 'Childe Roland' are obvious: there too is a vision of dispossession ('penury ... [was] the land's portion' (61–2)) and a movement within a wasteland ('such starved ignoble nature' (56)) toward a site that is no longer a site – the ambiguous genitive of 'the Dark Tower's search' (40) means that the very tower might just be seeking, might just be itinerant. Roland himself is seeking, or moving towards, an *exhalation* – 'the slug-horn to my lips I set, / And blew' (203–54); moreover, his whole quest is haunted by the Hebraic 'other of the Greek', in particular the then-popular legend of the Wandering Jew.[15] Roland, 'one more victim' (6) of 'world-wide wandering' (19), speaks of 'Tophet' (143) and travels in hope of a promised land – 'Now for a better country' (128). As Roland wanders towards that country he, like Derrida, mimics the detours of not just the Jew but writing: he fears that the cripple will 'write my epitaph ... in the dusty thoroughfare' (11–12), 'turn[s] aside / Into that ominous *tract'* (13–14: my italics) and, finally, goes where other 'strugglers [are] ... penned' (129–34). 'I had', he declares, 'been writ / So many times' (37–9).

For all this writing, however, 'Childe Roland' finally challenges Derrida's prioritising of the written over the spoken; but in so doing, ironically, the poem only confirms its correspondence to 'Metaphysics and Violence'. For just as Roland's final blowing of his slug-horn returns his quest to the site of breath and, therefore, the possibility of speech so, in 'Metaphysics', there is a movement 'toward ... an *exhalation,* [and] ... prophetic speech'. Though this phonocentric moment or telos is, strictly speaking, Levinas's it is, nevertheless, a moment to which Derrida's Jewish inheritance necessarily commits him by virtue of its especial stress upon prophecy, the root of which is *phetes,* 'speaker'. In this same essay Derrida goes so far as to write of the 'inspiration which opens speech'.[16] But then, Derrida's grammatology has always admitted the possibility of prophecy – as early as 1963 he declared that 'writing is the anguish of the Hebraic *ruah'*.[17] By 1981 Derrida is prepared to remark that 'the style of [his] ... questioning as an exodus and dissemination in the desert might produce certain prophetic resonances. It is possible', he adds, 'to see deconstruction as being produced in a space where the [Old Testament] prophets are not far away'.[18]

They *are,* though, far away in the even lonelier world of 'Childe Roland'; the poem's Hebraism, unlike Derrida's, has no prophetic resonance. Even as Roland's final and dramatic breath looks forward to a 'Christian' dispensation, or 'better country', of the spirit (*spirare,* 'to breathe') the *King Lear* quotation looks back to a 'Jewish' dispensation of the letter. This backward glance is characteristic; just as, for Derrida, speech is only ever an inflection of a generalised notion of writing so, in Browning, Christianity is only ever an inflection of a generalised notion of the writing that is Hebraism. Though we read in *The Ring and the Book* (1868–69) of the 'foolish Jew / Pretending to write Christian history'[19] in 'Cleon' we are reminded that much of Christian history *was* written by a Jew, namely Paulus. In 'Childe Roland' it is only the disreputable slave-master who 'pits ... Christian against Jew' (138); indeed, the Jews in 'Holy-Cross Day' call on Christ to '"join sides with us!"' (116, 98). There could hardly be a more dramatic inversion of

Schleiermacher's influential claim that 'in the Christianity of us Western nations there was … much more of Plato and Socrates than of Joshua and David'.[20]

Schleiermacher's boast is, in a sense, Derrida's accusation. Time and again he seeks to disrupt the Hellenism at the 'origin' of not only the West's philosophy but also its Christianity. This becomes most obvious in 'Circumfession' (1991), where, as the title suggests, Derrida makes a Jewish incision on the 'Christian body'[21] of St Augustine's text. Like Browning, Derrida acknowledges the possibility of a Christianity outside the 'Greek domination of the Same and the One' – in an 1981 interview he argues that

> the original, heterogeneous elements of … Christianity … perdure throughout the centuries, threatening and unsettling the assured "identities" of Western philosophy.[22]

Monstrous angels

Identities are, for Derrida, always already unsettled by the play of writing, or archi-writing – a play, or movement, which is altogether prior to the seeming stability of meaning. This, the groundless ground of language, is also a preoccupation of Browning's. His often bizarrre diction is, as Hillis Miller observes, 'close to the inarticulate noise which is the source of all words … the inexhaustible murmur of the language behind language'. In Herbert Tucker's words, 'the proper end of Browning's poetry is to foster an awareness of the means whereby meaning may happen'.[23]

Derrida's key, though self-questioning, term for the means of meaning is *différance*, that 'non-full, non-simple, structured and differentiating origin of [the] differences'[24] which constitute language. This term also 'names', for Derrida, 'the displaced and equivocal passage of one different thing to another, from one term of an opposition to the other'.[25] So described, *différance* is most obviously approached in Browning by his recurring interest in the play, or movement, between monster and angel, ape and god. Such oppositions mean intensely for post-Darwinian Victorians; witness Disraeli's declaration in 1864 that 'the question now placed before society … is this – Is man an ape or angel?'[26] This same question stalks what one Victorian critic of Browning called 'the perplexing borderland of beauty and deformity'.[27] What makes this borderland so like Derrida's *différance* is not just that Darwin had made it so problematic but also that it was haunted by the figure of the Jew. It is no accident that the 'ape or angel?' question is most famously expressed by Disraeli; nor that it is echoed in 'Browning's *opus magnum Hebraicum*, "Jochanan Hakkadosh"'[28] (1883): '*Wherein*', asks Tsaddick, 'differs Man from beast?' (377). This question is begged with especial force by the Jew simply because of his brutalisation; he *was* the man made brute. In the nineteenth century 'the Aryan or real man was defined', argues Poliakov, 'by comparison with brother Shem, the Jew ... half-man ... half-animal'.[29] Half-animal are the Roman Jews in 'Holy-Cross Day', compelled as they are to substitute for horses in an annual race – 'a herd of us / ... spurred through the Corso ... / Jew brutes' (51–3).

Browning is himself, in a sense, a Jew brute; for just as the indirection, or endlessness, of his writing marks itself with a certain Jewishness so the difficulty and unreadability of his writing is, with remarkable frequency, declared monstrous. As Armstrong observes, 'Walter Bagehot slides from talking of Browning's style as grotesque because it is coarse and grotesque because it is complicated'.[30] Other contemporary readers described Browning as 'a barbarian' or 'semantic stutterer'; even Hillis Miller sees him as 'a kind of swamp poet wallowing in an almost pre-verbal state'.[31] Monstrosity raises its head still higher with Swinburne's reference to the 'unnatural tortures ... inflicted ... on our patient mother-tongue by the ... unsparing author of *Sordello*'; and again, with George Steiner's description of the unreadable 'intralingua' of Browning's translation of Aeschylus as 'a centaur-idiom'.[32] Though 'Agamemnon' is an extreme case of Browning's monstrous difficulty, the poem represents for Yopie Prins 'a process of deformation that happens even in the most familiar Browning poem'.[33] In this sense the 'cripple' who 'lie[s] in every word' (1–2) – the sign of semantic as well as physical deformity – stands at the outset of not just Childe Roland's quest but all the other 'adventure[s] of the trace'[34] that are the poems of Browning.

A cripple, or rather deformity, also stands at the outset of the great (mis)adventure of deconstruction. 'Structure, Sign and Play', the 1966 lecture that both made Derrida and *un*made structuralism, culminates in the declaration that

> the as yet unnameable is proclaiming itself ... as is necessary

> whenever a birth is in the offing, only ... in the formless, mute, infant, and terrifying form of monstrosity.[35]

Likewise, *Of Grammatology*, the 1967 book that declared the 'End of the Book' does itself begin with monstrosity:

> patient meditation[s] ... on ... what is ... called writing ... are the wanderings of a way of thinking that is faithful ... to the ineluctable world of [a] ... future which ... can only be proclaimed, *presented* as a sort of monstrosity.[36]

This is the beginning of an almost Gothic scene, or plot, in Derrida – a plot which develops into Derrida's fascination with ghosts. As Derrida himself remarks, as early as 1967, 'this is not an extraordinary tale by Poe but the ordinary story of language'.[37] One name for this story surfaces in *Of Grammatology*, where, soon after the monstrous opening, we read that 'deconstruction always ... falls prey to its own work';[38] the name, of course, is *Frankenstein*. The monster, though, might just be Derrida, for in *Of Grammatology* he is turning on Saussure, his structuralist maker. In fact, as Michael Payne points out, the very trope of the monster is taken from Saussure – he it is who first calls writing a 'monstrosity'.[39] Even in his rebellion Derrida is derivative, is playing the monster; or is it, more precisely, the infant? Like Mary Shelley's original narrative, Derrida's account of monstrosity reads, in part, as a 'birth myth', as testimony to the strange otherness of the newly-born.[40] In 'Structure, Sign and Play' monstrosity has to do with 'a birth' and arises from '*conception* ... *gestation*, and *labor*' – words which Derrida admits to using 'with a glance toward the operations of childbearing'.[41]

It is in this same maternal direction that, many years later, the monstrous Derrida again glances when, in 'Circumfession', his own deformity reminds him of his dying mother:

> for several days now my face has been disfigured by a facial paralysis holding my left eye fixed open like a glass-eyed cyclops ... and my twisted mouth from which water falls a little onto my chin when I drink, recall[s] ... me to my mother each time that, one hand holding up her head, I pour water into her mouth ...[42]

Derrida the cyclops has, it seems, 'a monster mother'.[43] So too does Swinburne's monstrous Browning – do not forget 'the violence [he 'inflicted'] on our ... *mother*-tongue' (my italics). This Browning *is*, in a sense, the monstrous Caliban of 'Caliban upon Setebos' (1864) – to quote the poem's motto: 'I was ... such a one as you' (805). Caliban's monstrous discourse upon Setebos, 'that other, whom *his dam* called God' (170: my italics), is also a sustained violation of a mother-tongue – in this case, the tongue of his monstrous 'dam' Sycorax, she who has already 'called', or articulated, Caliban's world.

In both Browning and Derrida monstrosity refers beyond, or before, itself to the prior figure of a woman who is herself monstrous. This figure is, though, more nuanced in Browning than Derrida. It is true that, in 'Circumfession', Derrida writes of mothers as not only 'monster[s]' but saints – Augustine's mother, 'Saint Monica', is both; nevertheless, Derrida contests such hagiography: 'my mother', he writes, 'was not a saint'.[44] By contrast, Browning inhabits a culture in which a woman's capacity to play the monster is only ever the reverse side of her capacity to play the angel. In Browning the two roles are especially close, for his angels are marked by a difficulty or undecidability that is, finally, monstrous; like biblical angels, they are neither male nor female, God nor man, light nor dark. 'The traced ... and outlined angel' (34–55) of 'One Word More' (1855) is neither absent nor present; as such, it is undecidable in the same way as is Derrida's *différance*. And, like *différance*, this angel names a kind of pre-text, or non-originary origin; the poem retells the story of how Dante's *Inferno* was only written as a departure from a prior attempt 'to paint an angel' (32).

The outline, or trace, of an angel again locates the enigmatic 'before' of discourse in 'Porphyria's Lover' (1836); here the angel-trace is Porphyria – she who 'worship[s]', has 'yellow hair' (33, 18) and, by lighting the fire, 'performs', as Bristow remarks, 'the function of the perfect angel in the house'.[45] When her lover, having strangled Porphyria, remarks that 'all night long we have not stirred, / And yet God has not said a word!' (59–60) it is, *inter alia*, as if an angel has been killed merely in an attempt to break the silence, to make words possible. If here the angel-trace plays the part of *différance* as language's condition of possibility, in 'Fra Lippo Lippi' (1855) the angel-trace plays the part of '*différance* ... [as] the ... *unfolding* of Being',[46] the loophole within the metaphysics of presence. Lippi has just described his *Coronation of the Virgin*, in one corner of which the painter-monk himself appears; suddenly embarrassed by such self-portraiture he is rescued by one of his female admirers:

> I, in this presence, this pure company!
> Where's a hole, where's a corner for escape?
> Then steps a sweet angelic slip of a thing
> Forward ... [and]
> – Addresses the celestial presence 'nay –
> He made you and devised you ...'
>
> (363–73)

This angel is, quite literally, the way out of the closure of 'presence'; far from being the angel in the domestic house she is, more nearly, the 'hole' in the metaphysical 'house of Being'.[47] For Lippi's 'angelic slip' we may, for a moment, read the slippage of Derrida's *différance*.

We may also read, in Browning's other angels, something of the 'differing and deferring' of *différance*; whilst some angels isolate the very moment of difference – 'A second, and the angels alter that' ('How It Strikes', 113), others isolate the moment of deferral: 'Dear and great Angel ... suspending / Thy flight' ('The Guardian Angel', 1–6). In the case of the angels of *Sordello* it is 'the *dis* of *différance*'[48] that is achieved:

> songs go up exulting, then dispread,
> Dispart, disperse ...
> Like an escape of angels ...
>
> (I.881–3)

In 'The Boy and the Angel' (1844) it is the peculiar origin-ality of *différance* that is at stake; for as 'Gabriel ... sank to earth' 'like a rainbow's birth' (25–6) he gives his name to the source of the pure difference that is the spectrum. Like Derrida's archi-writing, Browning's arch-angel makes thinkable the unthinkable birth of the non-Same – the 'birth' that, in 1966, 'is in the offing'.

The birth was predicted, of course, to be 'monstrous' and, indeed, historical – 'let us still', wrote Derrida, 'call it historical'; and so it was in so far as it took the form of what Derrida would, much later, call that 'veritable mutation ... the "event" May '68'.[49] However, in so far as the 'birth in the offing' took the form of deconstruction it has been marked less by monsters than angels, figures that we might *not* call historical. Witness Geoffrey Hartman's 'wrestling with the angel of the unconscious'; or again, what Michael Haar calls 'Derrida's ... struggle with the angel of discourse'; or yet again, M. H. Abrams's 'deconstructive angel'.[50]

These angels are, though, largely casual metaphors. It is true that Derrida himself has, recently, written very knowingly of angels – in 'Circumfession' there is, most obviously, 'the angel that last night took hold of my computer'.[51] Previous to this, however, even in Derrida the appearances of angels seem almost accidental. In 'Of an Apocalyptic Tone' [1983] Derrida's reading of Revelation and its complex 'interlacing of [angelic] voices and *envois*' ends by calling this interlacing a 'completely angelic structure'[52] – this epithet is, though, left totally unglossed, seemingly unnoticed.

It is, I suppose, in the very nature of certain biblical angels to be unnoticed: 'some', we read, 'have entertained angels unawares' (Hebrews 13.2). Why, though, should deconstruction be *so* unawares? Is it because the angel, as *angelos* (literally, 'messenger'), embarrasses a discourse which has questioned the very idea of the message and, indeed, that its questioning is itself a message? Now that Derrida *does* acknowledge that his 'questioning … provoke[s] prophetic resonances', deconstruction might yet become more aware of the angels it entertains.

If so, those angels might themselves do more than entertain, more than merely embellish; perhaps then we *would* call them historical; indeed, after Walter Benjamin's reading of Paul Klee's 1920 painting *Angelus Novus*, we might call them 'angels of history'. Browning's angels, haunted as they are by the cruelties of history, might certainly be so called; witness, in particular, *Sordello*'s 'escape of angels' which, in begging the question 'escape from what?', come uncannily close to Klee's painting itself. Here, as Benjamin sees it,

> the angel [of history] look[s] … as though he is about to move away from something he is fixedly contemplating … His face is turned toward the past … The angel would like to stay … [b]ut a storm is blowing from Paradise … a storm [that] irresistibly propels him into the future.[53]

This same storm of history haunts Dante's Beatrice, the 'outlined angel' of 'One Word More' – her fate as the sketch abandoned to make way for the *Inferno* is shadowed by the self-effacement historically required of the mid-Victorian woman. In 'Porphyria's Lover' (1836) precisely the same historical imperative bears on the angel in-the-house who, in being murdered as if simply to provoke God into speech, functions as a kind of sacrifice. The historical force of *this* angel's fate would have been underlined, for the poem's first readers – readers for whom the Gospels were still, primarily, history – [54] by the cryptic and punning evocation of the last hours of Christ; witness her 'passion' (23, 26), the 'gay feast' (27), and how she 'kneeled and made the cheerless *grate*' (8: my italics).

Eating words

The long night of 'Porphyria's Lover', the night spent waiting for God to speak, is scarred, it seems, by the trace of not just an angel but the 'feast' that was the Last Supper. In Browning the eucharistic memorial of that supper characteristically marks the impossible 'before' of speech. In 'One Word More' Dante is imagined, in the very moment before composition, to 'bit[e] into the live man's flesh for parchment' (39). In 'Bishop Blougram's Apology' (1855) a parody of the eucharist is, again, a quite literal precondition of discourse:

> No more wine? then we'll push back chairs and talk.
>
> (1)

It is, of course, 'Corpus Christi Day' (34) and the act of drinking takes on almost sacramental significance: 'this *last* glass I pour you out in *sign* of amity' (919: my italics). In 'Bishop Blougram' we almost, like another of Browning's clergy, 'hear the blessed mutter of the mass' ('The Bishop Orders His Tomb', 81).

In crossing speech with eating, this muttered mass recalls Gerard Manley Hopkins's assertion that 'Browning has … a way of talking … with the air and spirit of a man bouncing up from table with his mouth full of bread and cheese.'[55] Hopkins, it seems, makes Browning eat his words. Though Hopkins refers this speaking-whilst-eating to Browning's vulgarity or monstrosity, such poems as 'Blougram's Apology' and 'The Bishop Orders' would, in turn, refer that monstrosity to the scene of the eucharist – to a man with his mouth full of bread and wine.

Such a scene may also be glimpsed in Derrida's work, and from an early stage. In *Of Grammatology* we read that

> our language, even if we are pleased to speak it … is already *eaten* by writing. Its accentuated features have been *gnawed* through by the consonants. (my italics)[56]

At work here is Derrida's fascination with the host-parasite relationship, whose eucharistic significance is marked by the very word 'host'. This was made clear, of course, by Hillis Miller back in 1977.[57] Still earlier, however, is Derrida's own discussion of the eucharist in the Hegel column of *Glas* (1972). Here, as Geoffrey Ulmer remarks, Derrida's 'interest ... [in] the Last Supper ... is that it offers a story of language',[58] or rather, the story of language according to Hegel. Remarking on the disciples' ingestion of the bread,

> Hegel proposes to read that movement [of 'resubjection'] as the tongue's, as language's hearing-understanding-oneself-speak ... [since] the voice ... annihilates the signifier's objective exteriority.[59]

Though opposed to this story of language, Derrida seems to endorse Hegel's reading of the eucharist in terms of the now-you-see-it-now-you-don't drama of signification. This confirms what is, for Derrida, Hegel's central insight into the eucharist: namely, that it is about the precariousness of God. 'Divinity', comments Derrida,

> stands ... between swallowing and vomitting ... it is neither ... outside nor in ... the divine has melted in ... [the disciples'] mouths.[60]

This precarious, melting God returns us to Browning, or at least to 'The Bishop Orders', where the churchman talks of 'see[ing] God made and eaten all day long' (82). What, though, distinguishes this line from Derrida's is irony, the irony that these are words spoken by a *trans*substantiationalist but written by a *con*substantiationalist. By contrast, in so far as the Francophone Derrida is writing within a Christian culture it is, of course, Catholic and, as such, founded on the doctrine of the 'real presence', the real presence of Christ in bread and wine. It is, then, a quasi-*Catholic* Derrida who sees the eucharist as a danger to God-as-presence; for the Protestant Browning there is no such danger, since there is no real presence in the first place. By virtue of his Protestant realism, Browning escapes something of not only the *metaphysics* of presence but also its displacement. Is, then, deconstruction a Catholic dis-ease? Certainly, what protects Browning the Protestant from the shock of deconstruction is not his belief but, as it were, his *un*belief.

Neither belief nor unbelief can, though, protect Browning from the disordering shock of *death*. Though the Bishop orders his tomb, Browning cannot; writing will not allow him to do so.

A grammatologist's funeral

In Browning death and writing forge a close relationship; witness 'A Death in the Desert', 'Childe Roland' and, most obviously, 'A Grammarian's Funeral'. The relationship is similarly intense in Derrida. Admittedly, Derrida often speaks of death in a generalised sense, as a trope for difference, the difference by which signs signify. 'The [very] possibility of the sign is', we read, '[a] relationship with death.[61] At other times, death is a more nearly literal aspect of the gaps and absences implicit in writing:

> it [*can*] be said that upon the death of the addressee ... the mark left ... is still a writing.[62]

Your death like mine is, for Derrida, part of the very structure of writing. This is particularly evident in the case of my name, which 'is destined to survive me [and] in this way announces my death' – so much so, in fact, that 'When I sign, I am already dead ... the structure of the "signature" event carries my death in that event.[63] The grammatologist, unlike the grammarian, conducts his *own* funeral:

> As for the one who organizes the *Funeral* – i.e. literary – *Rites* of J.D... he is ... the double of the dead.[64]

Writing, argues Derrida, will always remind me of my death. And to remember death is, for Derrida, nothing less than an ethical imperative. Speaking in the wake of Paul de Man's death, Derrida declares that

> even if th[e] ... metonymy of the other in ourselves already constituted the truth and the possibility of our relation to the living other, death brings it out into more abundant light.[65]

More abundant light? Is this really Derrida? Or is it an anachronistic Derrida reinventing the medieval tradition of *memento mori*?[66] After all, if to remember my death is to remember the future I am doomed to anachronism, doomed to an untimely death.

That is certainly the case with Browning, who, in remembering his death, is not quite Victorian; time and again he departs from the Victorian privileging of death as a kind of telos, or moment of truth.[67] Browning comes much closer to Derrida's sense that '*différance* … lasts … up to the end of (the) man. *Différance* till death, and for death, without end.'[68] For Browning, like Derrida, death is not excluded from the (dis)order of differing and deferring, death is itself a text. In 'Caliban' the 'sunbeams cross / And recross till they weave a spider-web' (12–13) – a web that is at once both a text (*texere*, 'to weave') and a death-trap. In 'Prospice' (1864) the scene of death is similarly crossed and recrossed, this time by the net-work of modern communications:

> I am nearing the place [of death],
> The power of the night, the *press* of the storm,
> The *post* of the foe …
>
> (4–6: my italics)

If death really is a kind of text does it lose the force, and indeed threat, of an ending? How close is the deconstructive interrogation of death to St Paul's? 'Death,' he *asks*, 'where is thy sting?' (1 Corinthians 15.55). Strangely, Derrida seems closer to Paul than is Browning, or at least 'The Bishop Orders'. Here the deconstruction of death-as-the-moment-of-truth takes a strangely negative turn: the dying Bishop talks of how 'I shall *lie* through [the] centuries' (80). By contrast, in Derrida's *Glas* the same deconstruction is more nearly affirmative:

> if death is the being of what is no more, the no-more-being, death is nothing.

For this 'reason',

> The *glas* is for (no) one. (No) one [*personne*].[69]

Given that *personne* can also mean 'someone' we sense here not only the resurrectionist question of St Paul but also the poststructuralist assertion of (St) Paul de Man: 'death is a displaced name for a linguistic predicament'.[70] Nevertheless, Derrida's recurring description of writing as 'living on', as a spectral, posthumous life, brings him, in 'Circumfession', so close to resurrection that it is as if he writes, or questions, from within it, or rather *them* – for Derrida seems to see double the resurrection that is not one: 'I write', he remarks, 'between two resurrections.'[71]

One such resurrection, or cheating of death, is to be found in Derrida's Levinas, in his 'summons … to move toward … an *exhalation*'. If this exhalation is the final breathing-out of death then this death '*toward*' (but not '*to*') which Levinas summons 'us' is never quite reached but always deferred. Indeed, if 'exhalation' implies there was once an *in*halation, or even in*spir*ation, then the movement towards it, the movement of deconstruction, never quite breathes its last, never quite rids itself of the possibility of its own inspiration. Deconstruction may well be, to redirect Derrida's own words, 'a discourse losing its breath'[72] but never, it seems, one that has finally *lost* either its breath or, therefore, the possibility of spirit. Derrida's more recent writings, in particular *Of Spirit*, are testimony to this.

There is, however, an older and counter impulse in Derrida, an impulse that *can* envisage the possibility of a final exhalation, or expenditure of self; and to this we are directed by Childe Roland, he who *does* lose his breath. Having come to the dark tower of death, Roland turns his final breath into a horn-blast even though it is to be heard by no living person. In so doing he makes his death a kind of gift or pure expenditure – Roland sounds the horn without any expectation of return, or sense of debt. This is not a death that 'in a minute pay[s] glad life's arrears' ('Prospice', 19); Roland's death is more like that of the Grammarian, he who 'would not discount life … / Paid by instalment … / [But] … ventured neck or nothing' ('A Grammarian's Funeral', 107–9). Still more reckless, however, and thus still more like Roland's death is what Derrida once called 'the absolute risk of [a] death … which … constitute[s] … an expenditure … *without reserve*' – death as an impossibly pure gift, a gift which somehow escapes the 'chain of restitutions',[73] or systems of exchange.

Perhaps, then, 'the glas is for *someone*'; for if death can be a gift it is just possible that someone might give himself. 'When *someone* gives *something* to *someone*,' writes Derrida, 'one is already long within calculating dialectics … [but] I give *me*, I make me the gift.'[74] As Derrida has more recently remarked, '"giving" must be neither a thing nor an act, it must somehow be someone'.[75] And that might just be what is accomplished with Roland's final and fatal breath-blast for it is an exhalation by which he names himself and thus becomes *someone*:

> Dauntless the slug-horn to my lips I set,
> And blew. '*Childe Roland to the Dark Tower came.*'

What Browning's poem finally locates in Derrida is the sense that, *because* 'writing [is] the becoming-absent of the subject',[76] there is always the possibility of someone other than the subject, the *im*possible someone whose death is a gift. Witness, of course, *The Gift of Death* [1992], where Derrida speaks of 'the other' as 'one whose infinite goodness *gives* in an experience that amounts to a *gift of death*.'[77]

> this is my body, which is broken for you.
>
> (1 Corinthians 11.24)

Spectres of Sludge, or Mr Derrida the Medium

Things that go thump

If Christ's death was a gift of bread then within the eucharist, the memorial of that death, we meet a *ghost* made of bread, a ghost who is to be eaten. This conceit haunts both Derrida in *Specters of Marx* [1993] and Browning in 'Mr Sludge the Medium' (1864). As our two authors turn to ghosts so they also imagine them to be eaten. In *Specters*, the Cartesian ego encounters the other as a spectre to be consumed: '[the] unique Ego … [is] visited by its own apparition … [and] gives to himself his "this is my body"'[78] – this Ego, adds Derrida, is 'a eucharistic Narcissus', a Christ who eats his own ghost. Derrida himself would not, of course, eat ghosts but he does eat *with* them in the sense that he commends 'the companionship … of ghosts' (xviii/15) – a companion is, literally, 'one with whom I share my bread'. In 'Mr Sludge' the eucharistic play between ghost and Host, spectre and bread, is heightened as belief in ghosts is figured as a kind of cannibalism. Those that believe David Sludge are said to have 'gulped [him] down … whole' (213) and he, in turn, has 'swallowed down [his] … bread of shame' (662), the shame of ghosts, one of whom – the radical 'Tom Paine' (37) – so nearly goes by the French name for bread. Paine, though, is *not* quite *pain*; this is one ghost whom Sludge cannot swallow, one ghost who remains indigestibly militant:

> Thumping the table [he swore] …
> He'd do me … a mischief.
>
> (38–9)

With Paine, the medium's table is turned – it is no longer a table to be rapped but one to be thumped; the table no longer of a medium but of a political radical.

At Derrida's table the reverse occurs; here Marx the radical becomes a kind of medium. In reading the *Manifesto* in terms of manifestations, what he calls the 'manifestations of the manifest' (103/169), Derrida undoes the manual force of *manifestus* – literally, 'hand-struck'. Derrida's Marx is, by contrast, sleight of hand; even as he denounces Max Stirner for perpetuating such spectres of idealism as God and Man, Marx turns out to be himself obsessed with spectres *per se*. He does not so much strike the table as rap it. 'What', asks Derrida, 'is Marx's hand doing here ...?' (142/225). The revolutionary's fist is unclenched. This, though, has happened before; in Browning's 'Apparent Failure' (1864) an English visitor to the Paris Morgue, addressing one particular corpse, declares: 'You ... a socialist ... / Be quiet, and unclench your fist!' (41–5).

Derrida replays this scene within the morgue of the late twentieth-century academy: 'now that Marx is dead,' writes Derrida, '[many] enervat[e his] ... *corpus*, by silencing in it the revolt' (31–2/61). For Derrida, the revolt will not be silenced, but it must be reinterpreted. For Derrida, the most militant spectres of Marx are, ironically, the *victims* of Marx, or rather Marx*ism*; alluding, *inter alia*, to Stalinist atrocities, Derrida speaks of these victims as '[the] millions and millions of supplementary ghosts who will keep on protesting in us' (30/59).

Ghosts that protest are, though, spectres of not only Marx but also Luther, that founding protest-ant.[79] Luther's manifesto, his *95 Theses*, was quite literally mani-fest (hand-struck) when nailed to the door of the church in Wittenberg; this was thumping, not tapping. But then Luther *is* a spectre of Marx in the sense that, as Marx himself acknowledges,

> Germany's revolutionary past is ... the Reformation. Once it was the monk's brain in which the revolt began, now it is in the philosopher's.[80]

This haunting by Luther is redoubled by what Derrida sees as Marx's preoccupation with *Hamlet*, a play beset by the ghost of not only Claudius but Luther or at least Wittenberg, Hamlet's university town. 'Go not to Wittenberg', says Gertrude,[81] but it is too late; for to go to *Hamlet* is to go to Luther. And this Derrida has always already done simply in talking of 'deconstruction', a term that comes, in part, from Heidegger's *Destruktion*, which in turn comes, as John D. Caputo observes, from 'Luther's notion of a *destructio*' – a hermeneutic that breaks 'through the crust of scholasticism to the life of the New Testament'.[82] According to Alice Jardine,

> Derrida's work is 'protestant' in its battle against any *katholikos* [or universal] ... Derrida doth protest – religiously.[83]

In tracing Derrida back to Luther via *Hamlet*, or at least Gertrude's 'the lady doth protest too much' (III.ii.225), Jardine speaks better than she perhaps knows.

However, Jardine doth also protest too much in the sense that the Derrida of *Specters* tends not so much to protest religiously as *refer* religiously; in *Specters* Luther is not so much a protest-ant presence as a ghostly reference.[84] But then, for Derrida, religion cannot be separated from reference, literally 'carrying-back': 'Religion,' he writes, 'we will come back to this' (42/76). Derrida is speaking of his lecture, but to approach re-ligion, literally 'tie-back', may well entail some kind of coming-back or carrying-back, some kind of re-ference. When Derrida speaks, in passing, of 'the reference to the religious world' (165/262) we sense a near-tautology. For Derrida, reference is religious – or at least marked by ghost, or spirit – because it implies a kind of waiting, a weak form of messianism:

> if there is some ghost, it is to be found precisely where ... reference hesitates. (107/175)

For Browning, reference is no less ghostly, or spirited. Mr Sludge, when charged with faking ghosts, suggests we '*refer* / The question to this table' (66–7). But 'this dear old table' (76) is an unlikely table for critical debate; in Derrida's phrase it is 'a table of ghosts' (142/226). Derrida has in mind that Marxian table, the exemplary 'ordinary sensuous thing' (160) which, under capitalism, is 'haunted by its other, namely [its] ... commodity-form' or exchange-value (160/254–5). Sludge's 'dear old table' is similarly haunted: 'dear' can mean 'expensive', and besides the table represents his 'trade'. Such a table makes strange the table of symposium, the table of the 'philosophic diner-out' (776). And it was around precisely this table that Victorian thinkers were soon to gather when, in 1877, *The Nineteenth Century* conducted a debate on 'The Soul and Future Life' as part of what it called a 'Modern Symposium'.[85] It is a very contemporary philosophic table that

Sludge nudges; 'tables do tip' (195), he observes.

The unstable table of philosophy is also a feature of *Specters*: 'the table,' writes Derrida,

> erects its whole self like an institution, it stands up and addresses itself to others … from Plato to Heidegger … [And yet] with all of them, the same ceremony: a séance of the table. (151/241)

Though the table of philosophy is standing it also entails the 'sitting' that is the literal meaning of 'séance'. Once Derrida turns to Marx we have a table that is not even upright: stressing the *caput* ('head') in *cap*ital, Marx argues that the commidified, capitalised table 'stands on its head … [*auf den kopf*]' (152/241). At this point in *Specters* deconstruction becomes *destructio* as another religious spectre of Marx is raised[86] – that 'most spectral of specters … Jesus' (144/229), Jesus the carpenter for whom a table was a piece of work and who, upon entering the Temple in Jerusalem, overturns the tables of the money-changers (Mark 11.15). In a topsy-turvy Marxian sense, Christ thereby uprights the already inverted tables of exchange-value.

Christ in the temple is another spectre who does not so much tap tables as thump them; he is another protest-ant ghost, and in that sense another spectre of Luther. The two spectres were, though, fated to meet since both knock at doors: for Christ's 'Behold, I stand at the door, and knock' (Revelation 3.20) read Luther's hammering on the Wittenberg door and his famous 'Here I stand; I can do no other.'[87]

It is this double-ghost that haunts Browning's poem 'La Saisiaz' (1878). Here Browning confronts the death of a friend whilst on holiday near Geneva – 'where Calvin', Luther's great student, 'preached' (104); the poem recounts the experience of reaching the top of the mountain which Browning and the deceased had planned to climb on the day of her death:

> Climbing, – *here I stand*: but you – where?
>
> (139: my italics)

In a strange and moving twist the standing ghost of Christ-cum-Luther is implicated in the very moment of loss. To put it another way, Browning *stands* to mourn. Mourning is thus made strange; for this is not the familiar mourning of sitting, of séance, the mourning that seeks the comfort of ghosts. Here I stand; I *can*, therefore, do other – I can mourn otherwise. In particular, I mourn other than the Jew; for in the tradition of 'sitting Shivah' the Jew takes a stool and *sits* to mourn. But then Browning, for all his Jewish themes, is not a Jew. Derrida, of course, *is*; thus his concern with the 'séance of the table' of philosophy might, in the end, have more to do with mourning than ghosts. Derrida's subtitle refers not only to 'the State of the Debt' but also 'the Work of Mourning'.

Given that 'State' derives from *status* ('standing'), Browning's mournful 'here I stand' effectively conflates the two parts of Derrida's subtitle to produce the '*State* of Mourning'. And national, or State, mourning *did* coincide with Browning's own, personal grief – Elizabeth Barrett Browning died in the same year as Prince Albert. For the next forty years Queen Victoria, the Head of State, remains in mourning clothes. In Victoria's State of mourning what space is left to mourn otherwise, what space is left for private grief? Its relative scarcity in Browning's verse suggests that, for him, there is little or none.

Mourning becomes

A State of mourning, a State in black, is a possibility or conceit that runs through *Specters* – at one moment it might just be 'the State of Israel' (58/101); at another it might be a State burdened by the 'foreign debt' that 'holds a mass of humanity … in … slavery' (94/155); at yet another it might be that '"Negroid state"' which names, for Marx, Stirner's dark 'obscurantism' (137/226). Marx intends no reference to the actual negroid States of Africa; it is different, however, for Derrida. He does not forget the *black* spectres of Marx. The most obvious is Chris Hani, the black South African Communist who was killed just a few days before Derrida gave his lectures and to whom they are dedicated. The least obvious is Derrida himself or rather the young North African Derrida, that 'little black and very Arab Jew' of whom he writes in 'Circumfession', the 12-year-old who was 'expelled [for being Jewish] from the Lycée de Ben Aknoun in 1942'.[88] Marx's 'Negroid state' names, for Derrida, a stateless State, a people without citizenship.

Ironically, Derrida's reading of Statehood *is* marked by citizenship; for it is, as he himself remarks, an 'ingenuous reading' (149/238) – a reading that, in its original, Latin sense, is 'in-born' or 'native, not foreign' and thus 'free-born, not slave'. According to Marx, '"ghosts from … Rome watched over [the] … cradle"' of the

French Revolution' (111/182); they also, it seems, watch over the cradle of Derrida's revolution. 'Lend an ear', declares Derrida (114/186), which, after his injunction to 'remember the specter of Caesar' (11/32), conjures up Mark Antony's famous: 'Friends, Romans, countrymen, lend me your ears!'[89] Antony speaks, of course, both *as* a citizen and *to* citizens. For all his talk of aliens, Derrida seems to acknowledge a difference between himself and Marx, he who 'remains ... a glorious accursed immigrant' (174/276). In 1943, following the liberation of Algeria, the little black Jew returned to his lycée to prepare for what became a whole life within the academy. In this sense, deconstruction owes a very simple debt *to* the State. Derrida acknowledges that ghosts can, to some extent, be reappropriated: hence, the 'repatriated specters [that] run [to] the forum' (129/206), the site of citizenship. '[A]n immigrant', writes Derrida, '[is] accursed ... and [o]ne should not rush [t]o ... neutralize him through naturalization' (174/276). He seems to suspect, however, that this has, in a sense, happened to himself.

By contrast, Browning's Mr Sludge, though based on the real-life Daniel Dunglas Home, is never quite homely. Whilst Sludge also echoes Mark Antony – 'lovers, friends and countrymen' (307) – the medium is himself accused of being a 'hybrid' (567), literally the child of a slave and a freeman. To mediate between the living and the dead is, it seems, to mediate between master and slave. 'Mr Sludge' is not only written by the son of a former master of a West Indian plantation[90] but published within eighteen months of Abraham Lincoln's emancipation of slaves. Just occasionally, the poem makes its ghosts work as a metaphor for slaves:

> '... you spirit come, go, fetch and carry,
> Read, write, rap, rub-a-dub, and hang yourself!'
>
> (301–2)

If this spirit is itself haunted, haunted by the figure of the slave, then the slave is, in its turn, doubled by the figure of the negro; very early on we read that:

> There's a thick
> Dusk undeveloped spirit ...
> Owes me a grudge – a negro's, I should say.
>
> (30–2)

The poem never returns to this spirit; in this sense too he is 'undeveloped'. What *is* developed is merely the 'dusk' of the negro spirit; his blackness no sooner appears than it disappears into the motif of the evening – in particular, the 'evenings' (80) in which the medium plies his trade. Erased is any trace of the negro himself, for these are the 'shiny night[s]' (1247) of the making of dollars – American nights made shiny *white* by the 'star[s]' (276) of, as it were, the '"Stars and Stripes"' (346).

This critique of Mr Sludge might also, though, apply to the Derrida of *Specters*. The 'blackness' (137/218) that here so interests him is, finally, the blackness not of Hani or the young Derrida but of 'this evening' (51/89), the evening in which he gives his lecture, this 'essay in the night' (xviii/14). Though Derrida writes of the 'rattle of chains ... in the middle of the night' (135/216), *his* night, like that of Sludge, is literally American[91] – he is lecturing at the University of California. But then Derrida has always belonged, in a sense, to America: he was christened not as 'Jacques' but as 'Jackie', an Americanisation; he is most enthusiastically read in America; and he has himself '"risk[ed], with a smile, the ... hypothesis [that] America *is* deconstruction"'.[92] Despite all this, however, the night of *Specters* is, symbolically, European:

> It is still evening, it is always nightfall ... along the ... battlements of ... old Europe.
>
> (14/37)

Europe is, for Derrida, what Browning calls 'the evening country' ('Too Late', 29). It is a version of Europe that allows Derrida to evoke a night of profound and almost lyrical belatedness, a night haunted by the ghosts of high culture – not only Shakespeare but Baudelaire, Gide, Hölderlin, Hugo, Mallarmé and Valéry. It is, moreover, a night of vigil, the 'vigil of philosophy:'[93] 'read with ... philosophical ... vigilance' (74/125); 'vigilance therefore' (97/160). By contrast, Mr Sludge gives us an all-American night of unabashed commodification, low cunning and sheer novelty; a night in which Europe's high-cultural and philosophical ghosts are reduced to table-rapping. Here 'Shakespeare writes you songs' (1408), 'Locke / Reason[s] ... in gibberish, Homer writ[es] ... Greek / In noughts and crosses' (589–91) and Beethoven becomes an organ-grinder:

> Suppose, the spirit Beethoven wants to shed
> New music ... why, he turns
> The handle of this organ, [and] grinds with Sludge.
>
> (339–41)

For all Derrida's claims to disrupt Western thought, there is a sense in which the shades of Locke *et al.* are more bewildered by Sludge's new night than Derrida's old evening. As Sludge puts it, 'it's a "new thing" that philosophy fumbles at' (410). Philosophy does not seem to fumble on 'the … [haunted] battlements of … old Europe'; for here we find not only the philosophers Derrida and Hamlet but Horatio the 'scholar'. In the words of Browning's Napoleon III, one who knows Europe's battlements well:

> Be Kant crowned king o' the castle in the air!
> ('Prince Hohenstiel-Schwangau', 1108)

What makes the philosopher king of the castle of Europe is not simply that it is a castle *in the air*, an idea, but also that it is a site of violence. Sludge is brought to the table of reason by violence – 'your thumbs', cries Sludge, 'are through my windpipe' (17); it is, though, a violence overlooked by philosophy: 'with … philosophers', continues Sludge, 'you're on your best behaviour!' (124–5). If philosophers are, for Sludge, guilty by association then for Browning's Napoleon III they are guilty by definition:

> Be Kant crowned king o' the castle in the air
> Hans Slouch, – his own, and children's mouths to feed
> I' the hovel in the ground, – wants meat, nor chews
> 'The Critique of Pure Reason' in exchange.
> ('Prince Hohenstiel-Schwangau', 1108–11)

Philosophy, implies Browning, might have a bad conscience. Is that why Derrida stages philosophy as a vigil, as an avoidance of sleep? The belief that Marxism is but a ghost 'awakens us', he writes, 'where it would like to put us to sleep' (97/160). Given Derrida's injunction to 'think … of Macbeth' (11/32), we must ask if Derrida 'doth murther Sleep'.[94] For to sleep is perchance to dream, perchance to dream out of guilt, if only the guilt of survival. And *Specters* is a book about survival; 'the question of [ghosts]', writes Derrida, 'open[s] onto a dimension of irreducible *sur-vival*' (147/235–6). Besides, it is the evening and the hour is getting late: it is '"since Marx"'; since 'the end of history'; even 'since the future' (16–17/41). But Derrida still asks, '"Why so late?"' (88/145). One answer is that *Specters* is a work not just *about* mourning but *of* mourning. Spivak describes this *Hamlet*-obsessed book as 'a how-to-mourn-your-father book';[95] however, it might just be about mourning a mother. If so, it is a continuation of 'Circumfession', where Derrida declares: 'I am writing *for* my mother, perhaps even a dead woman.'[96] By the time of *Specters*, she *is* a dead woman. At the very end, Derrida asks if one can speak to a ghost; 'Peut-on', he asks, '[parler] à *ça*?' (175/278). For *ça*, as in *Glas*, read *sa*? Read 'her'? And, as in 'Circumfession', for *sa*, or 'SA', read '*Sa*far',[97] the maiden name of Derrida's mother? (Derrida elsewhere confesses to such circumfession.)[98]

'Mr Sludge' is certainly about one who has survived his 'mother' and seeks to speak to her – Hiram has contacted Sludge precisely for this purpose. Survival, however, is in this case very clearly marked by guilt; Hiram has survived his mother simply because he killed her: 'you throttled your … mother' (1506). In this sense 'Mr Sludge' brings to the surface the very same guilt that remains buried in *Specters*.

David Sludge, whose 'Christian name' (144) is, of course, Jewish, talks of 'explain[ing] … my life / The Jews' way' (884–5); given the history of the Jews this is, perhaps, to explain my life as survival. And this Sludge does in a way that, uncannily, chances upon what it might be for a Jew to survive in mid twentieth-century Europe:

> oh, you've told me, sir,
> Of … How yourself
> Once, missing on a memorable day
> Your handkerchief – just setting out, you know, –
> You must return to fetch it, lost the train,
> And saved your precious self from what befell
> The thirty-three whom Providence forgot.
>
> (931–7)

David the medium here conjures up a ghost train, a ghost of the death trains that would be crammed with *the race* whom Providence forgot. It is a ghost which Derrida cannot lay: having just described the evening in which he speaks as an extension of the 'evening … of … Europe at war', Derrida asks: '[is] it … possible to take … the last train after the last train – and yet be late to an end of history[?]' (15/38). Perhaps; it is certainly possible for a French-Algerian Jew born in 1930 to be just too late for the last train to that end of history which was the death camp.[99] *Specters* cannot forget the 'ghosts in … the charnel houses of all the camps' (105/171).

Even as Derrida explores the ironies of the 'end of history' he is also, it seems, explaining his life; this is autobiography without an 'I' or, as Derrida himself puts it, 'self-confession that *confesses the other*' (21/46). To quote Browning's Napoleon III: 'A plague of the return to "I – I – I" / ... / Autobiography, adieu!' ('Prince Hohenstiel-Schwangau', 1118–20). Though *Specters* flirts with a return to 'I – I – I', though the vigil of philosophy very nearly becomes a monodrama in which '*I* mourn' and '*I* stay awake',[100] the ghosts finally lead elsewhere: 'ghosts ... are where *there is* watching [*où ça veille*]' (175/277) – not where *I* watch and wake but where *it* watches and wakes. In the long vigil that is *Specters* Derrida eventually disappears to be replaced by *ça*. And it is with *ça* that Derrida ends. 'Can one', he asks, 'address oneself to a ghost? To whom? To him? To *it*? [*À ça*?]' (175/278). Is this *ça* the impersonal, ever vigil-ant *ça* that wakes and watches? If so, this is confession *to* the other, a God-like other. It is, in this sense, 'autobiography *à Dieu*'. To address my autobiography to God is, of course, to explain my life the Augustinian way, the way that Derrida went in 'Circumfession'; here he writes, 'I am addressing myself ... to God.'[101]

SA/Ba

> Dommett writes 'Who?'; Browning replies 'Sa.'
>
> (note to *Sordello*)[102]

Though Derrida may speak *à Dieu*, or *à ça* 'like SA' – his acronym for Saint Augustine – *un*like Augustine Derrida simultaneously addresses his mother: 'I address her like him, my God'.[103] Derrida's relationship *à ça* is beset by the homonymic 'SA' of not only Saint Augustine but also Safar. The declaration 'ghosts are where there is watching [*où ça veille*]' is haunted by *ça vieille*, that old woman whom Derrida may be mourning.

In 'Mr Sludge' Browning also may be mourning a woman – not SA but 'Ba', Browning's name for Elizabeth Barrett; as one who believed in ghosts and whom Robert scorned for doing so,[104] Elizabeth *is* – in a sense – Mr Sludge. The medium is, in a sense, the woman: his 'tricks emasculate the soul' and Elizabeth is, for Robert, 'my mind's ... medium'.[105] Sludge may not have succeeded in raising the ghost of Hiram's 'sainted mother' but he does raise the ghost of Robert's sainted wife. Browning's ghosts, like Derrida's, are not necessarily male;[106] there is a Ba, there is a SA. When Spivak says 'woman ... is nowhere in *Specters*'[107] she is only right in an unintended sense. When, at the very end, Derrida remarks that 'specters ... give us to rethink the "there" [*le 'là'*]' (176/279) we might just read *le 'la'*, the feminine article. Ba and SA certainly give us to rethink the question 'Who's there?' The straight answer to Marcellus' question is, of course, the ghost of Hamlet's father, but for Derrida and Browning *there* might just be a woman. It was, as Browning reminds us, the same for Dante:

> 'Certain am I – from this life I pass into a better, *there*
> *Where that lady lives* of whom enamoured was my soul.'
> ('La Saisiaz', 214–15: my italics)

Like Dante's lady, the ghosts that haunt Browning and Derrida make us rethink *le 'la'* in that they turn *la mort* into *l'amour*. For each writer, mourning becomes desire – 'becomes' in both senses of the word: 'Can we love', asks Browning, 'but on condition, that the thing we love must die?' ('La Saisiaz', 311); 'whenever I love,' answers Derrida, 'a law *engages* me to the death of the other'.[108] This, though, is not simply a philosophical point; the rapid movement from *la mort* to *l'amour*, from death to desire, is also the Oedipal point of Hamlet's obsession with the death of his father and the sexual activity of his mother. Conscious of this and other 'analogies', Derrida hesitates before painfully relating, in 'Circumfession', how his dying and confused mother

> when ... alone with me ... had several times ... exposed herself naked ... [and when] asked why ... replied ... 'Because I'm attractive.'[109]

'Suppose we let her write?', remarks Sludge of Hiram's 'sainted mother'; if that, in a sense, is what Derrida does here then *his* sainted mother seems doomed to 'write', or speak, as patriarchy dictates. But then so too does the dead woman whom Browning lets speak in 'Eurydice to Orpheus' (1864):

> But give ... me ... the eyes ...
> Let them once more absorb me! ...
> ...
> ... no past is mine, no future: look at me!
> (1–8)

Browning's Eurydice anticipates Derrida's mother not only in demanding to be looked at but also in dying – it was, of course, because Orpheus *did* look at Eurydice that she disappeared back into Hades.

What distinguishes Browning's Eurydice is that she seems to *will* her death, to will the gaze that shall consign her to Hades. Unlike Pluto, she is not distracted or overcome by Orpheus' music; she is one spectre whom the poet cannot raise. In this sense she gives us to rethink *le 'la'* of music, in particular the music of male poetry, a music which she will not follow.

'Fol-lol-the-rido-liddle-iddle-ol!' (83) sings Mr Sludge the medium-cum-'poet' (1184). But *does* Hiram's sainted mother follow? Does Browning's sainted wife? Perhaps not, if only because the music he mediates is so appalling – it passes through a musical mill in which

> … [Beethoven's] Thirty-third Sonata …
> Comes from the hopper as …
> The Shakers' Hymn in G, with a natural F,
> Or the 'Stars and Stripes' set to consecutive fourths.
>
> (343–6)

Put through Sludge's mill, Beethoven's sonata becomes not just American (a 'Shakers' Hymn') but America-set-to-music. Precisely the same music, suggests Derrida, is still to be heard at the 'American end … of History' (71/121), which, 'singing the advent of … liberal democracy' (85/141), proclaims 'Marx is dead' 'to the rhythm of a cadenced march' (52/90). As Derrida puts it, 'Fukuyama sing[s] … but Koyève [does] … not' (71–2/121). Neither does Derrida: 'instead of singing,' he writes, 'let us never neglect th[e] … fact … of suffering' (85/141).

This not-neglecting does, though, itself raise the spectre of another kind of music – the music encoded in Derrida's translation of 'the time is out-of-joint' (71/88) as 'contretemps'; in French, this means not only mishap but syncopation, whilst the phrase *à contretemps* suggests, in a musical sense, being out-of-time or in counter-time. Still more disjointed, even pained, is the music evoked by Derrida's talk of the 'nocturnal noise … and rumbling sound of ghosts chained to ghosts' (5/23) and, again, 'the rattle of chains … in the middle of the night' (135/216). If Derrida merely hints at a music, or percussion, of pain and torture, a music of the literally out-of-joint, Browning goes further. After all, the world of

Sludge is one in which '*Stripes* are set to consecutive fourths' and the strangled throat is almost an instrument: 'Aie-aie-aie! / Please sir! Your thumbs are through my wind*pipe* … !' (16–17: my italics). A more generalised suffering is set, or linked, to music in the person of

> [The] foreigner, that teaches music here
> And …
> … says [a hunchback] fellow … informed of him
> And made him fly his country …
>
> (520–3)

Ironically, the informer is himself suggestive of a music of displacement: '[the] hunchback cobbler sat, stitched soles and sang, / In some *outlandish* place' (524–5: my italics).

As well as the music that comes through Sludge's psychic mill there is, it seems, the music of those who have themselves gone through the mill. There is also the music of those who have simply *gone*. As if testifying to this, Mr Sludge hints at a spectral poetry that is itself marked by disappearance, the disappearance of letters: this he does when declaring himself ''ware o' the spirit-world' (1249). Sludge's 'wareness o' absent spirits is here mimicked by *our* awareness of absent, apostrophised letters. In '"Transcendentalism"' (1855) Browning summarised the motto of the prosy poet as: 'Speak prose and hollo it till Europe hears!' (11); nine years later the new-world Sludge speaks prose and *hollows* it till old Europe hears it as spiritual awareness. The (il)logic at work is a parody of the Transcendentalist, or Hegelian, thesis that where there is spirit the letter will, eventually, be sublated; the letters 'a' and 'f', it is implied, have been spirited away. This, though, is *not* Herr Hegel the philosopher but Mr Sludge the medium, whose letters are not so much spirited away as merely purloined, gone elsewhere; for elsewhere the poem is littered with stray or excess letters: at one point with 'a *y* and a *k*' (311), at another with a 'G' and an 'F' (345), and at still another with 'l's and 'r's:

> [I've] …
> Lost all-l-l-l …
> …
> … Bl-l-less you, sir!
> R-r-r, you brute-beast …
>
> (1485–1500)

Here is no operation of spirit, simply a moving around of letters.

This, though, for Derrida *is* the spirit of Marxist critique, a 'spirit that [in not denying its own materiality] ... supposes the very movement of its letter' (172/272). This lettered, or literal, movement becomes literal in the more usual sense as Derrida rereads 'Ma*r*x' as 'Max', Max Stirner:

> In *The German Ideology* ... [in response to] Stirner['s] ... 'Man, there are specters in your head!' Marx thinks it is enough to turn the apostrophe back against Saint Max.

Marx's obsession with Max's obsession with ghosts is itself an obsession with ghosts; for 'Marx' read 'Max'. The letter 'r' has moved; it too has been apostrophised – literally, 'turned away'. At work before our eyes is that 'spirit which supposes the very movement of its letter' and not even the 'proper name' (17/41) is safe; in this sense the movement is *im*proper, an affront to property, a purloining.[110] The spirit of Marxist critique here becomes a thief in the night of *Specters*, a thief made more – we suspect – in the image of Derrida than Marx. The thief, however, is made still more in the image of Christ, the *good* 'thief in the night' (2 Peter 3.10); for a thief of letters in the night of mourning might mean, of course, that 'mo*u*rning' becomes 'morning', the coming of light and tomorrow. This good possibility dawns on both writers: Browning's elegy for Elizabeth, 'Prospice', looks forward to 'the black minute's ... end ... / Then a light' (22–6); whilst *Specters'* end hints at light with its talk of 'the intellectual of *tomorrow*' (176/279).

The morrow's intellectual is, though, given the nocturnal task of speaking to ghosts; *Specters* ends with: '*Thou art a scholar: speak to it Horatio.*' And this is no simple task; for to '*apostrophiz[e]* ... the ghost' (12/34) is not only to address it but also, at a literal level, to 'turn it away'. For this reason, 'Come!' – the apostrophe implicit in *Specters'* weak but insistent messianic[111] – is haunted by impossibility; if 'Come!' only succeeds in turning away we are confronted with an impossibility in which coming is also somehow a going. This, though, *is* to some extent made possible; first, by what Derrida calls the 'coming and going' (11/32) of the ghost in *Hamlet*; and then by the future tense of Derrida's own ghosts: 'the revenant is going to come' (4/22); 'is it going to come back?' (37/69). Prior, however, to this 'going to come' is Hamlet's 'coming to go', his 'nay, come let's goe together', the final line of the quotation with which Derrida opens *Specters* (3/20). Where exactly they are to 'goe' is a question that connects with Derrida's 'original' question, 'Whither Marxism?'; the connection is not only the question of destination but also the fact of being together: 'whither Marxism' is, as Derrida puts it, 'the question that brings us together' (14/37). We are at least together – even back together, back to what Derrida in 1967 called 'a community of the question'.[112]

Who, though, is in this community? It is a question we dare not answer; for to do so would be to no longer belong. We would, in effect, be turned away; but to be turned away is to be apostrophised, which is also to be spoken to. Whereas the community of the question excludes, the community of the apostrophe includes its own outside; its power to turn away, or exclude, is identical to its power to address and, therefore, *in*clude. As Derrida speaks to the question of the ghost, the question gradually recedes and only the *speaking to* remains – the book's very last words are: *'speak to it, Horatio'*. Mr Derrida the medium leaves the community of the question for what we might call the community of the apostrophe. Though the ghost may not actually be there, Derrida does at least speak *with* Marcellus and *to* Horatio.

By contrast, for Mr Browning the monologist there is always the possibility that there is no *Horatio* to speak to, never mind ghosts. For Browning, the movement away from the question may lead not to apostrophe but, more terrifyingly, to an unaddressed cry. Witness the case of Sludge, for whom the question of God is no sooner asked than discarded for an exclamation:

> But, for God?
> Ay, that's a question!
>
> (793–4)

Though Sludge refuses to speak to the question of God, in doing so with an exclamation we glimpse what it might just be to speak to the mystery, or shock that is God. As Hopkins will put it, '(My God!) My God.'[113]

Notes

My title is, in part, a glance towards Derrida's recent book, *Adieu* (Paris: Seuil, 1997). The chapter itself is a response to W. David Shaw's fascinating suggestion that, in *The Ring and the Book*, Browning 'reads and writes like a Victorian Derrida' – see his *Victorians and Mysteries: Crises of Representation* (Ithaca:

Cornell University Press, 1990), 319. Other extremely important work in connection with Derrida and Browning includes Herbert F. Tucker, Jr, *Browning's Beginnings: The Art of Disclosure* (Minneapolis: University of Minnesota Press, 1980); L. M. Findlay, 'Taking the Measure of *Différance*: Deconstruction and *The Ring and the Book*', *Victorian Poetry*, 29 (1991), 401–14; and Yopie Prins, 'Elizabeth Barrett, Robert Browning, and the *Différance* of Translation', *Victorian Poetry*, 29 (1991), 435–51.

1 *Robert Browning: The Poems*, ed. John Pettigrew (Harmondsworth: Penguin, 1981), 837.392–5. All subsequent references to Browning, with the exception of *The Ring and the Book*, are to this edition with line numbers appearing parenthetically in the text.
2 Jacques Derrida, *Writing and Difference*, tr. Alan Bass (London: Routledge, 1978), 82 / *L'Écriture et la différence* (Paris: Seuil, 1967), 122.
3 Joseph Bristow, *Robert Browning* (Brighton: Harvester, 1991), 115.
4 Jacques Derrida, *Glas* (Lincoln: Nebraska University Press, 1986) / *Glas* (Paris: Galilée, 1974).
5 See A. F. Cheskin, *Robert Browning and the Hebraic Tradition*, as quoted in *Dissertation Abstracts International*, 42 (1981–82), 1643; and J. Berlin-Lieberman, *Robert Browning and Hebraism* (Azriel, 1934).
6 Shaw, *Victorians and Mysteries*, 319.
7 Jacques Derrida, *Writing and Difference*, 68, 64 / 104, 99.
8 See Kevin Hart, *The Trespass of the Sign: Deconstruction, Theology and Philosophy* (Cambridge: Cambridge University Press, 1989), 50; as Hart pointed out, in 1989 the only two exceptions to this rule were Susan Handelman, *The Slayers of Moses: The Emergence of Rabbinic Interpretation in Modern Literary Theory* (Albany: State University of New York Press, 1982), 164, and Andrew J. Mckenna, 'Biblioclasm: Joycing Jesus and Borges', *Diacritics*, 8 (1978), 16.
9 Jacques Derrida, *Of Grammatology*, tr. Gayatri Chakravorty Spivak (Baltimore: Johns Hopkins University Press, 1976), 6 / *De la grammatologie* (Paris: Minuit, 1967), 15.
10 Roland Barthes, *Image–Music–Text*, ed. Stephen Heath (London: Collins, 1977), 157.
11 See Jacques Derrida, *Dissemination*, tr. Barbara Johnson (Chicago: University of Chicago Press, 1981), 65–172 / *La Dissémination* (Paris: Seuil, 1972), 69–198.
12 Anti-Semitism within Victorian Britain was such that the Jew was also an accused figure for many of Browning's readers. See Anne Aresty Naman, *The Jew in the Victorian Novel: Some Relationships Between Prejudice and Art* (New York: AMS, 1980), 42.
13 Patricia Parker, *Inescapable Romance: Studies in the Poetics of a Mode* (Princeton: Princeton University Press, 1979), 224; Derrida, *Writing and Difference*, 66/102.
14 Derrida, *Writing and Difference*, 82/122.
15 As Naman observes, 'one of the myths that became more prominent in the nineteenth century was that of the wandering Jew' (*The Jew in the Victorian Novel*, 41).
16 *Writing and Difference*, 98/145.

17 *Ibid.*, 9/19.

18 Jacques Derrida, 'Deconstruction and the Other', tr. Richard Kearney, in Kearney (ed.), *States of Mind: Dialogues with Contemporary Thinkers on the European Mind* (Manchester: Manchester University Press, 1984), 169.

19 Robert Browning, *The Ring and the Book*, ed. Richard D. Altick (Harmondsworth: Penguin, 1971), IX.1040.

20 This is Matthew Arnold's version of Schleiermacher – *Letters of Matthew Arnold, 1848–1888*, ed. G. W. E. Russell, 2 vols (New York: Macmillan, 1895–1900), 1.442.

21 Geoff Bennington and Jacques Derrida, *Jacques Derrida*, tr. Geoff Bennington (Chicago: Chicago University Press, 1993), 170 / *Jacques Derrida* (Paris: Seuil, 1991), 160.

22 *Writing and Difference*, 83/123; 'Deconstruction and the Other', 167.

23 J. Hillis Miller, *The Disappearance of God* (Oxford: Oxford University Press, 1963), 90; Tucker, *Browning's Beginnings*, 188.

24 Jacques Derrida, *Margins of Philosophy*, tr. Alan Bass (London: Harvester, 1982), 11 / *Marges de la philosophie* (Paris: Minuit, 1972), 12.

25 *Ibid.*, 17/18.

26 Speech at the meeting of the Society for Increasing Endowments of Small Livings in the Diocese of Oxford, 25 November 1864.

27 F. A. Paley, review of Browning's *Agamemnon*, in B. Litzinger and D. Smalley (eds), *Browning: The Critical Heritage* (London: Routledge, 1970), 439.

28 The poem is so described by Cheskin (see no. 5).

29 Léon Poliakov, *The History of Anti-Semitism*, tr. Miriam Kochan, 3 vols (London: Routledge, 1970–75), 3.319.

30 Isobel Armstrong, 'Browning and the Grotesque Style', in Armstrong (ed.), *The Major Victorian Poets: Reconsiderations* (London: Routledge, 1969), 95.

31 *Ibid.*, 94; in *The Disappearance* Miller opens his chapter on Browning thus: 'At the beginning Browning is a huge sea … shapeless, fluid, and capricious … But it is not enough to say that Browning is pressed in on all sides by a great bulk of matter. He *is* that matter, that ocean, that "protoplasm"' (81).

32 Algernon Charles Swinburne, 'The Chaotic School', in Litzinger and Smalley, *Browning: The Critical Heritage*, 215; George Steiner, *After Babel: Aspects of Language and Translation* (London: Oxford University Press, 1975), 315.

33 Yopie Prins, '"Violence bridling speech": Browning's Translation of Aeschylus' *Agamemnon*', *Victorian Poetry*, 27 (1989), 157.

34 Derrida speaks of 'the … adventure of the trace' toward the end of 'Structure, Sign and Play' – *Writing and Difference*, 292/427.

35 *Ibid.*, 293/428.

36 *Of Grammatology*, 4–5/14.

37 Jacques Derrida, *Speech and Phenomena and Other Essays on Husserl's Theory of Signs*, tr. David Allison (Evanston: Northwestern University Press, 1973), 97 / *La Voix et le phénomène* (Paris: Presses Universitaires de France, 1967), 108.

38 *Of Grammatology*, 24/39.

39 See Michael Payne, *Reading Theory: An Introduction to Lacan, Derrida,*

Kristeva (Oxford: Blackwell, 1993), 18, 25. Saussure refers to writing as 'a genuine orthographic monstrosity' – Ferdinand de Saussure, *Course in General Linguistics*, tr. Roy Harris (La Salle, IL: Open Court, 1983), 31.

40 See Chris Baldick, *In Frankenstein's Shadow: Myth, Monstrosity and Nineteenth Century Writing* (Oxford: Oxford University Press, 1987), 31.

41 *Writing and Difference*, 293/428. Payne is also interesting in this connection – see *Reading Theory*, 17–18.

42 Bennington and Derrida, *Jacques Derrida*, 98/95.

43 *Ibid.*, 104/100.

44 *Ibid.*, 19/20.

45 Bristow, *Robert Browning*, 48.

46 Derrida, *Margins of Philosophy*, 22/23.

47 This is Martin Heidegger's phrase – see *On the Way to Language*, tr. Peter D. Hertz (New York: Harper and Row, 1971), 63.

48 Derrida, *Margins of Philosophy*, 25/26.

49 *Writing and Difference*, 293/428; Jacques Derrida, *Points ...: Interviews, 1974–1994*, ed. Elisabeth Weber, tr. Peggy Kamuf *et al.* (Stanford: Stanford University Press, 1995), 348 / *Points de suspension: Entretiens* (Paris: Galilée, 1992), 359.

50 Geoffrey Hartman, 'The Interpreter's Freud', in David Lodge (ed.), *Modern Criticism and Theory: A Reader* (London: Longman, 1988), 417; Michael Haar, 'The Play of Nietzsche in Derrida', tr. Will McNeill, in David Wood (ed.), *Derrida: A Critical Reader* (Oxford: Blackwell, 1992), 52; M. H. Abrams, 'The Deconstructive Angel', *Critical Inquiry*, 3 (1977).

51 Bennington and Derrida, *Jacques Derrida*, 238/221.

52 Jacques Derrida, 'Of an Apocalyptic Tone Recently Adopted in Philosophy', tr. John P. Leavey, Jr, *Oxford Literary Review*, 6 (1984), 27 / *D'un ton apocalyptique adopté naguère en philosophie* (Paris: Galilée, 1983), 77.

53 Walter Benjamin, *Illuminations*, ed. H. Arendt, tr. H. Zuhn (London: Fontana, 1992), 249.

54 As an example of the degree to which even the most educated Victorians read the Bible as detailed and precise history, see Clough's diary entry for 7 April 1838 which reads: 'On this day ... 1800 Years ago, – our Lord was in Bethany, just arrived; – this His last sabbath day ... Found historically only in St John's Gospel' – *The Oxford Diaries of Arthur Hugh Clough*, ed. Anthony Kenny (Oxford: Oxford University Press, 1990), 38.

55 *The Correspondence of Gerard Manley Hopkins and Richard Watson Dixon*, ed. C. C. Abbott (London: Oxford University Press, 1935), 74.

56 *Of Grammatology*, 226/322.

57 'The word "Host" is of course the name for the consecrated bread or wafer of the Eucharist' – J. Hillis Miller, 'The Critic as Host', in Harold Bloom *et al.*, *Deconstruction and Criticism* (London: Routledge, 1979), 20.

58 Gregory L. Ulmer, 'Sounding the Unconscious', in John P. Leavey, *GLASsary* (Lincoln: University of Nebraska Press, 1986), 103a.

59 Derrida, *Glas*, 69a/81a.

60 *Ibid.*, 71a–72a/83a–84a.

61 *Speech and Phenomena*, 54/60.

62 *Margins of Philosophy*, 315/375.

63 Jacques Derrida, 'Aphorism Countertime', tr. Nicholas Royle, in Jacques

Derrida, *Acts of Literature*, ed. Derek Attridge (London: Routledge, 1992), 432 / *Psyché: Inventions de l'autre*, (Paris: Galilée, 1987), 532; *Glas*, 19b/26b.

64 *Glas*, 6b/12b.

65 Jacques Derrida, 'Psyche: Inventions of the Other', tr. Catherine Porter, in Lindsay Waters and Wlad Godzich, *Reading de Man Reading* (Minneapolis: University of Minnesota Press, 1989), 31 / *Psyché*, 20–1.

66 Henry Staten talks of 'the pursuit of the *memento mori* that Derrida finds contaminating all forms of presence' – *Wittgenstein and Derrida* (Oxford: Blackwell, 1985), 121.

67 See, for example, the death of John Barton in *Mary Barton* (ch. 35) or that of Barkis in *David Copperfield* (ch. 30).

68 Jacques Derrida, 'Before the Law', tr. Avital Ronell and Christine Roulston, in *Acts of Literature*, 204 / 'Devant la loi', in A. Phillips Griffiths, *Philosophy and Literature* (Cambridge: Cambridge University Press, 1984), 184.

69 *Glas*, 133a, 79b / 151a, 92b.

70 Paul de Man, *The Rhetoric of Romanticism* (New York: Columbia University Press, 1984), 81. The complex relationship between Derrida and resurrection is also discussed in my essay 'The Hostage of the Word: Poststructuralism's Gospel Intertext', *Religion and Literature*, 25 (1993), 1–16.

71 Bennington and Derrida, *Jacques Derrida*, 54/53. This begins, of course, with Derrida's essay 'Living On/Borderlines', where he speaks of 'writing, of triumph, as *living on*' – Bloom *et al.*, *Deconstruction*, 176 / *Parages* (Paris: Galilée, 1986), 218.

72 *Writing and Difference*, 257/368. For further discussion of Derrida and inspiration see Timothy Clark's excellent *The Theory of Inspiration: Composition as a Crisis of Subjectivity in Romantic and Post-Romantic Writing* (Manchester: Manchester University Press, 1997), 238–81.

73 *Ibid.*, 257–9/378–80; Jacques Derrida, 'At this Very Moment in this Work Here I Am', in Robert Bernasconi and Simon Critchley (eds), *Re-reading Levinas* (Bloomington: Indiana University Press, 1991), 14 / *Psyché*, 163.

74 *Glas*, 243a/271a.

75 'At this Very Moment', 15/164.

76 *Of Grammatology*, 69/100.

77 Jacques Derrida, *The Gift of Death*, tr. David Wills (Chicago: Chicago University Press, 1995), 3 / *L'éthique du don, Jacques Derrida et la pensée du don* (Paris: Transition, 1992), 13.

78 Jacques Derrida, *Specters of Marx: The State of Debt, the Work of Mourning, and the New International*, tr. Peggy Kamuf (London: Routledge, 1994), 133 / *Spectres de Marx: L'État de la dette, le travail du deuil et la nouvelle Internationale* (Paris: Galilée, 1993), 212. All subsequent page references will appear parenthetically in the text, with the reference to the English translation appearing first; this order is reversed when I quote the French.

79 The spectre of Luther also haunts Derrida's 'Circumfession' in the sense that its '59 periods, 59 respirations, 59 commotions, 59 four-stroke compulsions' (Bennington and Derrida, *Jacques Derrida*, 127/122) is a precise numerical inversion of Luther's *95 Theses*.

80 Karl Marx, *Critique of Hegel's 'Philosophy of Right'*, ed. J. O'Malley (Cambridge: Cambridge University Press, 1970), 137–8.

81 William Shakespeare, *Hamlet*, ed. Harold Jenkins (London: Routledge, 1982), I.ii.119. All subsequent references to *Hamlet* will appear parenthetically in the text.

82 John D. Caputo, *The Prayers and Tears of Jacques Derrida: Religion without Religion* (Bloomington: Indiana University Press, 1997), 139. I am much indebted to this fine book.

83 Alice Jardine, *Gynesis: Configurations of Woman and Modernity* (Ithaca: Cornell University Press, 1985), 234.

84 His name appears only twice, and in both cases only because he plays a very minor role in a passage from Marx – see 109–10, 113 / 178, 184.

85 Browning refers to this symposium in 'La Saisiaz', where he speaks of 'Sundry minds engaged in "On the Soul and Future Life"' (164).

86 Aijaz Ahmad locates still another religious spectre of Marx, or rather Derrida: for Ahmad, Derrida's 'quasi-religious tone' makes the spectral Claudius and his son Hamlet suggestive of 'the *Holy* Ghost and his famous Son' – see 'Reconciling Derrida: "Spectres of Marx" and Deconstructive Politics', *New Left Review*, 209 (1994), 92.

87 Tradition has it that Luther thus concluded his defence at the Diet of Worms in April 1521 – see G. R. Elton, *Reformation Europe* (London: Fontana, 1963), 51.

88 Bennington and Derrida, *Jacques Derrida*, 58/57.

89 William Shakespeare, *Julius Caesar*, ed. T. S. Dorsch (London: Routledge, 1982), III.ii.73.

90 See Donald Thomas, *Robert Browning: A Life within a Life* (New York: Viking Press, 1982), 2–3.

91 Interesting in this connection is Gayatri Chakravorty Spivak's response to *Specters* in an essay which, to some extent, sets Derrida alongside the contemporary Algerian writer Assia Djebar. The essay concludes by quoting Djebar's question 'How shall I name you Algeria?' and remarking: 'For the specters of Marx to be able to ask questions of that genre, the *Specters of Marx* must travel in terrains that it seems not yet to know' – 'Ghostwriting', *Diacritics*, 25 (1995), 82.

92 Anselm Haverkamp (ed.), *Deconstruction is/in America: A New Sense of the Political* (New York: New York University Press, 1995), 3.

93 *Writing and Difference*, 118/127.

94 William Shakespeare, *Macbeth*, ed. Kenneth Muir (London: Routledge, 1964), II.ii.35.

95 Spivak, 'Ghostwriting', 66.

96 Bennington and Derrida, *Jacques Derrida*, 25/26–7.

97 *Ibid.*, 170/160; 'SA' is, primarily, Derrida's acronym for Saint Augustine but it also works, *inter alia*, as an encoding of his mother's maiden name.

98 See *Points* ..., 120/128.

99 In 'Circumfession' Derrida circumfesses ('one always confesses the other') to 'remain[ing] guilty of ... [not] doing enough to save Jews' – Bennington and Derrida, *Jacques Derrida*, 147, 312 / 139, 289.

100 Interesting in this connection is Simon Critchley's assertion that '*Specters* is an event, a performance, a staging which is ... utterly pervaded by its own *theatricality*' – 'On Derrida's *Specters of Marx*', *Philosophy and Social Criticism*, 21 (1995), 28.

101 Bennington and Derrida, *Jacques Derrida*, 56/56; see Robert Smith's fascinating *Derrida and Autobiography* (Cambridge: Cambridge University Press, 1995).

102 *Robert Browning: The Poems*, I. 1059n.

103 Bennington and Derrida, *Jacques Derrida*, 58/57.

104 See Thomas, *Robert Browning*, 159.

105 This line appears only in the manuscript version of 'Mr Sludge' – see *Robert Browning: The Poems*, I.1167n.; letter to E. B. B., February 1846, *The Letters of Robert Browning and Elizabeth Barrett Browning 1845–46*, ed. Elvan Kintner, 2 vols (Cambridge, MA: Belknap Press of Harvard University Press, 1969), 1.455.

106 According to Margaret Homans there *is* something peculiarly male, or masculine, about Derrida's ghosts – see my earlier discussion of Irigaray's critique of ghosts, pp. 17–18.

107 Spivak, 'Ghostwriting', 66.

108 *Acts of Literature*, 422 *Psyché*, 524; for further discussion of this see Nick Royle's excellent *After Derrida* (Manchester: Manchester University Press, 1995), 139–40.

109 Bennington and Derrida, *Jacques Derrida*, 25, 24 / 27, 26.

110 Frederic Jameson alludes to something of this in giving his discussion of *Specters* the title 'Marx's Purloined Letter', *New Left Review*, 209 (1994), 75–109.

111 Derrida speaks of 'a messianic without messianism' (59); for a good discussion of this see Ernesto Laclau, 'The Time is Out of Joint', *Diacritics*, 25 (1995), 86–96.

112 *Writing and Difference*, 80/118.

113 'Carrion Comfort', *The Poems of Gerard Manley Hopkins*, ed. W. H. Gardner and N. H. Mackenzie (Oxford: Oxford University Press, 1970), 100.

4

'No one dreams': where Hopkins was, there Lacan will be

> Where id was, there ego will be.
>
> (Freud)[1]

God's sleep

> The task [of interpreting the unconscious] is made no easier by the fact that we are at the mercy of a thread woven with allusions, quotations, puns, and equivocations.
>
> (Lacan)[2]

> It seems true … that you can trace your dreams to something or other in your waking life … But the connection may be capricious, almost punning: I remember in one case to have detected a real pun but what it was I forget.
>
> (Hopkins)[3]

To read Hopkins's poems as, in some sense, dream-texts requires no special pleading; overdetermined, difficult, punning and radically ambiguous, they seem, at times, to *be* Lacan's complex, woven thread. Recent commentators on Hopkins have written of the rule, or misrule, of the signifier; we should now follow the Lacanian lead and refer that rule, albeit tentatively, to the unconscious. Hopkins himself writes of the 'mind['s] … cliffs of fall', of the 'heart in hiding', and of an 'underthought, conveyed chiefly in … metaphors … [and] only half realised by the poet'.[4] Moreover, if 'I wake [only to] … feel the fell of dark not day' (101), 'wish day come' (99), and 'not breed one work that wakes' (107) to what extent am 'I', or indeed my poetry, ever fully conscious? Given the poet's 'aspirations to anonymity',[5] we might take from 'Andromeda' the formula 'no one dreams' as an epigram for Hopkins.

That, in effect, is what several critics have done. Daniel Harris remarks that the terrible sonnets 'verge … towards nightmare'; Robert Martin talks of the 'chaos of [the] … unconscious within … an exigent verse form'; and Hillis Miller observes that, 'as in the opium dreams of De Quincey, Hopkins' time of desolation is elastic'.[6] In his work on *The Wreck of the Deutschland* Walter Ong also lays, or breaks, the ground for our discussion. Ong puts much stress on the telegraphic communications that made possible *The Times*'s day-by-day on-the-spot reports of the disaster which in turn made possible Hopkins's highly detailed poem. *The Wreck*, declares Ong, is a 'telegraphically conditioned poem'.[7] But is it also, therefore, tele*pathically* conditioned? As Nicholas Royle observes, 'telepathy … is necessarily related to other nineteenth-century forms of [tele]communication … including … telegraphy'.[8] Given Derrida's observation that 'it is difficult to imagine a theory of … the unconscious without a theory of telepathy',[9] there is a sense in which *The Wreck* is a telegraphically-dreamed text. The distance between the Kentish coast and the 'pastoral forehead of Wales' (st. 24) is mediated by a telegraphy, an 'electrical horror' (st. 27), that is also telepathic, dream-like.

One critic who certainly prompts us to read *The Wreck* as a dream-text is David Shaw, who points out moments in which it is 'as if [the poet] … were suffering from … aphasia'[10] – at times a similarity-disorder ('where, where was a, where was a place?'), at other times a contiguity-disorder ('the Master, / *Ipse*, the only one, Christ, King, Head'). According to Lacan, these disorders constitute – as metaphor and metonymy, respectively – characteristic features of the unconscious.[11] In *The Wreck*, the unconscious most obviously surfaces through the biblical story of Christ asleep in the midst of a terrible storm:

> [the men]
> Woke thee with a *We are perishing* in the weather of
> Gennesareth.
>
> (st. 25)

If the unconscious, namely Christ's, is in some sense crucial to the sea-storm, might it not also have to do with the poem's aphasic storm of metaphor and metonymy? Might not both storms be, to some extent, a function of Christ's unconscious – an encounter with 'the dark side of the bay of thy blessing' (st. 12)? Does the poem confront not only 'the storm of his strides' (st. 33) but the storm of his dreams?

To represent God, albeit in Christ, as unconscious is to make a radical departure from traditional, Enlightenment representations of God. 'Always thinking', writes Locke, 'is the privilege of the infinite Author ... who never slumbers nor sleeps.'[12] For the Victorians, however, it was possible, in the wake of Romanticism's privileging of the irrational, to imagine a quite different God. Thomas Carlyle talks of 'the domain of the Unconscious ... from [which] ... all Religions ... have proceeded'; Sir William Hamilton claims that 'spiritual treasure lies ... hid in the obscure recesses of the mind'.[13] In this context, Hillis Miller's claim that 'Hopkins' linguistic underthought undoes his Christian overthought'[14] is too oppositional. That faith might be strengthened, rather than undone, by what we could call the unconscious of language was R. C. Trench's insight: 'God', he writes, '[has] pressed such a seal of truth upon language that men are continually uttering deeper things than they know ... it may be asserting them against themselves.'[15]

Hopkins, however, is not as affirmative as this; unlike Matthew's Gospel, *The Wreck* does not tell of a Christ who wakes to calm the storm. Moreover, for Hopkins the point is not just that God is identified with the unconscious but, more radically, that he *is* unconscious. In Thomas Hardy's poetry this conceit will serve, only a few years later, to express profound agnosticism. Hardy's God characteristically allows the human race to slip both his mind and the grasp of his 'too oft unconscious hand'.[16] In the work of Lacan the same conceit is even further from faith – 'the true formula of atheism', he declares, 'is not *God is dead* ... [but] *God is unconscious*'.[17] In Hopkins, this may not be a formula for atheism but neither is it purely or simply a formula of faith. To be more precise, Hopkins's unconscious Christ points up the latent piety of Lacan's atheism. In 'Andromeda', for instance, the eponymous heroine and type of Christ – she is bound, '*forsaken*' by her father the king and left, as a sacrifice, to a dragon – is saved by a Perseus who both 'hangs / His thoughts on her' and treads '*pillowy* air'. This is a rewriting of the Passion in which Christ – as Andromeda – is saved by one who, as a pillowy visitation of thoughts, may be read as Christ's unconscious. It is as if, in the moment of crucifixion, the moment in which 'he made himself of no reputation'

(Philippians 2.7), Christ dreams; or as the poem itself puts it, '*no one* dreams'. For Hopkins, the formula 'God is unconscious' does indeed mark out a moment of atheism, a moment of *sacred* atheism: the moment of Christ's 'My God, my God, why hast thou *forsaken* me?' (Matthew 27.46: my italics).

Hopkins negotiates what Lacan describes as 'a corridor of communication between psycho-analysis and the religious register'.[18] Consider the case of the split subject. In *The Wreck*, Christ possesses not only a 'double-natured name' but is 'mid-numbered ... in three' (st. 34); again, when, in 'Carrion Comfort', we read that 'I ... lay wrestling with (my God!) my God' we cannot but echo the poem's earlier question, 'which one?' As Miller observes, 'the intimate life of the Trinity ... is characterised for [Hopkins] ... by the act whereby God divides himself from himself'.[19] In 'I wake and feel' this is particularly obvious if, reminded of Psalm 22, we interpret the 'I' as that of the God-forsaken Christ:

my lament
Is cries ... like dead letters sent
To dearest him that lives alas! Away.

To adapt the Isaiah text in 'Nondum', 'Verily, Thou art a God that hidest Thyself' *from thyself*.

In so far as Hopkins also hides from himself, is also a split subject, he too inflects the doctrine of the Trinity. As Miller comments, 'Hopkins, in his deprivation, experiences a horrible parody of the reflexive relation of God to himself.'[20] Something similar may be said of Lacan, in his theorisation; most obviously, when he refers to 'the decomposed trinity of the ego, the superego, and the id', but also when he rewrites *milieu* as 'mi-dieu'[21] – thereby opening up the notion of a mid-God or between-God. The possibility of a split, or even schizophrenic, deity again surfaces when Lacan asks whether 'Freud's discovery [of 'the self's radical ex-centricity to itself'] represent[s] the confirmation, on the level of psychological experience, of Manicheism?'[22]

That Hopkins and Lacan should so converge raises their Jesuit connection – Hopkins became one, whilst Lacan was educated by them. As Geoffrey Hartman has argued, we might well 'read ... Lacan ... in the light of what Sartre called "la grande affaire" – the scandal of theological survivals in even the most secular thinkers'.[23] Catherine Clément goes so far as to describe Lacan as a 'profoundly Christian spirit', whilst Antoine Vergote writes that 'Lacan believes he finds the rationality of theology in the structure of the unconscious'.[24] To reverse the equation, there are moments in Hopkins which recall the familiar observation that confession is like psychoanalysis, moments when Hopkins as priest appears charged with the *talking* cure of souls and, like the passing-bell, with 'summoning men from speechless day' (23) – the speechless day of consciousness. In 'Felix Randal', the 'im*patient* soul' is that of the sick and dying parishioner in whom 'reason rambled'; most often, however, the soul is the poet's own, engaged as it is in an apparently free association of words only interrupted by the occasional interpretation: 'where I say / Hours I mean years, mean life' (101).

God's (m)Other

If Hopkins's God is doubled by an unconscious – which, for Lacan, is 'the discourse of the Other' – then since, traditionally, 'the place of the Other is also the place of God',[25] Hopkins arrives at the possibility of an Other that has an Other. In strictly Lacanian terms, 'there is no Other of the Other';[26] nevertheless, that is precisely how we should theorise the unconscious of Hopkins's God, particularly when expressed in terms of the Mother of God – that is, the (m)Other of the Other.

The Other that is the unconscious of God is most nearly the Mother of God in *The Wreck*. Here the 'dark side of the bay of thy blessing', the dark or night side of God, is marked by distinctly *mothering* violence. Witness the 'unfathering deeps' (st. 13), the 's*mother* of sand' (st. 14) that wrecks the ship, and the decapitated sailor, suspended from the rigging, '*dandled* the to and fro' (st. 16). This mothering storm's strange Othering of God climaxes in the paradoxical figure of the tall nun. She is, at once, not only a hysterical bride of Christ – one of 'the wild woman-kind below' (st. 16) – but also the ecstatic mother of Christ. Even as her 'new born'-Christ is 'conceived' (st. 34, 30) she cries to her 'lover'-Christ. The cry is at once that of both a mother and a lover: 'O Christ, Christ, come quickly' (st. 25, 24). In this storm of a poem the Mother of God is hopelessly entangled with the Other that is *jouissance*. She is, however, no less entangled in the calm of 'The May Magnificat'; here the poet declares, of 'Spring's universal bliss', that 'this ecstasy all through mothering earth / Tells Mary her mirth till Christ's birth'.

What then, of Lacan's claim that, under the domination of the phallic term, 'we [have] ended up in Christianity by inventing a God such that it is he who comes'?[27] It is true that, the Christological vision of the hawk in 'The Windhover' climaxes in '*his* ecstasy' (my italics); it is true that, in *The Wreck*, Christ 'hadst glory of this nun' (st. 30). The same poem, however, also declares: 'Not out of *his* bliss' (my italics); and this, along with the tall nun's ecstatic conceiving, is part of a counter-thought that concerns not just the Mother of God but also the Other that is the unconscious of God. As Lacan declares, 'in the sexual relation [the woman] is radically Other, in relation to what can be said of the unconscious'. To put it more simply, 'there is a *jouissance* proper to her ... of which she herself may know nothing'.[28]

Lacan goes on to support this claim by reference to female mystics – 'it is clear', he writes, 'that ... they are experiencing ... [*jouissance*] but know nothing about it'.[29] Like Hopkins, Lacan is interested – to quote the seminar's title – in 'God and the *Jouissance* of the Woman'; indeed, as in Hopkins, that *jouissance* can appear to relate to God not simply as sign, or intimation, but as the Other: 'It is', writes Lacan, 'insofar as her *jouissance* is radically Other that the woman has a relation to God greater than all that has been stated in ancient speculation.'[30]

If Lacan and Hopkins meet at the point of the *jouissance* of the Woman, they begin to separate in so far as the Woman is, for Hopkins, the Mother of God. This way, of course, lies the Other of the Other. According to Lacan, what is meant by this is that 'no metalanguage can be spoken',[31] that the Other that is language, and the unconscious which it structures, admit of no final guarantee, or vantage point. On this definition, Lacan's aphorism is most obviously gainsaid in the very last stanza of *The Wreck*. For here the poem's long storm of language at last gives way to a transcendental, and, as it were, metalinguistic, signifier: namely, the Christ that is the long-deferred but eventual and Lordly subject of the final line:

> Our heart's charity's hearth's fire, our thought's chivalry's
> throng's Lord.

This may be what Lacan means by the Other of the Other; but it is not the Other of the Other that Hopkins imagines via the doctrine of the Mother of God. The latter has nothing to do with metalanguage but everything to do with the outer limits of alterity and, indeed, the thinkable. Nevertheless, here at the end of *The Wreck*, as Hopkins moves from the Mother to the Son of God, he does arrive at the end that is metalanguage. For Lacan that end is an *im*possible closure; for Hopkins, or at least the earlier Hopkins of *The Wreck*, it is not only possible but a kind of opening, an almost unending ending, an astonishing straining towards a horizon that is not quite forever-receding.

Though Hopkins may depart from Lacan on the possibility of metalanguage, the possibility of an End to meaning, the two writers come together again with respect to origins, or rather the absence of origins. Witness Lacan's insistence that 'the unconscious is neither primordial nor instinctual',[32] it being always already structured by language. This insistence returns Lacan to Hopkins in that *his* insistence on the Mother of God also problematises the notion of origin – above all, the notion of *God*-as-origin. To say that God has a mother is to say the beginning is not the beginning. This paradox surfaces in *The Wreck*, where the traditional notion of Christ as the primal Word, the 'arch and original Breath' (st. 25), is countered by the rival claims of Mary. First, there is the reference to the voice of the tall nun (the Mary-to-be) as 'a virginal tongue' (st. 18); then there is the poet's declaration that the tears of the 'mother of being in me' – namely his heart – 'make words break from me', thus giving speech 'a madrigal start' (st. 19). 'Madrigal' is rooted etymologically in *matricalis*, meaning 'mother.'

This rivalling, or contesting, of the 'arch and original Breath' recalls Miller's observation that 'Hopkins' poetry never quite restores language to an originary … Word.'[33] This failure in turn recalls Victorian theologians' increasing conviction that the Gospels were mythical rather than historical, texts without simple factual basis. This conviction, in *its* turn, recalls – or rather, anticipates – Lacan's account of the unconscious as a text that neither is, nor has, an origin. For Strauss, the nineteenth-century Higher Critic, the Bible was myth, 'unconscious fiction'; for Arnold, the strongest part of religion was its 'unconscious poetry'.[34] Even *The Wreck*'s fleeting résumé of faith's historical grounds – 'It dates from day / Of his going in Galilee' and so forth – is prefaced by not only 'here … the faithless fable' but also 'here the faithful waver' (st. 6).

Again, in 'Nondum' the poet declares that 'we clothe Thee, unseen King ... / Each in his own imagining'. Admittedly, as a Jesuit, Hopkins could not have been more committed to the historicity of the Gospel narratives. Nevertheless, the Ignatian practice of realising biblical episodes with 'the eyes of the imagination' – 'the aim ... [being] to bring ... the mind as close as possible to the primal scene'[35] – may, in fact, make the Jesuit peculiarly susceptible to Higher Criticism's critique of faith as the work of the unconscious. In his journal, Hopkins relates how one particular meditative exercise caused him to fall asleep and dream.[36]

Another quite orthodox aspect of Hopkins's faith that echoes Higher Criticism's heterodox questioning of Christianity's origins is, strangely enough, the Virgin Birth – a doctrine that leaves Christianity without a primal scene, without an original sexual encounter. In *The Wreck*, of course, Hopkins makes desperate efforts to recover, or invent, precisely this scene. But this very desperation is witness only to the scene's unthinkability; indeed, it is witness to the unthinkability of *any* sexual encounter. This point is, in one sense, biographical – Hopkins once declared he 'had never seen a naked woman'; in another sense it is theological – 'it is better', writes Hopkins, '[not] to have sexual intercourse with woman'; but it is also, and at the same time, Lacan's provocative, psycho-structuralist point that 'the relation between the sexes does not take place'.[37] Whether the doctrine of the Virgin Birth is merely a distant displacement of Lacan's provocation or vice versa is impossible to say. It is clear, though, that again Hopkins arrives at Lacan's radical distrust of origins directly via the doctrinal irony that is Mary. In Hopkins, the Mother of God is a dangerous and almost deconstructive principle.

Indeed, as a mother who conceives without a father, Mary opens up a gap within the very fabric of that most cherished Victorian institution, the family. She anticipates, in fact, what Hélène Cixous has identified as the subversive role of the maid, or servant-girl, within the recurring family romance of Freud's case-studies – most famously, 'Dora'.[38] This, though, is exactly the connection that Cixous, and indeed Lacan, do not make; it is not the servant girl but Dora that they both compare to the Madonna.[39] To this extent they duplicate the very error that Cixous locates in Freud: concerned 'to rewrite unconscious desire in closer conformity to the endogamous rules of the bourgeoisie', he overlooks the significance of the maid. And this is precisely because she is, as Cixous puts it, 'the hole in the social [and familial] cell'.[40]

By contrast, Hopkins, being focused on the manifestly *exo*gamous Mary, gives an account of desire that quite obviously ruptures the familial cell. In *The Wreck* the family is torn apart: first, by the 'unchilding [and] unfathering deeps' of the sleeping Christ's unconscious; and then by a tall nun who is at once both Christ's mother and bride. With the family cell so disordered a whole new meaning develops when we read, of this Madonna-type, that 'she rears herself' (st. 19).

For Hopkins, 'time's eunuch' (107), a distant and displaced family is a founding principle of discipleship: 'Father, and mother dear, / Brother and sister are in Christ not near' (101). We could not be further from a bourgeois endogamous code; and this is reflected by the way that, in Hopkins, the circuit of desire quite obviously includes the equivalent of Freud's servant-girl – witness the titular characters of 'Felix Randal' and 'Harry Ploughman'. Both poems are founded on a relationship between poet and subject that is, at once, explicitly socio-economic and tacitly, or unconsciously, homoerotic. That Felix Randal is 'hardy-*handsome*' repeats on the poem, phonetically, as first 'and some', then 'began some', and finally 'ransom'. Likewise, Harry Ploughman's manual labour or 'sinew service' has, for Hopkins, more than just economic value:

> Harry bends, look. Back, elbow and liquid waist …
> See his wind- lilylocks -laced …

Under the exogamous sign of Mary, unconscious desire in Hopkins betrays its implication in the extra-familial structures of class and economics; in this sense, she shows the unconscious to be structured not just by theology but also by society. The sign of Mary is the vehicle of its own abandonment; as such it reflects the more general way in which Hopkins's primarily theological account of the unconscious characteristically shades into a materialist one. For instance, in 'The Leaden Echo and the Golden Echo' we read of

> that side hurling a heavyheaded hundredfold
> What while we, while we slumbered.
>
> (93)

Here, the (il)logic of what happens during sleep is not only that of

Christ's parable ('and some ['seed'] ... bare fruit an hundredfold' (Luke 8.7–8)) but also of capitalism; it is supposed that capital multiplies autonomously while the investor sleeps, as it were. The unconscious again slides from the theological to the material in *The Wreck*, where the nun's ecstatic vision of Christ is beset by a strange sense of reification:

> Fancy, come faster –
> Strike you the sight of *it*? Look at *it* loom there
> *Thing* that she ... There then!...
> *Ipse*, the only one, Christ ...
>
> (st. 28: my italics)

Misreading 'loom' as noun, we here underwrite reification with a key symbol of fast-changing Victorian technology. To this extent the nun's vision rehearses the Victorian habit of conflating high technology with mind, or spirit. This is the habit which links telepathy to telegraphy, and finds its most concise formulation in the 'hard mechanic ghost' of Tennyson's *Maud* (1855).[41] This same ghost also hovers over the unconscious, or at least its suggestion, earlier in *The Wreck* when the poet's declaration that he is 'mined with a motion' (st. 4) carries the underthought of '*mind* with *e*motion'. In 'No worst there is none', Hopkins again works the mind/mined pun to remind us that both industrialisation and the unconscious undermine; when we read 'O the mind, mind has mountains; cliffs of fall', one way to make sense of the tacit semantic leap from 'mountains' to 'cliffs' – that is, from the mind's heights to its depths – is to reread the line as 'the mind, min*e*d ... has cliffs of fall'.

Technology also has its place in Lacan, whose talk of the 'mechanisms of the unconscious' is part of his more general belief that 'the machine embodies the most radical symbolic activity of man'.[42] Lacan's materialism does not, though, possess the developed political intelligence to be found in Hopkins.[43] This intelligence shows up in Hopkins's recurring fascination with the dissolution of the body – a dissolution that parallels not only Lacans' 'body-in-bits-and-pieces',[44] the body as experienced by the infant, but also the fragmentation of the body politic of late-Victorian Britain. We may be familiar with Hopkins as a kind of infant, but not as a political observer. Nevertheless, in 'Spelt from Sybil's Leaves' – a poem which first appears in Hopkins's

'Dublin Note-Book' in late 1884 – we are confronted with a 'Disremembering, dismembering' which, in a sense, is a *remembering* of that historic dismembering, Dublin's famous Phoenix Park murders of 1882 when both the chief secretary for Ireland and the permanent under-secretary were hacked to pieces by Republican extremists. The poem concludes:

> two flocks, two folds – black, white; right, wrong; ...
> ... ware of a world where ... these two tell, each off the
> other.

Of course, Hopkins's body-in-pieces is, in the first instance, a theological conceit; just before declaring 'This is my body' Christ or the priest *breaks* the bread (1 Corinthians 11.24). To make this connection is, though, to echo Lacan, who writes that

> [though] the unconscious ... is the censored chapter ... the truth can be rediscovered ... elsewhere. Namely: – in monuments: this is my body.[45]

The eucharistic drama begun by Lacan is completed by Hopkins, for whom the censored chapter of the unconscious is rediscovered in the inscription 'this is my body-*in-pieces*'. Witness 'I am gall, I am heartburn', which, as Harris remarks, shrinks the rational and conscious self, housed in an entire bodily shape, to separate and unconscious sensory phenomena'.[46] Again, in *The Wreck* the body, both 'asunder' (st. 5) and as-under, functions as a fragmented subtext, or unconscious:

> Warm-laid grave of a *womb*-life grey;
> Manger, maiden's *knee*;
> The dense and the driven Passion, and frightful *sweat*:
> Thence the *discharge* of it, there its *swelling* to be,
> Though felt before, though in high flood yet –
> What none would have known of it, only the *heart* being hard
> at bay ...
>
> (st. 7: my italics)

In the following stanza we read both of 'flesh burst[ing]' and, still more strangely, 'Christ,'s feet'; the bizarre punctuation all but separates Christ from his feet.

In completing Lacan's allusion as 'this is my body-*in-pieces*', Hopkins's account of the unconscious takes on all the tragic, negative force of the crucifixion – the breaking of Christ's body.

Hopkins thus foregrounds the Golgotha otherwise hidden in Lacan: witness 'this *passion* of the signifier' (my italics).[47] To express the same point in secular terms: Hopkins points up the 'not' in the 'knot' that is the Lacanian unconscious. Whilst Lacan talks of 'the unconscious [as] this knot of our being',[48] Hopkins declares 'Not, I'll not ... / Not untwist ... these last strands of man' (99). Unconsciousness, for Hopkins, can be a way of thinking negation *per se*: hence 'no one dreams'; or again, the beginning of 'The Loss of the Eurydice', where we read that,

> Some sleep unawakened, all *un*-
> warned, eleven fathoms fallen
>
> (72)

For all its eccentricity such negation still belongs to Hopkins's central, theological drama; the sequence which begins with 'unawakened' and 'un-' is later continued by not only 'unvisited' but also 'Unchrist'. At first glance, this latter negation carries an almost blasphemous force: the upper case of 'Un' quite dwarfs the lower case of 'christ'. A second glance, however, suggests that this same negation is the specific moment of crucifixion and, therefore, charged with the hope of resurrection. If crucifixion corresponds to the unconscious then resurrection becomes a waking-to-*consciousness*, a 'birth of a brain' (st. 30). And that is exactly what happens at the very end of *The Wreck*, where the poet declares, 'Let him easter in us, be a dayspring to the dimness of us, be a crimson-cresseted east' (st. 35). This resurrection-as-waking, easter-as-east, has, though, as much to do with patriarchy as faith. Christ, 'our King', 'prince', 'priest' and 'Lord', comes to 'brighten ... *her*' (my italics); he enters precisely as the 'dame at our door' exits. Where she was, he will be. Hence the shift from 'her' to 'hero' in successive lines. This is all very familiar: 'Through her we may see him' (Hopkins); 'this "her" ... does not exist' (Lacan).[49]

The Wreck's resurrection-as-waking proves to be as scarred by negation – the negation of 'her' – as is the crucifixion-as-unconscious. But then, in Hopkins, this particular crucifixion is a 'Disremembering, dismembering', and for that the only possible 'resurrection' is a *re-membering*. The consciousness that, in Hopkins, is most nearly a resurrection, most thoroughly privileged, is the consciousness of the body.

To privilege consciousness is, of course, a nineteenth-century habit of mind deriving, primarily, from Hegel, who argued that the movement of the absolute Idea towards self-consciousness constitutes nothing less than the very course of history. What, though, distinguishes Hopkins's privileging of consciousness is that it follows not so much Hegel as Marx, in particular his notion of 'sensuous consciousness'.[50] In Hopkins the conscious subject is not, necessarily, the mind, or spirit, but might just be the body. In 'The Caged Skylark', whilst 'Man's mounting spirit' is a 'bird beyond remembering' his body is not; the poem's very last words, 'his bones risen', articulate the hope of physical resurrection, the body's re-membering. That the body might remember *itself*, might become self-conscious, is also possible in Hopkins. In 'Harry Ploughman' the labourer's body, so long merely the object of the poet's gaze, becomes almost a subject when, as if with embarrassment, ''S cheek crimsons' – the peculiar contraction of 'his' to ''S' enforcing our sense of the body's autonomy. Again, in *The Wreck* the line 'Flesh falls within sight of us' invites misreading as 'Flesh falls with *insight* of us' (st. 11). Elsewhere, Hopkins writes that 'part of th[e] ... world of objects ... is ... man's ... own body'[51] – here it verges on the world of the object that becomes a subject, the thing that returns my gaze.

For Hopkins, the body in question is always, to some extent, the body of Christ – not just his actual body but also his metaphorical body, the Church. Witness Harry Ploughman's 'knee-nave'. This body's coming-to-consciousness is an event not only religious but political; the ecclesial body of Christ is a community, or collective, that shares Christ's suffering and alienation. In this sense, it is identical with those labouring classes which Marx had declared to be alienated and, as it were, somnambulant muscle and sinew. In Hopkins, it is a *labourer*'s cheek that 'crimsons'; a moment which mimics not just self-consciousness but also – with red (as Hopkins himself notes) being the colour of Communism – that arrival at 'Communist consciousness'[52] which, for Marx, would precipitate revolution. Hopkins once famously declared that 'in a manner I am a Communist', and there is certainly something Marxian about the poet's complaint that he produces 'not ... one work that wakes' (107) or, again, the quasi-Golgothan cry of the rural labourers in 'Binsey Poplars': 'O if we but knew what we do'. The voices of alienated labour are again encoded in 'The Loss of the Eurydice', where we read, of one particular corpse, that

Leagues, leagues of seamenship
  Slumber in these forsaken
Bones, this sinew, and will not waken.

(75)

What sleeps within this body is not only labour ('seamenship') but also the name of Victorian collectivism ('*Leagues*, leagues of seamenship').[53] That these 'leagues … will not waken' may well be the poem's sad wisdom, but it *is* contested; both by the Christian hope of resurrection and by Hopkins's clearly stated fear that 'some great revolution is not far off'.[54] The body's waking is, for Hopkins, as possible as hoped-for resurrection and half-feared revolution. Whether the body-in-question is finally ecclesial or political is impossible to say, but either way its coming-to-consciousness is so much a conceit as to be almost a dream. In this sense, it is a hope of consciousness that is always already returning to *un*consciousness. Like Lacan, Hopkins finally displaces the opposition between the two; unlike Lacan, this displacement occurs in both a moment, and the name, of hope.

Wo Es war

Wo Es war, soll Ich werden.

(Freud)

Whatever it is, I must go there.

(Lacan)

… who goes there?

(Hopkins)[55]

The name of hope, though present in Hopkins, does not come easily; it does itself belong to an opposition that is in question. In 'The Leaden Echo and the Golden Echo' the Leaden 'Despair, despair, despair, despair' is immediately answered by the Golden 'Spare!' – an echo that only speaks the golden name of 'hope' in its dim, homophonic evocation of the French *e-spère*. Inscribed, however, within this particular name for hope is the 'nom du *père*', which suggests a hope that has grown paternal, grown old; and such is, for Hopkins, the nature of hope – ever since *The Wreck* 'Hope had grown grey hairs' (st. 15).

In Lacan, of course, father and law are so closely identified that, at the level of concept, or signified, father and hope are totally unrelated. However, since they *are* related at the level of the signifier, the insistence of the letter is that the father might just become a figure of hope. And this is precisely what happens, as a radically intertextual trick, at the end of 'The Rome Discourse'.[56] Here, Freud's German *Da* – the positive, hopeful term of his grandson's game of loss and gain, '*Fort*! and *Da*!', '"Gone!" and "Here!"' – finds itself alongside the English 'Da' or 'Dadda' that haunts the Sanskrit 'DA … DA … DA' of T. S. Eliot's *The Waste Land* (1922), a poem that speaks of 'musing upon … my father'.[57] The *Da* that is 'Here' or gain becomes, via Eliot's Sanskrit 'DA', the 'Da' that is Dadda. There is more to Lacan's *nom du père* than simply the '*non* du père' of which we hear so much; the letter, unlike Lacan, insists on the possibility of *es-père*. This we cannot forget as we muse on fathers.

For Freud himself, however, musing on fathers belongs, if anything, to *Fort* rather than *Da*, 'Gone' rather than 'Here'; once his grandson could talk he no longer threw his toy down with 'o-o-o-o', or indeed *Fort*, but rather 'Go to the fwont!' where his father was fighting.[58] Another father goes when Lacan writes 'I, too, have seen with my own eyes … the child, traumatized by the fact that I was going away.'[59] The strict, psychoanalytic answer to Hopkins's question 'who goes there?' is: the mother; Freud believed that his grandson invented his game to cope with his mother's departures. However, the historical answer, the answer that comes more incidentally, or anecdotally, from both Lacan and Freud is: the father. Indeed, just as Hopkins's question echoes the cry of the soldier on guard ('Who goes there, friend or foe?') so the fuller, historical answer is the father-as-*soldier*. And this is as true for Hopkins as for Freud. In the same way as the child's initial 'o-o-o-o' becomes, according to Freud, 'G*o* t*o* the fw*o*nt' so, in *The Wreck*, it becomes 'T*o* her*o* of Calvary … / … men g*o*' (st. 8). Read alongside Freud, the 'hero' and 'go' of this quasi-military theology may be interpreted as the 'o-o-o-o' of not just a child but also a war. At the same time as being a psychoanalytic poet Hopkins is also a war poet.

As a Jesuit, an order founded by a knight-turned-priest, Hopkins was trained to see Christ as a soldier, as one who, to quote Hopkins, 'went before his troops to Calvary'. Hopkins's poetry is, therefore, full of the 'Alarms of war' (85); 'He knows war' (99),

'Wants war' (102), and is 'where wars are rife' (101), not only 'the war within' (106) but also the wars without – most obviously, when in Dublin, the Irish war of independence. There is, indeed, an uncanny sense in which Hopkins both 'knows war' and *fore*knows war – in particular, the First World War. After all, Hopkins was not really published, perhaps not really readable, until 1918, when Robert Bridges oversaw the first edition of the *Poems of Gerard Manley Hopkins*. This, 'one of the queerest [books] in the world', as Bridges called it, was prefaced with the hope that it would somehow answer to a world in which 'Hell wars without'.[60] And so it does, not so much as a cure but rather as a faithful reflection of one of the queerest wars in the world. Witness the 'hope' that is '*Trench*ed with tears' (st. 15); 'those lovely lads [that are] windfalls of war's storm' (98); and, above all, that 'Million-fuelèd ... bonfire' where

> Squadroned masks and manmarks ' treadmire toil ...
> Footfretted in it ...
> ...
> ... all is an enormous dark
> Drowned. O pity and indig ' nation!'
> ('That Nature is a Heraclitean Fire')

For 'Squadroned masks' read 'gas masks'; for 'Footfretted' read 'trench feet'; and for 'pity' read Wildred Owen's 'the pity of war'. As for 'nation!', read 'Deutschland'; for the Deutschland that, come 1918, was virtually wrecked by four years of war becomes the hidden subject of 'The Wreck of the Deutschland'. The new, anti-Catholic Falck Laws by which the nuns were exiled were very much part of the formation of Germany as the modern and homogenised nation that went to war in 1914.

Where I say 'for this read that' I mean, perhaps, 'misread'. But if Freud was right to claim that misreading is, more than any other parapraxis, a characteristic of war then Hopkins's very capacity to be misread – 'do not bother ... with the meaning', he tells Bridges[61] – does itself make Hopkins a war poet. In particular, it makes him a poet of the war that has been so closely identified with the 'no man's land' of the Freudian unconscious. As Lacan remarks, 'it was on the waves set up by the ... panic-stricken breath of war that Freud's voice reached us'.[62] And it was, of course, on precisely the same breath that Hopkins's voice first reached an audience; indeed, the two voices might be confused, particularly when Freud's association of war with the slips of misreading is set alongside Hopkins's talk of young soldiers as 'slips of soldiery' ('The Bugler's First Communion'). It is as if, for Hopkins as well as Freud, soldiers belong to a world of parapraxis – if so they may be numbered with 'those … windfalls of war's storms', the fair-haired slaves of whom, as the poem reminds us,[63] Pope Gregory famously punned: 'Non Angli sed angeli' ('Not Angles but angels'). Where there is war there is parapraxis; indeed, in this case, where there is parapraxis there is a nation, England. This is replayed in the 'pity and indig ' nation!' of Hopkins's heraclitean war-scape and, again, in the line, 'slips of soldiery Christ's royal ration' – or did I see '*n*ation'? For what is a nation but a slip of soldiery, an accident of war? The question of a nation is begged by the very hero of the poem: 'boy bugler, born … of Irish / Mother to an English sire' (82).

By making a link between the slips of parapraxis and the confusions of nationality, Hopkins anticipates Lacan's allegorial account of the arbitrary way in which language divides up reality: his story concerns a boy and a girl in a train who see, on a station platform, two signs: 'Ladies' and 'Gentlemen'.

> 'Look,' says the brother, 'we're at ladies!'; 'Idiot!' replies his sister, 'Can't you see we're at Gentlemen.' … Ladies and Gentlemen will be henceforth two countries … between which a truce will be the more impossible since they are actually the same country.
>
> ('The Insistence')[64]

'But enough,' adds Lacan, 'it … begin[s] … to sound like the history of France'; indeed, there is a strange sense in which, within the context of 'The Insistence', it begins to sound like that censored chapter of the history of France: the years of Nazi occupation. What connects the platform narrative with these years is the railway line, for just as 'the bar in the Saussurian algorithm [S/s]' is 'materialize[d]' in 'the rails in this story' so these rails might just, in turn, be historicised as Lacan proceeds to Freud's joke about 'the Jew [who complains] to his crony: "Why do you tell me you are going to Cracow so I'll believe you're going to Lvov, when you really are going to Cracow?"' Surrounded as it is by curious references to 'plan[s] of battle', 'peace negotiations' and 'troop movements', 'the sad plaint of the Jew' takes on something of that most apalling Jewish sadness – the Nazi death-train; from Cracow to Auschwitz it is just forty miles by rail.[65]

Like Lacanian desire, 'The Insistence' is itself 'caught in the rails of … metonymy';[66] more than that, it is caught in the rails of history. Lacan, however, is fully conscious of these rails, perhaps because they belong to a censored chapter of his own history – these were events in which he was himself involved. As Clément records, when Lacan's wife Sylvia declared herself Jewish he went personally to the Gestapo to retrieve her dossier, thereby almost certainly saving her life.[67] Lacan, indeed, nearly declares himself 'Jewish' in the sense that, as an analyst, he belongs to a community that he regularly describes in Jewish terms: witness 'the Pharisee', 'diaspora', 'synagogue', and 'kabbala'.[68] Paradoxically, as an analyst, Lacan is also cast in the role of collaborator; many French philosophers and scientists had initially resisted psychoanalysis on the grounds that it was not just German-speaking but, somehow, German-inspired.[69]

Whether Lacan is cast as Jew or collaborator, either way he is not a 'true' Frenchman; indeed, Lacan's relationship to his nation is as ambiguous as is Hopkins's who, for all his patriotic declarations, still owes a greater loyalty to the international community of Catholicism:

> Day and night I deplore
>   My people and born own nation.
>
> (87)

Part of the scandal of *The Wreck* is that the return of Catholicism to Britain is represented, through the wrecking of a ship that sounds like a nation, as a kind of landing or invasion:

> Our King back, Oh, upon English souls!
>
> …
>
> More brightening her, rare-dear Britain, as his reign rolls …
>
> (st. 35)

Knock, knock

> 'Knock, knock. Who's there …?'
>
> (*Macbeth*)[70]

The end of *The Wreck* is not just concerned with the invasion of a King; before the 'hero' there is that 'her', that 'Dame, at our door', to whom the final stanza is addressed. And it is with this dame that the poem at last finds a door to go with the 'Knock' upon which another 'her', the *Deutschland,* foundered: 'night drew her / Dead to the Kentish Knock' (st. 14). In Revelation, of course, it is Christ who declares 'Behold, I stand at the door, and knock' (3.20); in this sense Hopkins's Dame stands at a door marked 'Gentlemen'. Such unhinging of gender is repeated in 'The Bugler's First Communion', where Christ emerges from behind a door conventionally marked 'Ladies', the door of a kitchen cupboard:

> Forth Christ from cupboard [I] fetched.

This bizarre line has all the absurdity of a dream, as if Hopkins himself is 'dead to the ... Knock', dead to the world; he is not, as Lacan will pun, 'knocked up'. For Lacan, hearing a knock at the door has some specific connection with the moment in which sleeping becomes waking:

> The other day I was woken by knocking at my door just before I actually awoke. With this impatient knocking I had already formed a dream, a dream that manifested itself to me as something other than this knocking. And when I awoke, it is insofar as I reconstitute my entire representation around this knocking ... that I am aware of it ... that I know that I am waking up, that I am *knocked up* [*je suis* knocked].[71]

Knock, knock. Who's there? *Je suis. Je suis* who? *Je su(i)s* Jesus. This word-play, that Derrida will later exploit, is to be expected of one who was *Jesui*t-schooled.[72] Just as Christ emerges from Hopkins's cupboard so here he emerges, just as improbably, from Lacan's text; the result: Jesus knocked. As Hopkins writes, 'Christ plays in ten thousand places' (90) – even, it seems, in that everyplace in which, for Lacan, words can be otherwise.

Lacan knows this well. When, in 'The Insistence', the *barre* of the Sausserian formula (S/s), the line separating signifier from signified, is transformed, anagramatically, into the *arbre* of Saussure's diagram it branches into a whole wood of cultural associations, the very first of which is Christ's tree, the tree of Golgotha:

> Drawing on all the symbolic contexts suggested in the Hebrew of the Bible, it [*arbre*] erects on a barren hill the shadow of the cross.[73]

Although the first tree in Lacan's symbolic wood, the cross is by no means the greatest – indeed, it is the least in the sense that its barrenness is countered by a cryptic inscription of harvest that is set off by the last word of the last tree: *herbe* ('grass'). *Herbe* looks not only back to *arbre* but forward to *gerbe* ('sheaf') and in so doing gestures towards Heidegger's account of the origins of language as a kind of 'harvest or … gathering of fruit from the vine and soil'.[74] Lacan's own route to Heidegger's harvest is simple; as Michael Payne observes, just a year before 'The Insistence' he had been translating Heidegger. It is not, though so simple for the reader; in order to connect *arbre* with both *herbe* and *gerbe*, and thereby produce a harvest, the reader must follow Lacan to the letter, must follow what Lacan here describes as 'the double spectre of [*arbre*'s] vowels and consonants'.

A spectre, of course, implies a death – in this case that death or 'murder of the thing' by which, as Lacan writes elsewhere, 'the symbol first manifests itself'.[75] For Lacan, the Heideggerian harvest is no Eden; the primal scene of language is stained by a murder. The protest of Valéry's tree is, in a sense, the protest of the murdered thing:

> 'No! says the Tree, it says No!'[76]

There is another 'No' to be heard as Hopkins also turns the tree into a symbol – 'The Beginning of the End' is concerned with a 'tropic', or metaphorised tree, but declares:

> No, the tropic tree
> Has not a charter that its sap shall last.

The 'No' of the tree is even more forceful, albeit unspoken, in 'Barnfloor and Winepress', where the poet's eucharistic metaphorisation of the vine is gainsaid by the 'terrible' of

> Terrible fruit was on the tree
> In the acre of Gethsemane.

Like Lacan, Hopkins seems to know that the Heideggerian harvest, the harvest that is symbolism, is marked by a murder – the murder of not just Christ but also the thing. Witness that spectre of the thing which, for Hopkins as well as Lacan, haunts the harvest feast. In 'Barnfloor and Winepress' this is obvious:

> We scarcely call th[is] … banquet food
> But even our Saviour's and our blood.

For Hopkins, a transubstantiationalist, the eucharistic banquet is not simply symbolic; the real presence of Christ's suffering body and blood will always show through. In this sense, the thing for Hopkins turns out to be suffering; if 'Patience [is the] hard thing!' (102) then suffering, its etymological cousin, is the really hard thing. Indeed, suffering is also the thing whose spectre haunts the Lacanian banquet – according to Lacan, that 'Freudian thing' the unconscious is 'the stone guest who comes, *in symptoms*, to disturb the banquet of one's desire' (my italics).[77] What makes this Freudian thing here shade into the ghost of the murdered thing – normally, for Lacan, two quite different things – is, first, that this strange guest is made of that hard thing stone, and, second, that it conjures up that most famous spectre at the feast: the ghost of Banquo. As the haunted Macbeth asks, 'Can such *things* be ...?' Or is it, we might ask, merely an apparition, an effect of 'the madness that deafens the world with' – to quote Lacan quoting Macbeth – 'its sound and fury'?[78] The Lacanian answer is that Banquo's ghost is both, since madness is an aspect of the Freudian thing. To quote again the haunted Macbeth, and return to the thing that is stone: 'Stones have been known to move'; they have also, however, been known to cry out:

> It is the truth ... that the patient cries out through his symptom, as Christ said that the stones themselves would have cried out if the children of Israel had not lent them their voice.[79]

Again the Freudian thing, the painful truth that is the unconscious, is identified with that hard and *enduring* thing, stone – as if, for all Lacan's insistence on the letter, there is one thing that it can never finally murder: suffering. This is so if only because the Lacanian letter *is* so murderous – as Lacan says, 'it is said, the letter killeth'; he also says, of 'a man', that 'the signifier ... abolishes him'.[80] Hopkins speaks of the 'cipher of suffering' (*The Wreck*, st. 22), but for Lacan every cipher is the cipher of suffering.

Malcolm Bowie fears that the sheer 'welter of [Lacan's] theoretical speech can easily drown ... ordinary human suffering' but when Lacan declares, in 'The Purloined Letter', that 'we are ... dealing with ... a *letter in sufferance* [*en souffrance*]' the primary, theoretical meaning, 'in abeyance', cannot quite drown the secondary, pathological meaning: 'in pain'.[81] Pain also makes its presence felt even as Lacan seems to disappear into his wood of symbolic tress – for even there is a tree traced 'in the tortoise-shell cracked by the fire'. This excruciating image of immolation takes on a terrible historicity in so far as that final word *herbe* also looks back to *hébreu* ('Hebrew').[82] That Jews had become merely something to burn is a thing that repeats upon *Écrits* as, in 'The Freudian Thing', Lacan plays upon the name of his Jewish wife, Sylvia (literally, 'wood'). The essay, dedicated to this escapee of the Holocaust (literally, 'total burning'), speaks of not only 'the wood of ... theory' but also the desk that ends its life as 'firewood'.[83]

Footing it

Though Sylvia escaped this fate Hopkins, perhaps, does not – at the end of 'That Nature is a Heraclitean Fire and of the Comfort of the Resurrection', written in the last year of his life, Hopkins is no more than firewood, matchwood:

> I am all at once what Christ is ...
> This Jack, joke, poor potsherd, ' patch, matchwood, immortal
>   diamond,
>   Is immortal diamond.

Though matchwood, Hopkins is also the diamond that comes, eventually, from the carbon remains of matchwood; he is, the title implies, redeemed by the resurrection – this is the spirit of the poem. However, as if 'I am all at once what Christ is' were equivalent to Freud's 'Where id is ego shall be', the *letter* of the poem yields not the comfort of the resurrection but the discomfort of the unconscious. Note how the 'I am ... is' of '*I am* all at once what Christ *is*' endures a cryptic reversal in the 'Is ... i/am' of '*Is* immortal d*iam*ond'. For Lacan, this is the work of the unconscious, or discourse of the Other, that space in which 'I am where I do not think' and the subject 'receives ... his own message in reverse form'.[84] According to Lacan, the discourse of the Other, of the world 'outside' my conscious self, always already mediates my relationship to myself. Here in Hopkins's poem this complication of self and Other is encoded in the word 'diamond', where 'I am' shades into *mond(e)*, into world.

As not *monde* but 'mond' this 'world' is not quite right. In Hopkins's own terms, it is not straightforward: 'nothing', he once wrote, 'is so ... straight forward to the truth as simple ... *is*';[85] and if the 'Is' of 'Is immortal diamond' is straightforward the *mond(e)* of diamond is not. In Lacan's terms, it is not the straightforward totality of the mirror-stage, that illusory totality which, to quote Lacan, 'I shall call orthopaedic' – literally, 'straight-child'.[86] Of course, Hopkins himself was never 'straight'; only Manley by name, his manner was called 'effeminate' and his religion a 'perversion'.[87] As for his sense of totality, or world, that seems to grow out of a body that is certainly not straight. Witness the 'world' punningly produced by the 'whirled' of 'I whirled out wings' (*The Wreck*, st. 3), or again the universe of 'Thy wring-*world* right foot rock' ('Carrion Comfort': my italics). In this latter case it is specifically the foot (the foot *of* rock?) that is not straightforward, suggesting a limp that returns at the end of the poem, where 'I ... lay wrestling with (my God!) my God' – as Jacob discovered, to wrestle with God, with totality, is to end up limping (Genesis 32.24–32). For Hopkins, totality is dangerous, it can always leave you limping; it is no accident that, in Hopkins, 'fall' so often rhymes with 'all'. In 'Pied Beauty' the two words play together, as if each were an aspect of the other:

> For rose-moles *all* in stipple upon trout that swim;
> Fresh-firecoal chestnut-*falls*; finches' wings;
> Landscape plotted and pieced – fold, *fall*ow, and plough;
> And *áll* trádes, their gear and tackle and trim.

Again, in 'No worst, there is none' the phrase 'cliffs of fall / Frightful' is charged with the possibility of 'frightf*a*ll' – momentarily, we sense a whole world of fall, an all of fall; momentarily, we might just know what Hopkins elsewhere means by 'A noise of falls I am possessèd by' (164).

In Lacan there is also an all, or totality, to be imagined in terms of verticality, or height – witness what Lacan calls 'the open sky of omnicommunication'.[88] Unlike Hopkins, however, Lacan sees no danger or fall in this all; not for Lacan the free fall punningly inscribed in Freud's *frier Einfall* ('free association'). Lacan has no fear of falling because, quite simply, he does not fly; for all his polysemy and intertextuality he makes it clear that 'the open sky of omnicommunication' belongs to the future of psychoanalysis. It is not ready, in other words, to respond to Nietzsche's call to 'kill the Spirit of Gravity'; indeed, Lacan goes so far as to declare that 'psychoanalysis must rediscover its gravity'.[89] This unusually grave Lacan may, perhaps, be an illusion of the mirror-stage, a Lacan whose body seems no longer boundless, no longer capable of 'growing wings';[90] nevertheless, it is a Lacan with whom we must struggle. And this we do notwithstanding his brilliant levity, notwithstanding what he himself calls 'my acrobatics [in] ... the [Saussurean] tree', and notwithstanding his critique of the conventional, linear 'time of the fall of heavy bodies'.[91] By contrast, though Hopkins seems to give his very self to this fall – 'I am soft sift / In an hourglass' (*The Wreck*, st. 4) – his writing often witnesses to the defiance of gravity. Very often this takes the form of a cross between flying and walking: witness, in one poem, 'what wind-walks!' (70), in another 'a rainbow footing it' (71), in yet another 'Pillowy air he treads' (85), and in still another 'what we had lefthanded left ... / Will have ... walked with the wind' (93).

According to Freud, '"what we cannot reach flying we must reach limping"';[92] Hopkins, however, does both. His 'footing it' may always turn into limping, not only because he wrestles with God but also in the sense that the strange stresses of his poetry depend on what Hopkins himself called 'imperfect feet'.[93] After 'The Caged Skylark' we might say that Hopkins's feet, even when wind-walking, are dis-stressed:

> meadow-down is not distressed
> For a rainbow footing it nor he for his bónes rísen.

Equally distressed are the actual, non-metrical feet that preoccupy Hopkins in 'Tom's Garland: Upon the Unemployed' – a study of the 'garland of nails' hammered into the soles of the labourer's boots. What makes these booted feet so distressed, so imperfect, is their evocation of the feet of others; most obviously, the feet of 'Tom's fallowbootfellow' and the 'mighty foot' that appears, syntactically, as if from nowhere or, at least, elsewhere:

> What! Country is honour enough in all us – lordly head,
> With heaven's lights high hung round, or, mother-ground
> That mammocks, mighty foot.

These other, alien feet are, in one sense, the feet of the unemployed whose march in 1886 had led to 'Bloody Sunday'; in another sense, these are the feet of infantry – 'Tom' is already the generic name for a soldier';[94] in yet another sense, they are the feet of the crucified Christ, what Hopkins elsewhere calls, of course, 'Christ,'s feet' (*The Wreck*, st. 8); feet that, thus punctuated, thus nailed – as it were, are always already someone else's, always already somewhere else.

Indeed, in leaving their print upon 'Tom's Garland' they serve to animate the fallow boot trope in Lacan:

> the uncontrollable, infinite character of human desire [bears] … the mark of some divine clog [*sabot*] that has left its imprint on it.[95]

From *sabot* comes, of course, 'sabotage' – the sabot, or wooden clog, being the revolting peasant's first weapon. The divine uncontrollability of human desire may, then, turn into violent revolution – an insistence of the letter that is undeveloped by Lacan and completely overlooked by the translator who renders 'sabot' as 'slipper'. By contrast, Hopkins cannot forget that Christ may wear sabots – hence, the 'shéer plód [that] makes plough down sillion / Shine' (69) and, of course, the nailed feet that fall into step with nailed boots.

Just as the feet of the unemployed of 1886 were set towards Trafalgar Square and what became Bloody Sunday, so Christ's feet were set towards Jerusalem and what became bloody Friday. Both knew where they were bound, as does Lacan for whom 'the meaning [*sens*] of … a return to Freud' – or, if you like, the direction of that return – is, in 1955, an actual journey to Vienna to deliver what became 'The Freudian Thing': 'I have come here … to evoke the election by which this city will remain … the eternal city of Freud's discovery.'[96]

Vienna, Jerusalem, London – together Hopkins and Lacan return *us* to *The Waste Land*:

> Jerusalem Athens Alexandria
> Vienna London
> Unreal[97]

Where, though, is Hopkins going? Our only clue is that it is a place he felt he could not reach. When Bridges complained that he could not understand 'Tom's Garland', Hopkins's response began: 'I can go no further along this road.'[98] This road is, in a sense, Freud's road, that 'royal road to the unconscious' which Lacan shows to be the impossible, labyrinthine road of unreadability: 'I like … to leave the reader no other way out than the way in … I prefer to be difficult.'[99] Lacan's pursuit of Freud's royal road takes him, of course, to Vienna; in so doing Lacan responds to the insistence of not just biography but also, as Gallop observes, language: once in Vienna (*Vienne*) Lacan translates 'Wo Es war soll Ich werden' as 'Là ou c'était c'est mon devoir que je *vienne* à etre.'[100] Where Freud was, Lacan should be; but, just like the id with respect to the ego, Freud has gone before Lacan arrives – in 1939, in flight from the Nazis, he had emigrated to London. In this instance, the road of analysis, the road to the unconscious, is not royal but fugitive, a waste-land road uncannily anticipated by Eliot:

> Jerusalem Athens Alexandria
> Vienna London

Vienna to London completes, of course, the broadly westward movement of Eliot's strange itinerary and it is precisely the westwardness of psychoanalysis that Lacan seeks to reverse. As Gallop writes, 'when the center of analysis has moved decidedly westward, Lacan goes [east] from Paris to Vienna'; once there he declares that 'analysis must rediscover its centre', that it must cease to be 'disoriented'.[101] This attempt to, quite literally, re-orient analysis is, though, always already undermined by Freud's westward and disorienting movement to London. As Gallop writes, 'what eternally goes on in Vienna is the discovery that something is not where it is supposed to be'[102] – this, it seems, includes Freud. In his case, however, the work of the unconscious is tied to that of history.

If Freud is not where he is supposed to be then neither is Hopkins; for though converted to Rome he lives in Protestant Britain. And this alienation becomes dis-orientation as, in *The Wreck*, his desire that Britain should return to Rome becomes a desire for an east:

> Our King back, Oh, upon English souls!
> Let him easter in us, be a dayspring to the dimness of us, be a
> crimson-cresseted east ...
>
> (st. 35)

Though hope may come from the east, Hopkins himself is 'Away in the loveable west' (st. 24) and there he stays till, in his final Dublin years, it becomes an *un*lovable west:

> I am in Ireland now; now I am at a thírd
> Remove.
>
> (101)

This final and unalterable dis-orientation is curiously anticipated in the earlier 'Andromeda', where Hopkins describes the growing secularism of western Europe as 'a wilder beast from

West' – a formula charged with the underthought of a 'wilder *east* from west'. This particular disorientation is not, though, simply an alienation from some eastern origin, not simply a matter of the compass, but rather a loss of all sense of direction, a matter or effect of the signifier. Such linguistic displacement is, of course, precisely what both Hopkins and Lacan are after. In so far as the two writers *seek* a dis-orientation it is complete, linguistic confusion they have in mind – in particular, the multi-linguistic confusion of Babel, the confusion of non-translation. Both are concerned with German-speaking ships going to English-speaking America – for Hopkins it is the *Deutschland*, for Lacan it is the ship that took Freud and Jung to New York in 1909; neither, though, wants the ship to arrive. For Hopkins, the wrecking brings about a martyrdom to reconvert England; for Lacan, the fact that the ship *did* arrive in America, to find all-too-ready acceptance, led to ego psychology. In both cases the resistance to the movement from Germany to America, to the carrying-across of the German language, shades into a resistance to translation (literally, 'carrying across').[103] This resistance becomes, indeed, a positive celebration of that world without translation, the towered city of Babel. Witness, in *The Wreck*, the Babel that is the tall nun:

> a lioness arose breasting the babble,
> A prophetess towered in tumult …
>
> (st. 17)

Witness, in 'The Rome Discourse', the Babel that is the divided house of analysis:

> if we were to confront the principles in which each [analyst] believed his experience was based our walls would dissolve very quickly into the confusion of Babel.[104]

This, though, is precisely what happens as Lacan ends the 'Discourse' talking of the 'continued enterprise of Babel' and declaring that

> All I have tried to do is remind you of the misconstrued *a*, *b*, *c* of the structure of language, and to teach you to spell once again the forgotten *b-a*, *ba* of speech.[105]

This is also the *ba* of *ba*bble, or *Ba*bel; to be more precise, the *ba* or *Ba*bel of Freud in reverse, since here Lacan is responding, very specifically, to Freud's claim that

> it is a rule of pyschoanalytic technique that an internal connection which is still undisclosed will announce its presence by means of a contiguity ... just as in writing, if 'a' and 'b' are put side by side it means that the syllable 'ab' is formed out of them.[106]

This return to Freud is, then, a reversal of Freud which mimics that trick of the unconscious by which the subject 'receives ... his own message in reverse form' – in this case, the syllable 'ab'. To put it another way, here Lacan not only returns to Freud but also, as Gallop would stress, 'returns *something* to Freud'.[107] He returns 'ba' – an unintelligible thing of sound that, as such, plays the part of the Freudian thing. In so far, though, as 'ba' connotes 'Babel' – literally, 'gate of God' – it signifies a thing *of God*. This Roman 'ba' is, then, religious; Lacan's *ba*bble on Mons Vaticanus, his *vagitus* – as he himself etymologises – is not only 'an infantile cry' but also, as Bowie suggests, *vatic*, a prophetic cry.[108]

This returns *us* to Hopkins, for his tall nun is at once both Babel and 'prophetess'. She is also enduring an appalling martyrdom. In this sense she is not just a Babelic tower but a crucifix – or rather, that is the conceit which comes to the surface if we read the tall nun through Lacan. At the end of 'The Rome Discourse' Lacan presents a Babelic tower which somehow doubles as that improbable proto-crucifix, Moses' brass serpent-on-a-rod which to see was to be healed (Numbers 21.8–9). Immediately after referring to the 'enterprise of Babel' Lacan suddenly and cryptically declares:

> As for the darkness of the *mundus* around which the immense tower is coiled, let him leave to the mystic vision the task of seeing in it the putrescent serpent of life raised on an everlasting rod.[109]

If Babel is a tower that somehow doubles as a brass crucifix, when Lacan returns 'ba' to Freud he returns not only the gate of God, not only a thing of God, but also a thing that, however improbably, mediates the very healing of God.

In 'The Freudian Thing' Lacan, or rather 'the thing itself', declares that 'the trade route of truth no longer passes through thought: strange to say, it now seems to pass through things'.[110] Might the same, strange to say, be said of God? There is certainly much to suggest that God can pass through that gate of God that is the thing, both material and Freudian, that is the Babel that is so much of Hopkins and Lacan.

Notes

1 Sigmund Freud, *New Introductory Lectures, The Standard Edition of the Complete Psychological Works of Sigmund Freud*, 24 vols (London: Hogarth Press, 1953–74), 22.80.

2 Jacques Lacan, *Écrits: A Selection*, tr. Alan Sheridan (London: Tavistock, 1977), 169–70 / *Écrits* (Paris: Seuil, 1966), 521–2.

3 *The Journals and Papers of Gerard Manley Hopkins*, ed. Humphrey House and Graham Storey (London: Oxford University Press, 1959), 194.

4 *The Poems of Gerard Manley Hopkins*, ed. W. H. Gardener and N. H. MacKenzie (Oxford: Oxford University Press, 1967), 100, 69. (Subsequent page references, where needed, appear parenthetically in the text. In the case of *The Wreck of the Deutschland*, however, the references are to stanzas.) *The Further Letters of Gerard Manley Hopkins*, ed. C. C. Abbott (London: Oxford University Press, 1956), 252.

5 Geoffrey Hartman, *Beyond Formalism* (London: Yale University Press, 1970), 234.

6 Daniel A. Harris, *Inspirations Unbidden* (Berkeley: University of California Press, 1982), xiii; Robert Martin, *Gerard Manley Hopkins: A Very Private Life* (London: Flamingo, 1992), 384; J. Hillis Miller, *The Disappearance of God: Five Nineteenth Century Writers* (London: Oxford University Press, 1963), 354.

7 Walter J. Ong, SJ, *Hopkins, the Self, and God* (London: University of Toronto Press, 1986), 50.

8 Nicholas Royle, *Telepathy and Literature: Essays on the Reading Mind* (Oxford: Blackwell, 1991), 5.

9 Jacques Derrida, 'Telepathy', tr. Nicholas Royle, *Oxford Literary Review*, 10 (1988), 14.

10 David Shaw, *Victorians and Mystery: Crises of Representation* (Ithaca: Cornell University Press, 1990), 91.

11 See *Écrits*, 156–7/505–6.

12 *The Works of John Locke*, 10 vols (London, 1823), 1.87.

13 Thomas Carlyle, *The Works*, ed. H. D. Traill, 30 vols (London: Chapman and Hall, 1896–1901), 28.40; Hamilton cited in Ekbert Faas, *Retreat into the Mind: Victorian Poetry and the Rise of Psychiatry* (Princeton: Princeton University Press, 1980), 37.

14 J. Hillis Miller, *The Linguisitc Moment: From Wordsworth to Stevens* (Princeton: Princeton University Press, 1985), 265.

15 R. C. Trench, *On the Study of Words* (London: Macmillan, 1878), 7.

16 I discuss this point further in 'Waiting in "Unhope": Negation in the Early Poetry of Thomas Hardy', *Critical Survey*, 5 (1993), 174–9; 'By the Earth's Corpse', *The Complete Poems of Thomas Hardy*, ed. James Gibson (London: Macmillan, 1976), 126.

17 Jacques Lacan, *The Four Fundamental Concepts of Psychoanalysis* [1964], tr. Alan Sheridan (London: Hogarth Press, 1977), 59 / *Le Séminarie XI: Les quatre concepts fondamentaux de la psychanalyse* [1964] (Paris: Seuil, 1973), 58.

18 *The Four Fundamental Concepts*, 8/13.

19 *The Linguistic Moment*, 262.

20 *The Disappearance of God*, 355.

21 *Écrits*, 71/282; see Juliet Mitchell and Jacqueline Rose, *Feminine Sexuality:*

Jacques Lacan and the École Freudienne (London: Macmillan, 1982), 167, 171.

22 *Écrits*, 171/523.

23 Geoffrey Hartman, *Saving the Text: Literature/Derrida/Philosophy* (Baltimore: Johns Hopkins University Press, 1981), 99.

24 Catherine Clément, *The Lives and Legends of Jacques Lacan*, tr. Arthur Goldhammer (New York: Columbia University Press, 1983), 32; Antoine Vergote, 'Confrontation with Neutrality in Theory and Praxis', in Joseph H. Smith and Susan A. Handelman, *Psychoanalysis and Religion* (London: Johns Hopkins University Press, 1990), 79.

25 Lacan, *Écrits*, 193/549; Mitchell and Rose, *Feminine Sexuality*, 50.

26 Lacan, *Écrits*, 311/813.

27 Mitchell and Rose, *Feminine Sexuality*, 146 / *Le Séminaire XX: Encore* [1972–73] (Paris: Seuil, 1975), 70.

28 *Ibid.*, 151, 145/75, 69.

29 *Ibid.*, 147/71.

30 *Ibid.*, 153/77.

31 *Écrits*, 311/813.

32 *Ibid.*, 170/522.

33 *The Linguistic Moment*, 263.

34 'On Poetry', *The Complete Prose Works of Matthew Arnold*, ed. R. H. Super, 11 vols (Ann Arbor: University of Michigan Press, 1973), 4.63.

35 *The Sermons and Devotional Writings of Gerard Manley Hopkins*, ed. Christopher Devlin, S J (London: Oxford University Press, 1959), 173.

36 'As Father Rector was giving the points for meditation I shut my eyes, being very tired, and without ceasing to hear him began to dream' – *Journals*, 193.

37 See Norman White, *Hopkins: A Literary Biography* (Oxford: Clarendon Press, 1992), 385, 63; Mitchell and Rose, *Feminine Sexuality*, 138 / *Le Séminaire XX*, 63.

38 See Hélène Cixous and Catherine Clément, *The Newly Born Woman*, tr. Betsy Wing (Manchester: Manchester University Press, 1986), 150–2 / *La Jeune Née* (Paris: Union Générale d'Éditions, 1975), 276–7.

39 This observation is made by Jane Gallop in *Feminism and Psychoanalysis: The Dangerous Seduction* (London: Macmillan, 1982), 147.

40 Peter Stallybrass and Allon White, *The Politics and Poetics of Transgression* (London: Methuen, 1986), 159; Cixous and Clément, *The Newly Born Woman*, 150/276.

41 *The Poems of Tennyson*, ed. Christopher Ricks (London: Longman, 1987), 569 (II.ii.82).

42 Lacan, *Écrits*, 169/521; cited in John Forrester, *The Seductions of Psychoanalysis: Freud, Lacan and Derrida* (Cambridge: Cambridge University Press, 1990), 135.

43 As Malcom Bowie writes, '[although] Lacan's "chain of signifiers" … do … bind the individual mind to the ambient social world in which the chain has been forged … this does not mean – *pace* many Lacanian disciples – that psychoanalysis has come of age as a social theory' – *Freud, Proust and Lacan: Theory as Fiction* (Cambridge: Cambridge University Press, 1987), 176.

44 See Harris, *Inspirations Unbidden*, 55; Lacan, *Écrits*, 4/97; and Elizabeth

Grosz, *Jacques Lacan: A Feminist Introduction* (London: Routledge, 1990), 34.

45 *Écrits*, 50/259.

46 *Inspirations Unbidden*, 68.

47 *Écrits*, 284/688.

48 See Mitchell and Rose, *Feminine Sexuality*, 171 / Jacques Lacan, *Le Séminaire XXI*, 1973–4 (unpublished typescript).

49 Mitchell and Rose, *Feminine Sexuality*, 145 / *Le Seminaire XX*, 69.

50 'The whole of history', writes Marx in 1844, 'is a preparation, a development, for "*man*" to become the object of *sensuous* consciousness' (*Economic and Philosophical Manuscripts*, in *Karl Marx: Early Writings* (Harmondsworth: Penguin, 1975), 355). The conceit of the conscious body, I am suggesting, is latent in the writings of the early Marx. As Terry Eagleton has recently argued, Marxism is very much part of the modern attempt 'to ... think everything through again ... from the standpoint of the body' (*The Ideology of the Aesthetic* (Oxford: Blackwell, 1990), 196) – a claim that again finds support from the *Economic and Philosophical Manuscripts* when Marx asserts that 'the suppression of private property is ... the complete *emancipation* of all human senses' (351).

51 *Sermons*, 127.

52 Hopkins writes, in a letter to Robert Bridges, 'I have little reason to be Red: it was the red Commune that murdered five of our fathers lately' – *Letters of Gerard Manley Hopkins to Robert Bridges*, ed. C. C. Abbott (Oxford: Oxford University Press, 1955), 29; Karl Marx, *Selected Writings*, ed. David McLellan (Oxford: Oxford University Press, 1977), 71.

53 Victorian working-class movements, of various kinds, often used the name 'league', e.g. 'The Labour Representation League'.

54 *Letters to Bridges*, 27.

55 Freud, *Gesammelte Werke* (London: Imago, 1940), 15.86; Lacan, *Four Fundamental Concepts*, 33/34; Hopkins, 'The Lantern out of Doors'.

56 More formally known as the 'The Function and Field of Speech in Psychoanalysis'.

57 See Sigmund Freud, *Beyond the Pleasure Principle* [1920], *Standard Edition*, 18.14–17; *The Complete Poems and Plays of T. S. Eliot*, 74, 67

58 Freud, *Standard Edition*, 18.16.

59 *Four Fundamental Concepts*, 63/61.

60 *The Selected Letters of Robert Bridges*, ed. Donald E. Stanford, 2 vols (1983–84), 2.735; 'Hell wars without' is part of Bridges' prefatory poem – see 44.

61 See Freud, *The Psychopathology of Everyday Life* [1901], *Standard Edition*, 6. 112–13; Hopkins, *Letters to Bridges*, 44–6.

62 *Écrits*, 115/402; see Michael Payne, *Reading Theory: An Introduction to Lacan, Derrida, and Kristeva* (Oxford: Blackwell, 1993), 60.

63 The poem is 'To What Serves Mortal Beauty?':

> Those lovely lads once, wet-fresh ' windfalls of war's storm,
> How then should Gregory, a father, ' have gleaned else
> from swarm-
> èd Rome? But God to a nation ' dealt that day's dear chance.

64 *Écrits*, 152/500.

65 *Ibid.*, 173/525 (translation modified; Sheridan translates 'mouvement de troupes' as 'flock-movement'). On 13 March 1943 two thousand Jews from Cracow were sent by train to Birkenau, otherwise known as 'Auschwitz II'. On 1 June 1942 seven thousand had been deported by rail to the death camp at Belzec; and in March 1944 the remaining Jews of Cracow were sent by rail to Plaszow, where thousands were murdered – Martin Gilbert, *The Holocaust: The Jewish Tragedy* (London: HarperCollins, 1986), 548, 348, 700.

66 Lacan, *Écrits*, 167/518.

67 Clément, *Lives and Legends*, 19.

68 *Écrits*, 38, 115/246, 402; *Four Fundamental Concepts*, 3, 5 / 9, 11.

69 See Madan Sarup, *Jacques Lacan* (London: Harvester Wheatsheaf, 1992), xv.

70 William Shakespeare, *Macbeth*, ed. Kenneth Muir (London: Methuen, 1951), II.iii.7.

71 *Four Fundamental Concepts*, 56/56.

72 '"Jesus" is *Je suis*, without the I' – John P. Leavey, *GLASsary* (Lincoln: University of Nebraska Press, 1986), 71a.

73 *Écrits*, 154/504.

74 *Ibid.*, 156/506; see Martin Heidegger, *Early Greek Thinking* [1954], tr. David Krell and Frank A. Cappuzzi (New York: Harper and Row, 1975), 61; and Payne, *Reading Theory*, 76. Lacan had, in fact, been translating Heidegger's 'Logos', a paper on the origins of language – see Payne, *ibid.*, 75.

75 *Ecrits*, 104/319.

76 *Ibid.*, 155/504.

77 *Ibid.*, 143/433.

78 *Macbeth*, III.iv.110, V.v.27; *Écrits*, 7/99.

79 *Macbeth*, III.iv.122; *Écrits*, 167/518–19.

80 *Écrits.*, 158/509, 508.

81 Malcolm Bowie, *Lacan* (London: Fontana, 1991), 201; Jacques Lacan, 'Seminar on "The Purloined Letter"', tr. Jeffrey Mehlman, *The Purloined Poe: Lacan, Derrida and Psychoanalytic Reading*, ed. John P. Muller and William J. Richardson (Baltimore: Johns Hopkins University Press, 1988), 43 / *Écrits*, 29.

82 Lacan, *Écrits*, 154/504.

83 *Ibid.*, 114, 118, 133 / 114, 406, 422.

84 'On "The Purloined Letter"', 53 / *Écrits*, 41.

85 *Journals*, 127.

86 *Écrits*, 4/97; this etymological point is made by Payne, *Reading Theory*, 32.

87 See Norman White, *Hopkins: A Literary Biography* (Oxford: Clarendon Press, 1992), 34, 44, 139.

88 *Écrits*, 56/265.

89 Friedrich Nietzsche, *Thus Spoke Zarathustra* (Harmondsworth: Penguin, 1961), 68; *Écrits*, 143/434.

90 *Écrits*, 4/97.

91 *Ibid.*, 156/505.

92 Freud, *Standard Edition*, 18.64.

93 'Author's Preface', *Poems*, 45.

94 This point is made by Bernard Richards (ed.), *English Verse 1830–1890* (London: Longman, 1980), 526, n. 1.

95 *Four Fundamental Concepts*, 30 (translation modified) / 32.

96 *Écrits*, 114/401.

97 *The Complete T. S. Eliot*, 73.374–6.
98 *Letters to Bridges*, 272.
99 *Écrits*, 159, 146/509, 493.
100 See Jane Gallop, *Reading Lacan* (Ithaca: Cornell University Press, 1985), 96.
101 *Ibid.*, 95; *Écrits*, 143.
102 Gallop, *Feminism and Psychoanalysis*, 96.
103 *Écrits*, 116; Gallop is very good on the question of trans-lating Lacan to America – *Feminism and Psychoanalysis*, 58–9.
104 *Écrits*, 32/239.
105 *Ibid.*, 106/321.
106 This response is noted by Sheridan – see *Écrits*, n. 118.
107 'What … if the return to Freud were … transitive? Not a return to Freud's presence but a return by Lacan to Freud's text of what Freud was saying that never got recognized' – Gallop, *Feminism and Psychoanalysis*, 109–10.
108 *Écrits*, 31/238; Bowie, *Lacan*, 47.
109 *Écrits*, 106/321.
110 *Ibid.*, 122/410.

5

'The ends of being': between *Aurora Leigh* and Hélène Cixous

Ends

> My soul can reach, when feeling out of sight
> For the ends of Being and ideal grace.
> (Elizabeth Barrett Browning, *Sonnets from the Portuguese*)[1]

> She is not the being-of-the-end ... But she is how-far-being-reaches.
> (Hélène Cixous and Catherine Clément, 'Sorties')[2]

For a poem which opens with 'Of writing ... there is no end' and whose eponymous heroine names the beginning that is dawn, *Aurora Leigh* (1857) is strangely preoccupied with ends and in particular the End revealed in the Book of Revelation. The poem not only concludes with St John's vision but includes at least sixteen further references or allusions to Revelation.[3] The contemporary commentator who declared the book 'a Revelation'[4] spoke better than she perhaps knew. It is as if Barrett Browning cannot think her 'new oeconomies, new laws / [and] ... new societies'[5] without also countenancing a whole number of ends including, at one point, 'the end of woman' (7.883). The irony with which we are confronted is that woman – at least as a self-determining figure – does not survive the very renewing of the world that she herself initiates. Though the poem's concern with change and reform centres, for the most part, on Marian and Aurora, at the last it is Romney rather than Aurora who speaks of 'new economies and new societies'. Aurora may finally speak of the 'first foundations of that new, near Day' (9.956) but she does so only after accepting the marriage she had earlier rejected. It is not, then, a future to which she has independent access; even her sight of 'that new ... Day' is mediated by *his* inner gaze: 'I saw his soul saw' (9.962). The I and eye of the utopian vision is, finally, male.

To see the new, to see a beginning, is not, of course, the role of the idealised Victorian woman – she is too thoroughly inscribed in the end, in particular the end that is death; in her role as nurse to the dying, 'the nineteenth-century angel-woman becomes', write Gilbert and Gubar, 'an "Angel of death"'.[6] Aurora, however, is preoccupied with not the end of life but the end of the world. She is an enlarged and apocalyptic version of the house-trained angel; as Mary Carpenter comments, 'Barrett Browning's story of a female prophetic figure with shining golden hair ... alludes to the apocalyptic "woman clothed with the sun"'.[7] It is not for nothing that Aurora and Marian threaten Lady Waldemar with a noise to compare with 'the last trump's' (7.367). Barrett Browning's heroines might well escape the end that is domesticity – witness Marion; however, the apocalyptic scale of the End that these same women announce, or 'trump[et]', inevitably entails the possibility of 'the end of woman' herself.

A very similar irony both informs and deforms the work of Cixous. Even here, amidst all the intimations of a new world ('the New Woman ... [entails] the beginning of a new history') and declarations of the endlessness of the feminine ('[a] feminine textual body is ... always ... without ending),'[8] women are marked by the trace of an ending. 'I have always dreamed', writes Cixous, 'about ... [a] text written with final energies';[9] and, in a sense, Cixous's woman is herself just such an end-text. As Cixous reminds us, in French 'end' is a feminine noun.[10] Even if 'not the being-of-the-end ... she is how-far-being-reaches'; she marks the very limit of all identities and categories, even the category of 'woman'. In Cixous's more recent writings on ends and endings 'woman' does indeed seem to disappear; in her Wellek Library lectures of 1990 Cixous declares that 'we need to experience the end of the world' in order 'to be *human*'[11] – not, we note, in order to be women; for Cixous there is no 'woman' in the End.

That 'the [contemporary] reflection on the feminine is', as Rosi Braidotti remarks, 'closely connected to ... the "death of man"'[12] is well known; but commentators have been slower to note that in Cixous this very same reflection is also connected to the 'death of woman'. The male commentator is right to hesitate, particularly given Cixous's remark that 'men ... need femininity to be associated with death'; nevertheless, since she seeks to 'unnerv[e] the world of being' it is no surprise that she declares that 'there is ... no general woman', that 'she does not exist, she can not-be'.[13] Thus Cixous in *The Newly Born Woman* in 1975; Cixous, it seems, has always been prepared to risk the very woman in whose name(s) she writes. Besides, her point is that to 'not-be' is women's strength rather than weakness; Cixous is concerned not with women as the end of being but rather as the other of being, or other than being – what she calls '[f]lashes of being' or, following Heidegger, 'being ... without shelter'.[14]

For Cixous's critics, such a distinction is perilously close to making a deconstructive virtue of women's marginalisation. But then the same accusation might be made of Barrett Browning, if only because for Victorian women the philosophical question of being was so obviously pre-empted by the political problem of being invisible; the possibility of being otherwise was always already framed by the danger of not being at all.[15] In 1850 E. P. Hood remarks of 'woman' that 'political existence has she none' whilst W. R. Greg writes of her that 'the [sexual] desire is dormant if not non-existent'.[16] Such non-existence most obviously issues in an attempt to think outside being just four years later in Christina Rossetti's 'From the Antique':

> It's a weary life, it is, she said: –
>   Doubly blank in a woman's lot:
> I wish and I wish I were a man:
>   Or, *better than any being*, were not.
>
> (my italics)[17]

Such a heterodox way with being also strays, almost by linguistic accident, into *Aurora Leigh*. It happens during Romney's insistence that, at the death of her aunt, Aurora should inherit both the sum stated in the will *and* any 'other sum' of which the aunt died possessed:

> ... the other sum (there *is* another sum).
>
> (2.996)

One other sum is the 'sum' of *ego sum*, and this Cartesian ghost reappears when, in the next book, Aurora talks of how 'so much liver, lung [and] integument ... make [up] ... the *sum of "I"*' (3.287–8: my italics). Like the 'eccentric sum' that so fascinates

Dickens in *Hard Times* just three years before,[18] 'the other sum' speaks, almost unwittingly, of being otherwise.

Aurora herself is otherwise in that she is a(n *ego*) sum that does not add up, a sum that resists both what Cixous calls 'the fantasy of "total" being'[19] *and* the laws of arithmetic. On this account Aurora is quite unlike the biblical figure of Adam, who, as a microcosm of God's newly created world, constitutes 'the adding up of works' (6.157). For Adam read Add-am? Or at least, that son of Adam, Romney – he who operates from within the emergent statistical science of sociology, 'talk[s] by aggregates' (8.801), and 'keep[s] God's books for Him' (3.748). In contrast, Aurora, who has no such empathy with sociological calculations, cannot 'weep for the rule of three / Or compound fractions' (2.217–18). Aurora is not, though, the only woman who resists arithmetic; in talking of 'we pitiful / Remainders of the world' (4.259–60), Marian unwittingly anticipates her eventual eccentricity to that patriarchal rule of two which is marriage. *Aurora Leigh*'s 'other sum' locates the point at which arithmetic is in collusion with both metaphysics and patriarchy. To sum up, Aurora does *not* 'keep God's books for Him', nor indeed for him.

But then God, perhaps, does not keep his own books. Romney roundly denounces those who deduce from the universe 'an algebraic sign / Called God', those who 'add up nature to a nought of God / And cross the quotient' (8.639–42). In dissociating God from a self-confident arithmetic Romney is eccentric; he steps outside of a mid-Victorian intellectual community that, for the most part, continued to live off the Enlightenment's identification of God with logic, including mathematical logic. As Joan Richards writes,

> in [nineteenth-century] British writing you could [still] find statements like: It is as certain that God exists as it is that the sum of the angles of a triangle is equal to 180°.[20]

With the nineteenth century's discovery of non-Euclidean geometry and the more general collapse of absolute confidence in mathematics' ability to make truth-claims,[21] both this and other sums were brought into serious question. If then *Aurora Leigh*'s 'other sum' – the 'sum of [the female] "I"' – is indeed a sum that does not add up it is part, knowingly or not, of a more general historical crisis at the intersection of mathematics with, respectively, metaphysics and religion, with being and Being. What, though, is specific if not unique to *Aurora Leigh* is its intuition that the collapse of mathematical certainty is also a rupture in the text of patriarchy. This intuition is more obviously replayed just nine years later in *Alice in Wonderland*, where Dodgson, the mathematics don, centres his world of arithmetical non-sense on the figure of a girl.

This same anti-arithmetical girl may well be behind a very similar intuition in the work of Cixous – a keen reader of the *Alice* books.[22] Launching us into 'a space-time whose co-ordinates are all different from those we have always been accustomed to',[23] Cixous writes of the hysteric, that 'she destroys their calculations'; of the 'world of "being"', that 'there is no place whatsoever for woman in the calculations'; and of a woman, that 'at the end of a more of less conscious computation, she finds not her own sum but her differences'.[24] The frailities internal to modern mathematics surreptitiously mark Cixous's interruption of the ways of patriarchy. For Cixous 'the other sum' is the female body, which, as a 'body without end',[25] is an affront to the metaphysics of both identity and arithmetic.

Here, though, we should listen to Helena Michie, who argues that, by centring her account of women on their reproductive organs, Cixous re-enacts modern pornography's fetishistic preoccupation with 'vital statistics'.[26] If this is so, Cixous's body without end will never escape the gaze of patriarchal numeration. Cixous certainly runs, and even flaunts, the risk of implicating herself in an eroticism that is calculable, that may be accounted for. Even as she speaks of 'a female libidinal economy … without … closure' or a 'libido [that] is cosmic',[27] Cixous is so privileging female *jouissance* as, inevitably, to risk fixing it to the centre of her libidinal poetics. Her very privileging of the remainder that is *jouissance* might just return it to the accountable realm of centres, limits and ends. Though she talks of a 'body without end' she also refers to 'the ends of my bodies'.[28]

Cixous's poetics again seem to add up to an end in 'Coming to Writing' [1977], where, by describing a coming that is not just sexual ('I am invaded … More! Encore!') but universal ('worldwide my body'),[29] Cixous makes her *jouissance* the *Second* Coming. This conceit does itself come again when, for a moment, the female writer becomes the apocalyptic figure of the thief in the night. In the night of the unconscious she not only writes but steals and –

since in French 'to steal' (*voler*) is also 'to fly' (*voler*) – she not only steals but comes, takes off:

> At night … books open and reveal themselves … I didn't earn my book by the sweat of my brow, I received it. Worse still: I stole … a thousand and one tales a night … How could you resist? All this forbidden writing?
>
> I stole …
>
> These pearls … these signifiers … I admit it, I have often filched them from my unconscious … Furtively, I arrive, a little break-in, just once, I rummage, ah! The secrets!…
>
> 'Thief!' 'Me, a thief?'[30]

By making an end, or even an End, of *jouissance* Cixous not only compromises her own 'body *without* end' but once again interrupts our reading of *Aurora Leigh*. Here too, in a startling inflexion of the standard marital closure of the Victorian novel, the erotic is a kind of end-text; most obviously when Aurora compares the soul, in its sheer mix of the spiritual and sexual, to 'the apocalypse [rewritten] by a Longus!' – in short, to an 'obscene [last] text' (1.828–9). Just such a text repeats upon the poem: first with Lady Waldemar's confession to an 'indecent heart … / As ready for *outrageous ends* and acts / As any distressed sempstress' (3.456–64: my italics); and then with Romney's account of

> our cruel streets [slurred] from *end to end*
> With eighty thousand women …
> Who only smile at night beneath the gas.
>
> (8.413: my italics)

What distinguishes *Aurora Leigh*'s 'outrageous ends' from Cixous's erotic ends is that the former are marked by the historical circumstance of female prostitution. If, though, Michie *is* right, if Cixous does, in a sense, reproduce pornography's fetishisation of women, then the obscenity of *Aurora Leigh*'s eroticised ends may simply be the dark underside of Cixous's libidinal poetics.

We might, though, advance a broader reading of these eroticised ends: namely, that they locate within traditional Western apocalypse a gaze which has woman as never its subject but always its object – an objectification which culminates in commodification. Barrett Browning's 'obscene text' of prostitutes from 'end to end' might just tell the uncomfortable truth about Revelation's apocalyptic women – not just the 'woman clothed with the sun' but, of course, the 'Mother of Harlots' (Revelation 12.1, 17.5).

Returning to Cixous's eroticised apocalypse we must ask whether it too is informed by a look or gaze that, in objectifying woman, effectively commodifies her and thus sells her off. Cixous may begin to acknowledge this when remarking, of herself as the thief in the night, not only that 'I stole' but also that 'I stole *myself*' (my italics).[31] Cixous seems to know that she is not just the heroine of her apocalyptic subtext but also its victim – not just its central presence but also, thereby, its most conspicuous absence.

Deserts

> the link of sand ... unites them
>
> (Cixous, *Manna*)[32]

What links the ends that inform, on the one hand, *Aurora Leigh* and, on the other, the work of Cixous is the figure, or trace, of the desert. Cixous talks of 'an arid millennial ground';[33] Aurora's vision of the New Jerusalem is set against a sky described as a 'tingling desert' (9.953). For all its sense of an ending, however, the desert is not – for either writer – confined to the End. Cixous 'receive[s] ... the desert in the cradle', hers is *always* 'a desert writing'; indeed, in 'The laugh of the Medusa' [1975] '[w]e are ourselves ... sand ... beaches'.[34] Likewise, Aurora not only talks of the poet's 'melancholy desert' (1.1021) and describes the Victorians' new world as 'this desert newly made' (2.960) but refers to 'the strand of life' (2.4) itself as 'these sands betwixt two tides' (7.1025). In both cases the desert, and its sense of an ending, is everywhere; to quote Cixous on Freud's Sandman, 'we get sand thrown in our eyes'[35] – even our 'breath', remarks Aurora, is 'choked with sand' (2.962).

It is not, though, exactly the same sand, not exactly the same desert or wilderness. Though both are, in some sense, the biblical wilderness through which Israel wanders, whilst Cixous is confident of reaching a Promised Land Aurora Leigh is not; only for Aurora is the desert a *dead* end. As a 'Jewoman' Cixous may be 'assigned to ... the diaspora of [her] ... desires' to the intimate deserts'; nevertheless there is, she declares, 'no Promised Land I won't reach someday'.[36] By contrast, Aurora Leigh's exodus describes a journey not just through but also towards a desert: 'O

... / My Cloud,' she exclaims, 'to go before me every day / While I go ever *toward* the wilderness' (9.703: my italics).

If Aurora's exodus does indeed *end* in the wilderness, if at the poem's end she only sees rather than enters the promised land, then she endures the fate of Moses. It is a fate of which the poem is mindful: Grimwald speaks of the view from 'the top of Pisgah-hill' (5.730), whilst Aurora asserts that 'every common bush [is] afire with God; / But only he who sees, takes off his shoes' (7.822–3) – by association with Pisgah, 'only he who sees' mutates into 'he who only sees'. Or perhaps we should read '*s*he who only sees' for, just like Charlotte Brontë's *Villette* (1853),[37] *Aurora Leigh* locates a feminine figure in the Moses of Pisgah – the patriarch whose gaze is marked by a frustration of what Cixous calls the 'boy's ... return to the native land'. 'A boy's journey', she remarks, 'is the ... nostalgia that makes man ... come back to the point of departure.'[38]

In feminising Moses – albeit momentarily – *Aurora Leigh* departs from Cixous, for whom Moses is always the Father of the Law, always the very type of the masculine refusal-to-lack: the *feminine* male, she observes, 'isn't afraid of wanting for water ... [so] does n't arm himself with his Mosaic rod to smite the rock'.[39] In focusing on the Moses of Pisgah Barrett Browning effectively breaks the Mosaic rod; it is a kind of castration.

It is not that Cixous overlooks this final Moses but simply that he represents for her the fate of the Jew rather than the woman:

> the Biblical exclusion from paradise is ... played out again in the story of Moses ... Judaism is much more tragic [than Christianity].[40]

In contrast there is 'no Promised Land [the Je*woman*] ... won't reach someday' – *she*, it seems, is exempt from the tragedy within Judaism. Paradoxically, it is Barrett Browning's Jewoman (the Christian's Jewoman) who 'go[es] ever toward the wilderness'. *Aurora Leigh* seems to anticipate something of the awfulness of Jean Baudrillard's postmodern account of the desert:

> You always have to bring something into the desert to sacrifice, and offer it to the desert as a victim. A woman.[41]

Whilst Cixous tends to follow Irigaray and Kristeva in making a deconstructive virtue of all the desert's negations, including its negation of the sign 'woman',[42] Barrett Browning finds the non-place of the desert still structured by patriarchy. She it is that 'hear[s] / My father's step on that deserted ground' (7.1110). Baudrillard's intuition that the absence of the desert is predicated on the disappearance of woman finds a punning echo when, soon after describing her son 'cry[ing] in the desert night' (9.383), Marian talks of how one day he will

> desert
> (Not miss) his mother's lap, to sit with men.
>
> (9.434–5)

That women are the victim of the desert is also encoded in Lady Waldemar's declaration that 'lion-hunters go / To deserts' (3.384–5) – 'Roar … at me' (3.388), she adds, addressing an A*roar*a who not only speaks of '[t]he lion in me' (2.561) but is described as 'my lioness' (3.529).

Beset as she is by 'a crowd of lion-hunters' (5.816) that come to 'secure [her] … with a trap / For exhibition in … drawing-rooms' (3.385–6), the poem's untamed heroine shares something of the historical fate of colonised Africa. Aurora is Freud's 'dark continent' *avant la lettre*. Indeed, the poem frequently entangles colonialism and patriarchy; whilst the 'fallen' Marian is offered 'instant passage to the colonies' (6.1129) Romney remarks to Aurora that 'you … write … as if / Your father were a negro' (2.192–5), or again that 'you read / My meaning backward like your eastern books, / While I am from the west' (2.818–20).

If *Aurora Leigh*'s desert-woman is also colonised woman, Barrett Browning and Cixous once again cross paths. Parodying the imperial rhetoric of what she terms the 'white continent' of phallogocentrism, Cixous declares to the women readers of 'The Laugh of Medusa' that 'you are Africa, you are black. Your continent is dark.'[43] This moment of coincidence between our two writers is, however, precisely that – a moment; in both cases the fit between the structures of colonialism and patriarchy is no sooner established than it is disrupted. So much is obvious in *Aurora Leigh*, where it is a *woman*, Lady Waldemar, who comes hunting our lioness whilst Aurora herself talks of 'my woman's empery' (8.65). If only because there is a woman – Victoria – at the centre of the British Empire, the poem seems unwilling to conceive of patriarchy purely and simply in terms of colonialism. Similarly, Cixous writes not just as the colonised but also, without always knowing it, as the colonialist: she may be 'Africa' but '[s]he writes with white ink'; she may declare that 'the ... bodies [of women] ... have been colonized' but she also exclaims, '[w]orldwide my unconscious, worldwide my body'; she may rage against 'the empire of the Selfsame' but she also asks, 'If I can be all my others, who could n't I be?'[44] Still more imperiously, Cixous proclaims woman's Imaginery to be 'this unique empire' – there is always, for woman, 'a[n] ... America to be discovered'.[45]

Cixous thus writes the ambiguities of colonialism in much the same way as she has lived it; born in French Algeria to a Jewish, German-speaking mother Cixous has gone on to speak and write the imperial tongue. Indeed, it seems that Cixous sets out to positively flaunt the ambiguities of all colonialisms in the name of a utopian future of collapsed distinctions. Such deconstruction of imperialism does, though, itself come very close to yet another imperialism: as Kadiatu Kanneh writes, 'Cixous ... slips dangerously and prematurely into the realm of ... dissolved differences'.[46]

As Cixous's critics might continue, one name for this realm of dissolved differences is her desert; her 'desert-writing', they might say, is no more than playing in the postmodern sand. For all the force of this claim, Cixous's desert-writing trope still bears the mark of subversion, or protest. This becomes obvious when, read alongside *Aurora Leigh*, the trope is returned if not to its source then at least to a crucial intertext: namely, the biblical scene of the woman taken in adultery, the scene in which – in tacit subversion of the Mosaic law that would have the woman stoned to death – Christ writes in the dust, or sand (John 8.6, 8). Of Marian, the poem's 'fallen woman', we read not only that Romney's rejected proposal of marriage 'might as well [have] be[en] written on the dust' (4.134) but also that she inhabits a 'world / Where men have stoned [her]' (9.223–4). The woman-taken-in-adultery is a very timely figure; 1857 is also the year of the Matrimonial Causes Act, which legalised a situation in which husbands could divorce wives on the grounds of adultery but not vice versa. And indeed the biblical adulteress is not just a subtext of *Aurora Leigh* but she is, in a sense, its very pre-text. The whole poem is a kind of sand-writing. Whilst Aurora writes *in* sand – 'my pastime [is] writing ... / My ... name too near ... the sea' (2.69–70) – Barrett Browning may herself be said to be writing *on* Sand, namely George Sand.

Sand's real Christian name was 'Aurore' and, as Cora Kaplan remarks, 'the whole Sand oeuvre ... plays into Barrett Browning's conception of her poet heroine'.[47] Just as Christ writes in response to a woman taken in adultery so Barrett Browning writes in response to this 'fallen woman' of French writing – Elizabeth herself describes this bisexual figure as not just 'shameless' and 'monstrous' but 'a fallen angel'.[48] Whilst Christ writes *in* sand and *on* the woman taken in adultery, *Aurora Leigh* is written *on* Sand who *is* the woman caught in adultery. That which made the poem so controversial – according to one reviewer it was 'tainted with Sand'[49] – is precisely that which also makes the poem a curious extension of the writing of Christ. The fallen woman is not simply the outrageous premise of the lawless writing that is *Aurora Leigh*; she is also, and at the same time, the founding point of that *re*writing of the Law which is Christianity. *Aurora Leigh* recalls us to the female if not feminist premise of Christ's own scripture; it recalls us to what one critic of the poem casually calls the 'gospel of Sand'.[50] In so doing *Aurora Leigh* foregrounds what is also happening in Cixous, whose 'desert-writing' momentarily shades into Christ's own gospel of sand when, in 'Coming to Writing', she too becomes the woman caught in adultery:

> there was no lack in my personal spaces, of guardians of the law, their pockets filled with the 'first stone' to hurl.[51]

Gospels

> This is the one sad Gospel that is true,
> Christ is not risen.
> (A. H. Clough, 'Easter Day', 62–3)

That Cixous's writing might gesture towards some kind of female gospel should not surprise in that *écriture féminine* may, of course, be translated as 'feminine *scripture*'.[52] In 'Coming to Writing' Cixous talks both of a 'clandestine Bible' and of her lung as 'a Torah without end'; in later essays she speaks of, on the one hand, a 'he-Bible' and, on the other, 'the woman's Bible' – a scripture founded not on the Mosaic 'No' but on the 'Yes' of Molly Bloom' (another woman caught in adultery).[53]

Such scripture is also implicit in *Aurora Leigh* – witness the very first line, which is at once both a quotation from Ecclesiastes

(12.12) and an anticipation of Cixousian *écriture*: 'Of Writing … there is no end.' Intimations of a Bible that might itself be just such an open, 'feminine' writing recur: praying her 'prayers without the vicar' (1.700), the young Aurora opens the window of her father's house and 'let[s] the airs … sweep … in', we read, 'gradual gospels' (1.664–5). Alerting us to the *gradus* in 'gradual' – 'with a gradual *step* … [nature] came in' (my italics) – the poem here intimates a 'stepping' or 'walking gospel'. This conceit is almost made real when Marian tells of her flight from the brothel, a story in which Christ becomes a marginal figure within the larger narrative of a woman's journey:

> Up and down
> I went, by road and village, over tracts
> … large and strange …
> …
> While every roadside Christ upon his cross
> … shook his nails in anger.
>
> (6.1239–49)

To speak of Marian's gradual, or walking, gospel as the gospel according to the *flâneuse*, or even the street-walker – the gospel, as it were, that the Magdalene (Marian's biblical ante-type) never wrote – may be going too far. Nevertheless, there is a preoccupation with the trope of the woman who walks[54] and indeed who, like Aurora, 'walk[s] at all risks' (2.106), above all the risk of a new or gradual scripture.

That is certainly the risk that Cixous runs; in *Three Steps on the Ladder of Writing* (1993) she returns to the story of Jacob's ladder, to that point at which 'the Bible start[s] … dreaming':

> I appropriated this dream … For me it was everything. What I particularly enjoyed was the fact that the angels went up *and down* … what interested me was their *climbing down*.[55]

The biblical angels step out at the risk of stepping *down* and so too does Cixous for she, it seems, is prepared to walk at the risk of walking like an animal. Though she initially asserts that 'poetry is about travelling on foot' she later speaks of 'writ[ing whilst] … straddling the mane at full gallop' and, finally, of 'walking across ['these sheets'] with my hand'.[56] By the time of *Rootprints* [1994] she declares 'I write on all fours.'[57] This, though, is a biblical descent – for Cixous falls into step with angels, as she has done since at least *To Live the Orange* (1979), where 'writing came with an angel's footstep'.[58]

Cixous also falls into step with *Aurora Leigh*, whose 'gradual gospels' again imply the possibility of descent, or at least *not* ascending – the *gradus* or 'step' in 'gradual' refers (by analogy with 'gradual psalms') to the steps of the altar, steps that a woman, of course, could never ascend. With a lioness for a heroine Barrett Browning also walks at the risk of walking on all fours. Writing just eight years after *The Origin of Species* (1859) and four years before *The Descent of Man* (1871), Barrett Browning gives us the descent of woman. In doing so, however, she like Cixous descends *with* the angels: 'my … novel-poem', she remarks, 'rush[es] … "where angels fear to tread"'.[59] In this sense she too descends with the Bible. One contemporary reader described *Aurora Leigh* as 'that girls' gospel';[60] as the poem itself hints at just such a gospel – a 'lady's Greek' (2.76), 'the lady's mark' (3.721), 'Mark, there' (1.702) – so Aurora becomes the lioness to St Mark's lion.

These hints of an estranged, defamiliarised scripture acquire a special force in a period in which, under the pressure of Higher Criticism, the Bible had become for many a 'broken scripture'.[61] Whilst many of her contemporaries are busy reassembling that scripture – busy, like Romney, 'keep[ing] God's books' – Barrett Browning might just prefer Aurora's 'gradual gospels', might just welcome the new brokenness of scripture as a 'feminine' disruption of the Father's Book. The poem, it seems, is concerned with not only 'the other sum' of being but also the feminine other of the gospels. It is guilty of what Romney sees as the contemporary offence of 'cry[ing for] … some other Christ' (8.673–5) – a Christ who is other to the extent of being female. According to Victorian typology, Aurora the lioness might well be read as a female version of Christ the lion of Judah.[62] If so, Florence Nightingale's prophecy, made at the beginning of the 1850s, is fulfilled – 'the next Christ', she had written, 'will perhaps be … female'.[63] The relation between women and Christ is, though, by no means so simple in *Aurora Leigh*: though '[m]ere women … / [may] give us … / Madonnas and … saints', declares Romney, 'We get no Christ from [them]' (2.221–4). Women, we are told, at best give us a 'no Christ'. In so doing, however, do they alone faithfully picture that negation of Christ which is the kenotic Christ? Do women alone constitute a sufficient gap within the patriarchal text to give us the Christ whose crucifixion is God choosing 'things which are not to bring to nought things that are' (1 Corinthians 1.28)? Whilst Kristeva argues that 'woman is that which cannot be represented'[64] Romney's assertion inadvertently suggests that woman is the (kenotic) Christ who, quite simply, cannot be.

This suggestion is rehearsed by the person of Marian who, in playing the transgressive part of a hysteric, becomes a radicalised or 'other Christ'. It is as a kind of hysteric that she violently resists her mother's attempt to sell her to the Squire: seeing 'through some wild gap' (3.1197), she flies in 'mad fear / ... stunned [and] half tranced' (3.1073, 1125); and it is as a kind of Christ that she is then 'healed' by Romney, whose

> voice broke through,
> As the ointment-box broke on the Holy feet
> To let out the rich medicative nard.
>
> (3.1221–3)

Marian here plays not only the part of the Golgotha-bound Christ but also, and more predictably, a patient. In doing so she sets off both the etymological link between 'passion' and 'patient' (*pati*, 'suffer') and the analogical link between the crucified Christ and the hysteric. This link is underlined by both Marian's 'blind hysteric passion' (7.777) and the poem's 'long-suffering and most patient God' (7.1027). *Aurora Leigh* hints at not just the passion of the hysteric but the hysteria of the Passion.

The pre-Enlightenment theme of the insanity of Christ is, of course, something which Foucault has made familiar, arguing that the theme was revived in the nineteenth century.[65] Less familiar is any correspondence between Christ and the 'female malady' of hysteria. Nevertheless, Elaine Showalter observes, of Arthur Hughes's 1852 painting of Ophelia, that 'her hair resembles a crown of thorns'; again, in *Saint Hysteria*, Cristina Mazzoni argues that in the Goncourts' 1869 novel *Madame Gervaisais*, 'the Passion is turned into a hysterical spectacle of [female] pain'.[66] Such twists and turns are also at work in Cixous's writing, and this is true well before the 'strange Christian moods' of *The Book of Promethea* [1983].[67] In *The Newly Born Woman* of 1975, despite asserting that 'the religious is something that consolidates', Cixous presents a Dora who rages because women's bodies are 'despised, rejected'[68] – a phrase that recalls that most feminine ante-type of Christ, the suffering servant (Isaiah 53.3). The spectre of Christ also haunts Cixous's celebration of

> those wonderful hysterics, who … bombard … [Freud's] … law of Moses with their … inaudible thundering denunciations.[69]

Just as 'Dora … bursts the family into pieces'[70] so Christ declares that 'If any man come to me, and hate not his father, and mother, and wife … he cannot be my disciple' (Luke 14.26). Again, just as Cixous's hysterics violate any neat separation of analyst from analysand so Christ, in addressing to himself the proverb 'Physician, heal thyself' (Luke 4.23), is momentarily styled as at once both healer *and* diseased. 'DORA … – MADAME GOD THE SECOND'[71] is, in a sense, Madame God the Son.

This is no simple theologisation of hysteria; rather, it is the suggestion that between the respective histories of Christ and the hysteric there walks a gradual intertext or even gospel. Belonging fully to neither history it walks a biblical no-woman's-land.

Crucial to this intertext is the correspondence between Christ's tomb and the fate of women in relation to their bodies. In 'The Laugh of the Medusa' this fate is strangely shadowed by the gospel account of how, at the empty tomb, the Magdelene encounters her risen Lord only to mistake him for a gardener who has taken the body away (John 20.15):

> woman will return to the body which has been more than confiscated from her, which has been turned into the uncanny stranger on display.[72]

'In woman', Cixous continues, 'personal history blends together with the history of all women';[73] and so it is that here the Magdelen's Easter relationship to the body of Christ (marked as it is by both removal and an uncanny stranger) blends with the more general drama of women's relationship to their own bodies. Something both like and unlike happens in *Aurora Leigh*, where the Magdelene Marian identifies the fate of her raped and appropriated body with the rotting corpse of Christ; she talks of how, after the rape, she is taken away like 'a corpse … [and left to lie], cheek to cheek / With him who stinks since Friday' (6.1194–8). Marian also tells how she later stares at a sunset

> as if it were …
> The great red stone upon my sepulchre,
> Which angels were too weak to roll away.
>
> (6.1272–4)

We recall Romney's earlier remark (albeit of the modern world) that 'savage, hungry dogs … hunt *her* down / To the empty grave of Christ' (2.164–5: my italics). For Marian, though, the grave is far from empty; Christ's body, identified as it is with hers, is not liberated – the angels cannot move the stone. The gradual gospel according to Marian Magdelene really does 'walk at all risks', even the risk of proclaiming, like Clough's 'one sad gospel', that 'Christ is not risen'. Weighed down by the fate of the *female* body (there are 'eighty thousand women' on 'our cruel streets'), Barrett Browning's feminine scripture cannot countenance the resurrection of *Christ's* body.

By contrast, Cixous's conviction that 'woman *will* return to the body which has been more than confiscated from her' (my italics) does seem to prompt a form of resurrection faith – 'writing', she continues, 'is … undoing the work of death'.[74]

Ecclesia

> on n'est pas sorti de l'église.
>
> (Derrida, *Éperons*)[75]

> The Church … is the Spouse and Body of Christ.
>
> (*Book of Common Prayer*)[76]

Though Barrett Browning's feminine scripture – structured as it is by the historical tragedy of the female body – cannot think the comedy of resurrection, this same scripture does achieve some kind of comedy through that figurative female body which is the Church. Recalling the German student's talk of 'that new church for which the world's near ripe' (5.714), Romney's final apocalyptic vision begins with the Church:

> New churches, new oeconomies, new laws
> … new societies …
> HE shall make all new.
>
> (9.947–90)

What contests this final 'HE' is the poem's own memory of the Church's New Testament figuration as bride, as SHE – here we have not only 'mother-church' (5.747) but also 'that fair church, Buonarroti's Bride' (8.54). In returning to Italy Aurora returns to churches[77] which might all be called 'Our Lady's church' (8.145):

'[in] the churches chiefly women ... knelt and prayed' (7.1222–5).

As Cora Kaplan remarks, '*Aurora Leigh* is the ultimate Victorian attempt to inscribe the female body';[78] it is also a remarkably self-conscious attempt to inscribe the female body of Christ. It is, in part, the Church that provides what Michie terms 'a gynocentric grid for Barrett Browning's poetics'.[79] Her concern to write and rewrite the Church is crucial to her attempt to renew the very structures and codes by which the Victorian world is produced – 'New churches, new oeconomies'.

To suggest that writing the body might ever shade into 'writing the Church' would, for Cixous, be fraught with difficulty; in *The Newly Born Woman* she declares herself 'suspicious of anything related to the Church and its ideological rule'.[80] Nevertheless, two years later, in 'Coming to Writing' there is one moment that might just escape this suspicion: expanding on the assertion that '[l]ife becomes text starting out from my body', Cixous suddenly refers to 'my breast ... the Tabernacle'[81] – an Old Testament site of worship thus shades unwittingly into the peculiarly New Testament figuration of the Church as female body. In her attempt, both here and elsewhere, to rewrite Judaism in terms of the female body is it possible that Cixous re-enacts something of the feminising movement of the Old Covenant into the New? (The movement feminises in that God as Christ is not only embodied in his bride the Church but inhabits a womb. When Cixous articulates the 'femininity' of the Jew by talking of the 'Jewoman' ('women,' she writes, 'maybe they are double-Jews, or semi-Jews')[82] does she push Judaism to the point at which it almost becomes its Christian, feminine other? Might Christians also be called semi-Jews? Perhaps; Cixous the Jewoman certainly has 'strange Christian moods' – not surprisingly given her belief that Jewishness is never purely or simply itself: 'the ... Jew is ... other, even other than Jewish'.[83] In *Rootprints* Cixous writes of how, in 1916, her Jewish German grandfather's grave was marked with the star of David and yet placed among 'other graves adorned with crosses'; the paragraph concludes: 'Star and cross together'.[84]

To read the feminine, bodily other of Cixous's Judaism as Christian or as Church is to return to *Aurora Leigh*; for here the Church bears the mark of an almost Cixousian hysteria. In this the poem anticipates the accounts of the Church as an asylum that are to be found in both Nietzsche and Foucault. *Aurora Leigh*, however, envisions madness as not so much a danger to be policed by the Church but rather a constitutive and defining principle *of* the Church. The poem thus leans towards not Foucault but Nietzsche, in particular his intuition that 'the Church itself ... is ... the Catholic madhouse as an ultimate ideal'.[85] Satirising Sir Blais's Tractarianism, the German student talks of that 'ancient mother-church [which] would fain still bite, / For all her toothless gums' (5.751–2); mocking contemporary materialist theology, Romney declares that 'there are many ... in the Christian Church / ... [who] diet on mud / And splash the altars with it' (8.642–5). The madness is, though, most specifically transgressive and hysterical in the scene immediately following Marian and Romney's abortive wedding ceremony: 'the church / Rocked ... like the sea in storm', 'men cried out / "Police"', and 'women stood and shrieked for God, / Or dropt and swooned / . . or madly fled / ... and screeched' (4.858–68). The church is hysterical; as is said of Marian, '"the bride has lost her head"' (4.701).

Earlier Marian fears lest 'God ... has a missing hand' (4.41); here the conceit is that the body of Christ has a missing head. Encoded in Marian-the-bride is a Church that is 'quite another body than St Paul / Has promised' (8.653–4). In particular, since for St Paul 'the head of the body' is Christ (Colossians 1.18), Marian encodes a Church *without* Christ. We here glimpse a parable of that radical agnosticism *within* Victorian Christianity which prompted the protagonist of Tennyson's *Maud,* published just two years before, to declare that 'the churches have killed their Christ'.[86] Like all other 'mere women', from even the bride that is the Church we finally 'get no Christ'; though only figuratively female the Church, it seems, is no less disruptive of conventional Christology. And herein lies the main significance of the hysteria of the poem's 'new church' – a hysteria that is as prized by Barrett Browning as ever it might be by Cixous.

In *Aurora Leigh* there are two kinds of ecclesial madness. Alongside the bride who loses her head, there is what Romney describes as the 'mad ... pain' of what we take to be orthodox, Pauline Christianity:

> Here's the world half blind
> With intellectual light, half brutalised
> With civilisation, having caught the plague

> In silks from *Tarsus*, shrieking east and west
> Along a thousand railroads, mad with pain
> And sin …
>
> (2.199–204: my italics)

For Romney, the institutional Church is mad with the madness of not just civilisation's 'intellectual light' but the infrastructure of empire – 'a thousand railroads'. Witness St Paul's exploitation of his citizenship of the Roman Empire to travel its various trade routes; witness the Victorian missionary availing himself of the privileges and railroads of the emergent British Empire.

Of these two pictures of Church-as-madness – the headless bridge and the Tarsus plague – the bride more nearly images the 'new church' of which both Romney and the German student dream. By losing her head, however, Marian describes a Church that is a broken and centreless structure. If the Church rivals the female body as Barrett Browning's 'gynocentric grid' it also undermines the very notion of such a grid, the very notion of woman as matrix, as whole. This the Church will always do, for her Greek name, as Barrett Browning would know, is *ecclesia,* meaning 'summoned out' – she is, by definition, summoned out of herself, beside herself. Witness the churches in Italy; in complete contrast to Sir Blaise's 'apostolic … church / Inside of which, are Christian[s] … / And outside … dogs' (5.747–9), Aurora's Italian churches leave the reader quite unsure as to when she is inside and when outside:

> Musing …
> I walked the narrow … streets
> …
> … and came wandering out
> Upon the churches with mild open doors.
>
> (7.1216–22)

> I … would not miss a vigil in the church,
> And liked to mingle with the outdoor crowd.
>
> (7.1275–6)

When Aurora goes *into* an Italian church it almost reads as if she is going *out*. Alternatively, it is as if the Church, the house of God, does herself go out; as Romney remarks, after the burning down of Leigh Hall, '"the House ['our father's house'] went out"' (8.1014,

1031). Either way, Aurora's Italian *ecclesia* questions the very distinction between outside and inside. We do well to recall Derrida's 'on n'est pas sorti de l'église', since how can one leave a Church that, as *ecclesia*, has already taken leave of herself? Just such reasoning informs the poem's antagonism towards the Tractarians; they, like Sir Blaise, believe in a Church whose borders must never be blurred by the secularising nineteenth century. Aurora's satirical reference to 'Tracts *against* the times' (1.394) is much to do with this.

Her reference is also, though, to do with the patrilinearity of the Tractarian vision, or *re*vision, of the Church – in particular, the stress upon apostolic succession. This tenet the poem both hints at and satirises as first Romney is termed '[a] chief apostle' (2.416) and then Marian insists that '*he*, he made the church with what he spoke' (3.1214). But if here the poem merely ironises the patriarchal foundation of the apostolic Church elsewhere it begins to undermine that foundation. As if drawing on the ambiguity that surrounds the grammatical gender of 'the rock' upon which Christ's Church was to be founded – 'thou art Peter [*petros*], and upon this rock [*petra*] I will build my church' (Matthew 16.18)[87] – Aurora identifies herself with St Peter. 'I walk these waves / [with] ... thou / ... who art the way, the truth, the life' (7.1034–6); 'I stood there fixed, – / My arms up, like the caryatid, sole / Of some abolished temple' (2.60–2). At such moments *Aurora Leigh* almost reads like a response to a question of Cixous's: 'What would happen to logocentrism ... if the rock upon which [men] ... founded this church should crumble?'[88] *Aurora Leigh*'s 'reply', it seems, is that this Church of (phal)logocentrism becomes an 'abolished temple' – 'our father's house' burns down, and Aurora returns to an Italy which is 'my father's house, / Without his presence' (7.491–2). This, though, is only part of *Aurora Leigh*'s 'reply', for the poem also hints at the fate of the rock itself, the rock which crumbles: namely, that it turns out to be not Peter but a 'caryatid', not *petros* but *petra*. If the Church of phallogocentrism has, all along, been founded upon a woman then it has, in a sense, always already been abolished. This is precisely the point of Cixous's assertion that 'the Church is built upon' 'its petrifying fear of castration'[89] – it is an institution that is always already uncertain of its own masculinity.

No such uncertainty undermines the Church of which Romney speaks. As 'the ['intellectual'] plague from Tarsus', Romney's

Church metaphysical runs upon the conventionally masculine lines of a 'thousand railroads'. However, though it denies any feminine 'before' Romney's Church may just imply a feminine 'after' – for, strangely, '"these [are] the last days of railroads"' (2.975). What will follow is not known but it is marked as 'feminine' in the sense that in *Aurora Leigh* the technological future is, time and again, identified with women. Aurora's writing possesses a 'galvanic life' (3.249); her 'very garments', when close to Romney, 'thrill ... / With strange electric life' (9.821–2); and there is, according to Vincent Carrington, an 'od-force ... which still from female finger-tips burns blue' (7.566–7). This electrification of the female body is a conspicuous departure from the Victorian woman's more conventional identification with the fixed, visible and centralised energy of the domestic fire, or hearth. Cixous makes precisely this contrast, declaring that her newly born woman possesses a '*feminine electricity*' and

> takes pleasure in being ... far from a 'center' ... far from the 'hearth' to which man brings her so that she will tend his fire.[90]

New technologies make thinkable, it seems, new economies – most obviously, new sexual economies. For *Aurora Leigh*'s 'new churches, new oeconomies' we may read, in Cixous, 'new *technologies*, new economies'; where Barrett Browning reimagines the female through the trope of the Church Cixous uses technology. In both cases a link is established between the psycho-sexual and the historical; there *is* – in Cixous's words – a movement 'from the scene of the unconscious to the scene of history'. The particular scene of history to which technology belongs is, however, a scene of privilege; Cixous's *écriture féminine* is put in touch with only, as it were, masculine history. By contrast, *Aurora Leigh*'s use of the Church offers access to an-other and, as it were, feminine history. For though the Church is implicated in the railroads and fortunes of empire she is also inscribed with the revolutionary histories of the exploited. Such histories are most vividly inscribed upon that body of women who, when Marian fails to arrive for her wedding, violently remove their head – the 'master[ful]' Romney. Upon this headless and hystericised body is inscribed the reversal of not just patriarchy but also both social and imperial hierarchies. Whilst they, the poor women of the parish, are at one moment 'the turbulent masses' and at another a 'black crowd' (4.849, 795) Romney is marked by 'his masterful pale face', indeed a 'white face' (4.850, 876). As Romney once says of Aurora, 'you ... will write of factories and slaves' (2.192–4).

And it is this that may finally distinguish *Aurora Leigh* from Cixous; for with the trope of the Church Barrett Browning has a grid, or rather text, by which she can begin to map the female body on to the revolutionary histories of the exploited and marginal. As the bride and body of Christ, the text that is the Church might just have both the power and the weakness to return contemporary female poetics to such *hystericised* history. This, by the way, Julia Kristeva seems to know.[91]

> These that have turned the world upside down have come hither also ... (Acts of the Apostles 17.6)

Notes

1 Elizabeth Barrett Browning, *Selected Poems* (London: Everyman, 1992), 237.

2 Hélène Cixous and Catherine Clément, *The Newly Born Woman*, tr. Betsy Wing (Manchester: Manchester University Press, 1986), 87 / *La Jeune Née* (Paris: Union Générale d'Éditions, 1975), 161.

3 This calculation is based on the explanatory notes in *Aurora Leigh*, ed. Margaret Reynolds (Athens: Ohio University Press, 1992).

4 Quoted in Reynolds (ed.), *Aurora Leigh*, 6.

5 *Ibid.*, Book 9, lines 947–8. Further references to Reynolds's edition of *Aurora Leigh* will be given parenthetically in the text.

6 Sandra M. Gilbert and Susan Gubar, *The Madwoman in the Attic: The Woman Writer and the Nineteenth Century Literary Imagination* (New Haven: Yale University Press, 1979), 24.

7 Mary Wilson Carpenter, 'The Trouble with Romola', in Thais Morgan (ed.), *Victorian Sages and Cultural Discourse: Renegotiating Gender and Power* (New Brunswick: Rutgers University Press, 1990), 116.

8 Hélène Cixous, 'The Laugh of the Medusa,' in Elaine Marks and Isabelle de Courtivron (eds), *New French Feminisms: An Anthology* (London: Harvester Wheatsheaf, 1981), 248, 252 / 'Le Rire de la Méduse', *L'Arc*, 61 (1976), 41, 45; Hélène Cixous, 'Castration or Decapitation?', *Signs: Journal of Women in Culture and Society*, 7 (1981), 53 / 'Le Sexe ou la tête?' *Les Cahiers du GRIF*, 13 (1976), 12.

9 Hélène Cixous, *Coming to Writing and Other Essays*, ed. Deborah Jenson, tr. Sarah Cornell *et al.*, (Cambridge, MA: Harvard University Press, 1991), 136 / *L'Heure de Clarice Lispector* (Paris: des femmes, 1989), 123.

10 Hélène Cixous, *Readings: The Poetics of Blanchot, Joyce, Kafka, Kleist, Lispector, and Tsvetayeva*, ed. Verena Andermatt Conley (London: Harvester Wheatsheaf, 1992), 104.

11 Hélène Cixous, *Three Steps on the Ladder of Writing* (New York: Columbia University Press, 1993), 10.

12 Rosi Braidotti, *Patterns of Dissonance* (Oxford: Polity Press, 1991), 10.

13 Cixous and Clément, *The Newly Born Woman*, 69 / 126; *Coming to Writing*, 27 / *La Venue a l'écriture* (Paris: Union Générale d'Éditions, 1977), 33; 'The Laugh of the Medusa', 245 / 39; *The Newly Born Woman*, 65 / 118.

14 *Coming to Writing*, 1 / *La Venue*, 9; *Readings*, 113.

15 For a Victorian discussion of the question of being see 'The God of Metaphysics', in *The Complete Prose Works of Matthew Arnold*, ed. P. H. Super, 11 vols (Ann Arbor: University of Michigan Press, 1960–77), 7.173–202.

16 E. P. Hood, *The Age and Its Architects* (1850), 135; W. R. Greg, 'Prostitution', *The Westminster Review*, 53 (1850), 456.

17 *The Complete Poems of Christina Rossetti*, ed. R. W. Crump, 3 vols (Baton Rouge: Louisiana State University Press, 1979–90), 3.231.1–4.

18 I refer, of course to the following passage: 'They [the people at Coketown] took De Foe to their bosoms, instead of Euclid, and seemed to be on the whole more comforted by Goldsmith than by Cocker. Mr Gradgrind was for ever working, in print and out of print, at this eccentric sum' – *Hard Times* (Harmondsworth: Penguin, 1969), 90. For a general discussion of the meanings of arithmetic in Dickens see Schad, *The Reader in the Dickensian Mirrors* (London: Macmillan, 1992), 93–124.

19 'The Laugh of the Medusa', 254 / 46.

20 Cited in Philip J. Davis and Reuben Hirsch, *Descartes' Dream: The World According To Mathematics* (New York: Harcourt Brace Jovanich, 1986), 207.

21 As Morris Kline writes, 'in the 19th century the equanimity of mathematicians with respect to their reasoning was shattered' as the 'creation … of … strange geometries and strange algebras, forced [them] … to realise that mathematics proper and the mathematical laws of science were not truths' – *Mathematics: The Loss of Certainty* (Oxford: Oxford University Press, 1980), 100, 4.

22 See, for example, Cixous's 'Introduction to Lewis Carroll's *Through the Looking Glass* and *The Hunting of the Snark*', tr. Marie Maclean, *New Literary History*, 13 (1982), 231–51; or again, *Readings*, where she writes of a 'mirror that – as in Lewis Carroll – does not simply refer to the side of the same, but opens onto the infinite registers of the other' (135).

23 Hélène Cixous and Mireille Calle-Gruber, *Hélène Cixous: Rootprints: Memory and Life Writing*, tr. Eric Prenowitz (London: Routledge, 1997), 9 / *Photos de Racine* (Paris: des femmes, 1994) 19.

24 Cixous and Clément, *The Newly Born Woman*, 155, 64 / 284, 117–18; 'The Laugh of the Medusa', 264 / 54.

25 'The Laugh of the Medusa', 259/54.

26 See Helena Michie, *The Flesh Made Word: Female Figures and Women's Bodies* (Oxford: Oxford University Press, 1987), 144–5.

27 'Castration or Decapitation?', 53/12; Cixous and Clément, *The Newly Born Woman*, 88/162.

28 Hélène Cixous, *Vivre L'orange / To Live the Orange* (Paris: des femmes, 1979), 14.

29 *Coming to Writing*, 53, 47 / *La Venue*, 58, 52.

30 *Ibid.*, 45–6 / 51.

31 *Ibid.*, 46 / 51.

32 Hélène Cixous, *Manna: For the Mandelstams – For the Mandelas*, tr. Catherine A. F. MacGillivray (Minneapolis: University of Minnesota Press, 1994), 241 / *Manne aux Mandelstams aux Mandelas* (Paris: des femmes, 1988), 270.
33 'The Laugh of the Medusa', 245 / 39.
34 Hélène Cixous, 'We Who Are Free, Are We Free?', *Critical Inquiry*, 20 (1993), 209; *Readings*, 130; 'The Laugh of the Medusa', 260 / 51.
35 Hélène Cixous, 'Fictions and Its Phantoms: A Reading of Freud's *Das Unheimliche*', *New Literary History*, 7 (1975), 532 / 'La Fiction et ses fantômes: Une Lecture de l'*Unheimliche* de Freud', *Poétique*, 10 (1972), 199.
36 *Coming to Writing*, 7, 4 / *La Venue*, 15, 12.
37 See Charlotte Brontë, *Villette* (Harmondsworth: Penguin, 1979) 310; for an excellent discussion of Brontë's feminisation of the Moses of Pisgah see Janet L. Larson, '"Who Is Speaking?": Charlotte Brontë's Voices of Prophecy', in Morgan, *Victorian Sages*, 66–86.
38 Cixous and Clément, *The Newly Born Woman*, 93 / 173.
39 *Coming to Writing*, 57/62.
40 *Readings*, 16.
41 Jean Baudrillard, *America*, tr. Chris Turner (London: Verso, 1988), 66.
42 For an excellent discussion of Irigaray's and Kristeva's respective celebrations of the emptiness of the desert see Philippa Berry, 'Woman and Space according to Kristeva and Irigarary', in Philippa Berry and Andrew Wernick (eds), *Shadow of Spirit: Postmodernism and Religion* (London: Routledge, 1992), 250–64.
43 'The Laugh of the Medusa', 255, 247 / 47, 41.
44 Cixous and Clément, *The Newly Born Woman*, 94, 68 / 173, 125; *Coming to Writing*, 47/ *La Venue*, 52; Hélène Cixous, 'The Character of "Character"', *New Literary History*, 5 (1973–74), 388.
45 'The Laugh of the Medusa', 246/39–40; 'An exchange with Hélène Cixous', in Verena Andermatt Conley, *Hélène Cixous: Writing the Feminine* (Lincoln: University of Nebraska Press, 1984), 161.
46 Kadiatu Kanneh, 'Love, Mourning and Metaphor: Terms of Identity', in Isobel Armstrong (ed.), *New Feminist Discourses: Critical Essays on Theories and Texts* (London: Routledge, 1992), 148, 145.
47 Cora Kaplan, 'Introduction' to *Aurora Leigh and Other Poems* (London: The Women's Press, 1978), 23.
48 *The Letters of Elizabeth Barrett Browning to Mary Russell Mitford 1836–1854*, ed. Meredith B. Raymond and Mary Rose Sullivan, 3 vols (Armstrong Browning Library of Baylor University, Browning Institute, Wedgeston Press, and Wellesley College, 1983), 2.85.
49 See Patricia Thomson, *George Sand and the Victorians* (London: Macmillan, 1977), 54.
50 Thomson, *George Sand*, 49.
51 *Coming to Writing*, 11 / *La Venue*, 18.
52 As Hart remarks, 'the tradition of Derrida interpretation, which includes the tradition of Derrida translation, has almost exclusively taken *écriture* to mean simply "writing"; its other meaning, "scripture", has been ignored' – *The Trespass of the Sign: Deconstruction, Theology and Philosophy* (Cambridge: Cambridge University Press, 1989), 50.
53 *Coming to Writing*, 170 / *L'Heure*, 157; *Coming to Writing*, 52 / *La Venue*, 57;

Three Steps, 113; Hélène Cixous, 'Reaching the Point of Wheat, or The Portrait of the Artist as a Maturing Woman', *New Literary History*, 19 (1987–88), 4.

54 See Ann Wallace, '"Nor in Fading Silks Compose": Sewing, Walking, and Poetic Labor in *Aurora Leigh*', *English Literary History*, 64 (1997), 223–56.

55 *Three Steps*, 68–9.

56 *Ibid.*, 64, 107, 156.

57 *Rootprints*, 45 / 55.

58 *Vivre l'orange / To Live the Orange*, 10.

59 Letter to Robert Browning, 27 February 1845, in *The Letters of Robert Browning and Elizabeth Barrett, 1845–1846*, ed. Elvan Kintner, 2 vols, (Cambridge, MA: Harvard University Press, 1969–72), 1.31.

60 Elizabeth Stewart Phelps, *The Story of Avis*, ed. Carol Farley Kessler (New Brunswick, NJ: Rutgers University Press, 1992), 31.

61 See Janet L. Larson, *Dickens and the Broken Scripture* (Athens: University of Georgia Press, 1985).

62 See David E. Joliffe, 'The Tall Nun in *The Wreck*: A Lioness in Her Own Right', *Victorian Poetry*, 21 (1983), 80.

63 Florence Nightingale, 'Cassandra', in *Suggestions for Thought to the Searchers after Truth among the Artizans of England* (London: Croom Helm, 1994), 230.

64 Julia Kristeva, 'La Femme, ce n'est jamis ça', *Tel Quel*, 59 (1974), 21 (as translated by Toril Moi, *Sexual/Textual Politics* (London: Routledge, 1985), 163).

65 See Michael Foucault, *Madness and Civilisation: History of Insanity in the Age of Reason*, tr. Richard Howard (London: Tavistock, 1965), 78–82.

66 Elaine Showalter, 'Representing Ophelia: Women, Madness, and the Responsibilities of Feminist Criticism', in Patricia Parker and Geoffrey Hartman (eds), *Shakespeare and the Question of Theory* (London: Methuen, 1985), 85; Cristina Mazzoni, *Saint Hysteria: Neurosis, Mysticism and Gender in European Culture* (Ithaca: Cornell University Press, 1996), 67.

67 Hélène Cixous, *The Book of Promethea*, tr. Betsy Wing (Lincoln: University of Nebraska Press, 1991), 105 / *Le Livre de Promethea* (Paris: Gallimard, 1983), 127.

68 Cixous and Clément, *The Newly Born Woman*, 157, 154 / 289, 283.

69 *Ibid.*, 95/176.

70 *Ibid.*, 154/283.

71 *Ibid.*, 149/274.

72 'The Laugh of the Medusa', 250/43.

73 *Ibid.*, 252/45.

74 *Ibid.*, 254/46.

75 Jacques Derrida, *Spurs: Nietzsche's Styles / Éperons: Les Styles de Nietzsche*, tr. Barbara Harlow (Chicago: Chicago University Press, 1979), 90.

76 *The Book of Common Prayer* (London: Collins, n.d.) 367.

77 For various references to specific churches, see: 7.536; 7.197; 8.1279; 8.145.

78 Kaplan's argument as summarised by Michie in *The Flesh Made Word*, 68.

79 *The Flesh Made Word*, 68.

80 Cixous and Clément, *The Newly Born Woman*, 77 / 142.

81 *Coming to Writing*, 52 / *La Venue*, 58.

82 *Ibid.*, 12/19; Hélène Cixous, 'Difficult Joys', in Helen Wilcox *et al.* (eds), *The Body and the Text: Hélène Cixous, Reading and Teaching* (London: Harvester, 1990), 13.

83 *Readings*, 147.

84 *Rootprints*, 185/187.

85 Friedrich Nietzsche, *Twilight of the Idols / The Anti-Christ* (Harmondsworth: Penguin, 1968), 177. 'For the Catholic church, as in the Protestant countries,' writes Foucault, 'confinement represents, in the form of an authoritatiran model, the myth of social happiness' – *Madness and Civilisation*, 63.

86 *The Poems of Tennyson*, ed. Christopher Ricks, 3 vols (Harlow: Longman, 1987), 2.577.

87 For an interesting discussion of the use of the two different Greek words, one masculine, one feminine, see W. D. Davies and D. C. Allison, *The Gospel According to Saint Matthew*, 3 vols (Edinburgh: T & T. Clark, 1991), 2.627. I am grateful to Stephen D. Moore for his help in this matter.

88 Cixous and Clément, *The Newly Born Woman*, 65 / 119.

89 'First Names of No One', tr. Deborah Cowell, in Susan Sellers (ed.), *The Hélène Cixous Reader* (London: Routledge, 1994), 30 / *Prénoms de personne* (Paris: Seuil, 1974), 7.

90 Cixous and Clément, *The Newly Born Woman*, 106, 91 / 198, 168.

91 See, in particular, *Black Sun: Depression and Melancholia* (New York: Columbia University Press, 1989), where Kristeva writes that 'the Church itself appears as a *soma pneumatikon*, a "mystery", more than an institution' (158).

Index

Note: 'n.' after a page reference indicates a note on that page.

Abrams, M. H. 88
adultery 159
Africa 99, 157–8,
Ahmad, Ajaz 114 n.86
Allott, Miriam 57
America 101, 106
angels 57, 87–90
Antigone 36
apocalypse 150–5 *passim*
ApRoberts, Ruth 74 n.7
arithmetic 151–3
Armstrong, Isobel 1, 2, 76 n.39, 85
Arnold, Matthew 1, 42–78, 123
  'Alaric' 66
  'Bacchanalia or, The New Age' 55
  'The Buried Life' 52
  'The Divinity' 48
  'Dover Beach' 42–5, 56–7
  'A Dream' 49
  'Empedocles upon Etna' 42, 54–5, 69, 72
  'Euphrosyne' 49
  'The Function of Criticism' 44, 48, 72
  'Heine's Grave' 61
  'Memorial Verses' 62
  'New Rome' 67
  Obermann Once More 60
  'The Progress of Poesy' 67
  'Rome Sickness' 65–6
  'Rugby Chapel' 64–5
  'St Brandan' 43–4
  'Shakespeare' 49
  'The Sick King of Bokhara' 59
  'Sohrab and Rustrum' 44–5
  'Stanzas from the Grande Chartreuse' 47, 57–8
  'Tristram and Iseult' 44, 53, 71–2
  'The Youth of Nature' 59
  'The Youth of Man' 45, 58–9
Augustine, Saint 87
autobiography 104

Babel 142–3
Bagehot, Walter 85
Barthes, Roland 4, 63, 69, 81
Bataille, Georges 69
Baudrillard, Jean 74, 156–7
Beckett, Samuel 55, 70
Beer, Gillian 39 n.8
being 25–6, 72, 88
Benjamin, Walter 89
Bernauer, James 1, 74 n.7, 77 n.68
Berry, Philippa 20, 33–5, 172 n.42
Bible, the 7, 81, 159–63
Bidney, Martin 76 n.38

Bowie, Malcolm 1, 136, 143, 145 n.43
Braidotti, Rosi 150
breath 93–4
Bridges, Robert 131
Bristow, Joseph 2, 76 n.38, 79, 87
Bronfen, Elisabeth 24
Brönte, Charlotte
  Villette 156
Brown, Ford Madox 34
Browning, Elizabeth Barrett 99, 104–5
  Aurora Leigh 149–74
Browning, Robert 2, 79–115
  'Agamemnon' 85
  'Bishop Bloughram's Apology' 79–80, 90
  'The Bishop Orders His Tomb' 90–1, 93
  'The Boy and the Angel' 88
  'Caliban upon Setebos' 87, 93
  'Childe Roland to the Dark Tower Came' 82, 94
  'Cleon' 79, 81–2
  'A Death in the Desert' 81
  'An Epistle …' 81–2
  'Eurydice to Orpheus' 105–6
  'Fra Lippo Lippi' 87
  'A Grammarian's Funeral' 94
  'The Guardian Angel' 88
  'How It Strikes a Contemporary' 82
  'Jochanan Hakkadosh' 85
  'La Saisiaz' 98, 105
  'Mr Sludge the Medium' 95–109
  'One Word More' 89–90
  'Porhyria's Lover' 87, 89–90
  'Prospice' 93–4, 108
  Sordello 88

Caputo, John D. 96
Carlyle, Thomas 118
Carpenter, Mary 150
Carroll, David 74
Carroll, Lewis
  Through the Looking-Glass 14, 23, 25, 153
Catholicism 91, 97, 133
Chapman, Alison 19, 38 n.7
Chidester, David 74 n.7
Christ, Jesus 10–13, 22, 36–8, 59–61, 98, 108, 159
Christianity 84, 166–7,
Church, the 164–70
Cixous, Hélène 2, 123, 149–74
Clark, Timothy 113 n.72
Clément, Catherine 119, 133
Clough, Arthur Hugh 45, 53, 61, 112 n.54, 159
colonialism 157–8, 169–70
condemned man, the 59–61
confession 50–2, 104
Copernicus 33
Crimean War 56
Critchley, Simon 114
cup 27

Damiens 60
dance 29–31
Dante, Alighieri 7, 38, 105
Darwin, Charles 161
death 63, 92–5, 150–1
Deleuze, Gilles 55
Dellamora, Richard 75 n.29, 76 n.40
Derrida, Jacques 2, 4, 7, 51, 79–115
Descartes, Renè 20, 54
desert 46–8, 80, 83, 155–9
Dickens, Charles 4, 21, 152
différance 84–5, 87–8, 93
disease 62–5
Disraeli, Benjamin 84
dissection 62
doors 10–14, 55
Douglas, Lord Alfred 53

During, Simon 78 n.78

Eagleton, Terry 146 n.50
electricity 169
Eliot, George
  Middlemarch 31
Eliot, T. S. 130, 140–1
Engels, Friedrich 12
eucharist 90–2, 95, 126, 135–6
Europe 62, 101–3
evenements, les 56, 88
evening 101–3
execution 60

Faas, Ekbert 144 n.13
fall 72–3, 138–9
feet 138–40
Findlay, L. M. 110
fire 34–7, 136–7
Flaubert, Gustave
  The Temptation of St Anthony 46
Foucault, Michel 2, 4, 42–78, 162
Freud, Sigmund 1, 16–17, 123, 130–2, 139–43

Gallop, Jane 1, 13, 140–1, 143, 148 n.103
ghosts 17–19, 86, 95–105 *passim*, 135
Gilbert, Sandra M. and Gubar, Susan 150
Goethe, Johann W. von 62
Gombrich, E. H. 40 n.39
Great Exhibition, the 25, 77 n.63
Greg, W. R. 151
Grosz, Elizabeth 14

Haar, Michael, 88
Hacking, Ian 75 n.32
Hallam, Arthur 2
Halperin, David 47
Hamilton, William 118
Hamlet 45, 96–7, 105, 108–9
Hani, Chris 99
Hardy, Thomas 118
Harris, Daniel 117
Hart, Kevin 80–1
Hartman, Geoffrey 88, 119
Hebraism 80–4
Hegel, Georg Wilhelm Friedrich 91, 128
Heidegger, Martin 35, 72–3, 74 n.11, 96, 135, 151
Heine, Heinrich 61
Hellenism 79–84
Hipple, Walter J. 75 n.29
history 4, 32–3, 169–70
Holocaust, the 35, 103, 132–3
Homans, Margaret 17, 22, 115 n.106
Homer
  The Iliad 6
Honan, Park 70, 76 n.40
Hood, E. P. 151
Hopkins, Gerard Manley 90, 109, 116–48
  'Andromeda' 118–19, 141–2
  'Barnfloor and Winepress' 135
  'The Beginning of the End' 135
  'Binsey Poplars' 128
  'The Bugler's First Communion' 132–3
  'The Caged Skylark' 128, 139
  'Carrion Comfort' 119, 138
  'Felix Randal' 120, 124
  'Harry Ploughman' 124, 128
  'The Leaden Echo and the Golden Echo' 124, 129
  'The Loss of the Eurydice' 127–9
  'The May Magnificat' 120–1
  'Nondum' 119, 123
  'Pied Beauty' 138
  'Spelt from Sybil's Leaves' 125–6
  'That Nature is a Heraclitean Fire' 131–2

'Tom's Garland' 139
'The Windhover' 123
The Wreck of the Deutschland 117–29 *passim*
Horton, Susan 8
Hughes, Arthur 162
Hunt, Holman 10, 33–4
hysteria 165–70

incest 15–16
Ireland 126, 131
Irigaray, Luce 156
Speculum 6–39

Jabès, Edmond 80
Jameson, Frederic 115
Jardine, Alice 97
Jew, the 61, 85, 99, 155–6, 165
Joseph, Gerhard 75 n.29

Kanneh, Kadiatu 158
Kaplan, Cora 159, 165
Klee, Paul 89
Kline, Morris 171 n.21
Knoepflmacher, U. C. 25
Kristeva, Julia 156, 162, 170

Lacan, Jacques 116–48
Laclau, Ernesto 115 n.111
Larson, Janet L. 172 n.37
laughter 50
leper, the 63–4
Levinas, Emmanuel 82
light 8–9,
Locke, John 118
Lucas, John 77 n.63
Luther, Martin 96–8, 113 n.79

Macbeth 102, 133, 136
Macey, David 76 n.35
Magdelene, the 60, 159–60, 163
'Man' 58–9
Man, Paul de 92–3
Marsh, Jan 15, 18
Martin, Robert 117
Marx, 95–109 *passim*, 128
Mary, the Virgin 23, 120–4
Mazzoni, Cristina 162
Michie, Helena 153–4
Miller, Andrew 25
Miller, J. Hillis 1, 84–5, 91, 111 n.31, 117–19, 122
monstrosity 84–7
Moore, Stephen D. 74 n.7, 174 n.87
Moses 71, 156
mourning 98–106
murder 135
Murray, Nicholas 39
music 106–7

Newman, John Henry 57
Nietzsche, Friedrich 44, 56, 72–3, 138, 166
Nightingale, Florence 161
Norris, Christopher 2
novel, the 2

Ong, Walter 117

Pascal, Blaise 42, 73
Pater, Walter 30
Payne, Michael 86, 112 n.41, 135, 146 n.62, 147 n.86
pharmakon 82
philosophy 102
pillory 60
Plato 6–39 *passim*
Poliakov, Léon 85
Pratt, Linda Ray 73 n.3
Pre-Raphaelites, the 33
Prins, Yopie 1, 85, 110
prophecy 83, 143
Protestantism 91, 97
psychoanalysis 33

question, the 48–50, 109

quotation 7

reading 53–4
Reide, David G. 73 n.3, 78 n.82
repetition 7
resurrection 93, 113 n.70, 127–9, 137, 164
revolution 33, 128–9
Richards, Bernard 2, 147 n.94
riots, Hyde Park 56
Rome 99–100, 141
Rosenblum, Dolores 7, 25
Rossetti, Christina 6–39
'A Better Resurrection' 27
'A Chilly Night' 18–19
'Commonplace' 24
'The Convent Threshold' 11
'Death' 20–1
'Despised and Rejected' 10–11
'Ellen Middleton' 26
'Enrica' 8
The Face of the Deep 8
'4th May Morning' 14
'From the Antique' 151
'The Ghost's Petition'
'Goblin Market' 28–9
'I have a message unto thee' 24
'An "Immurata" Sister' 36
'The Lowest Room' 6–7
'Noble Sisters' 10
'Only Believe' 32
'Repining' 15–16
'A Study. (A Soul.)' 28
'The Thread of Life' 26
'Young Death' 24
Rossetti, Dante Gabriel 30
Rossetti, William Michael 7
Royle, Nick 1, 115n.108, 117
Ruskin, John 21

saints 46–8, 87
Sand, George 158–9
Sappho 28
Sartre, Jean-Paul 51
Saussure, Ferdinand de 86, 132, 134
Schleiermacher, Friedrich 84
sea 42–6
séance 63, 98
Shaw, W. David 1, 80, 117
Shelley, Mary 86
Showalter, Elaine 162
Schaub, Uta Liebmann 74 n.7
sight 8–9, 12, 19–22,
silence 49–56
slavery 99–101, 169–70
Smith, Robert 115 n.101
Socrates 6, 55
sodomy 52–3, 57
Sophocles 44
Spivak, Gayatri Chakravorty 102, 105, 114 n.91
Stallybrass, Peter and White, Allon 12
Steiner, George 85
Stone, Donald D. 78 n.82
Strauss, David Friedrich 122
survival 102–3
Swinburne, Algernon 85

table 97–8
Taylor, Mark C. 74 n.7
Tenniel, John 14
Tennyson, Alfred 125, 166
theatre 44
Tiresias 58
train 103, 132–3, 169
tree 134–5
Trench, R. C. 118
Tucker, Herbert F. 1, 84, 110

Ulmer, Geoffrey 91
Utilitarianism 2

Vergote, Antoine 120

Veyne, Paul 76 n.48
Vienna 140–1
walking 160–1
Walsh, Susan 53
war 51, 56–7, 130–3
Whitford, Margaret 1
Wilde, Oscar
  Dorian Gray 4
Wolfreys, Julian 75 n.26
Wordsworth, William 58